$39.99

$25.00
great Book
mint cond.

# Featherwing & Hackle
# FLIES FOR SALMON & STEELHEAD

## Chris Mann

**STACKPOLE BOOKS**

Published in USA by Stackpole Books, 2006

ISBN 978-0-8117-0219-5

Text & Illustrations © Chris Mann

All rights reserved. No part of this publication may be reproduced, stored in a retrieval system or transmitted in any form or by any means, electronic, mechanical, photocopying, recording or otherwise, without the prior permission of Stackpole Books.

Stackpole Books
5067 Ritter Road
Mechanicsburg
PA 17055, U.S.A.

Originally published (2006) in the UK by Merlin Unwin Books Ltd, Palmers House, 7 Corve Street, Ludlow, Shropshire SY8 1DB, U.K.

The author assert his moral rights to be identified as the author of this work

Book design by Chris Mann
Printed in China by Leo Paper Products

# Contents

**INTRODUCTION & ACKNOWLEDGMENTS**    1

**HISTORY & DEVELOPMENT
of the FEATHERWING FLY**    5

**EUROPEAN FEATHERWINGS**    19
Great Britain & Ireland    20
Iceland & Scandinavia    44

**NORTH AMERICAN FEATHERWINGS**    51
Atlantic Salmon Flies    52
Steelhead Flies    71

**CATALOGUE OF DRESSINGS**    115

**BIBLIOGRAPHY**    216

**INDEX**    219

# Introduction and Acknowledgments

his volume looks at featherwing and hackle flies and is the third in the series (see also *Shrimp & Spey Flies for Salmon* and *Hairwing & Tube Flies for Salmon*). In the History & Development chapter, we will examine the historical roots and see how featherwing flies developed and changed over the years. Reference will be made to some of the famous flies of the last two centuries, but in general this book is not an historical treatise about the classic flies of yesteryear. Rather, it is about modern featherwing and hackle flies still in use today.

Although it is certainly true that hairwing flies have overtaken featherwings in terms of the numbers being used, it would be a great mistake to think that feathered flies have no place in modern angling. You may also be surprised at the number of featherwing and hackled patterns that remain in use. Whilst a few of these flies are hang-overs from a previous age, many of them are modern developments, devised in the last few years.

There is, I suppose, a small band of dedicated enthusiasts and traditionalists who will occasionally continue to fish the old, classically-built flies just for the sheer fun of it. I can well imagine the satisfaction to be gained by catching a salmon on a fully-dressed Jock Scott. However, the main aim of this book is to present the surprisingly large number and variety of featherwing flies which are quite as effective as any hairwings when used in the right circumstances and in the correct manner.

It is generally held that fully-dressed classical salmon flies had far too many frills: extras added by the flytyer to demonstrate his own virtuosity, which had little to do with the fly's effectiveness in the water, and which the salmon itself could not appreciate anyway. Moreover, fully-dressed flies lacked translucence and mobility. These points are true but they do not add up to an argument which proves that featherwings are inherently inferior to hairwings. All they show is that the type of featherwings tied in the past suffered from defects in their construction which are quite capable of

# Introduction

being rectified. It may fairly be said that simply dropping many of the superfluous elements (horns, butts, multiple tails, etc) of these flies does not make them any more mobile: this is true, but mobility is not necessarily always a good thing. The high slab-sided but narrow aspect of many of the classic built-wing flies can indeed be a distinct advantage when fishing in fast flowing, heavy water conditions, offering a stability and retention of form lacking in many hairwings.

*'The classic featherwing is a type of salmon fly that, sadly, is not fished enough these days. It is a fly that I use a great deal and, **in the right type of water**, it will outfish any modern hairwing. In the rough, fast water, often between pools or at the turbulent head of a pool, it is far easier to control than it is the hairwing. Its effectiveness in these situations is mainly because its wing, being more 'solid', acts as rudder and helps keep the fly upright.'*

These words were written by Dave Riding in an article in *Salmon, Trout & Seatrout* magazine (April 1991) in which he discussed fly choice and control. They remain true to this day.

The practice of building multi-layered wings of married feather strips may also be called into question and there is no doubt that in many cases it was taken beyond any sensible limit – there is, however, another side to the story. The prismatic mixing of colours has many advantages over the simple use of single colours and it may well be that in the huge range of colour combinations used in married wing flies, more than a few achieved their success due to the effect gained through the juxtapositioning of multi-coloured wing strips.

nother of the major strands running through the history of featherwing flies is the use of complete feathers for winging. One of the earliest of all salmon flies, the Kings Fisher, is of this type. Other classic examples of this category are flies such as the Durham Ranger from the United Kingdom and the Lady Amherst from the USA. These flies continue to remain effective, due to the fact that this type of fly has some inherently good properties. The high wing gives an image with presence but with little bulk as well as being stable in the water due to the keel-like shape. They are particularly effective if the fly can be presented in profile to the fish. The impressive signature that they produce also means that a smaller fly may be used than would otherwise be the case. Flies such as the Redwing (see page 110) and the Flag Wing Shrimp (*Shrimp & Spey Flies for Salmon,* page 89) are modern examples of such flies.

The use of pairs of hackle tips for winging is another major trend that has become popular, particularly over the last ten years. Such a construction has plenty of translucency and mobility and has the advantage of producing no bulk at all. Very slim flies that nevertheless have an extremely attractive fluttering motion in the water are the result. Prismatic mixing of wing colours can also be done simply by mounting enclosing pairs of hackle tips of differing colours – some stunning effects can be achieved in this way – gold over red or dark brown, red over purple etc.

Geoffrey Bucknall wrote an article about this type of winging in the November 1969 issue of *Trout & Salmon* magazine so it is a concept that has been around quite a long time. Hackle tip winging of this type was also pioneered in the United States by Sydney Glasso as one of the major attributes of his stunning recreations of the classic Spey flies which he made so popular for steelhead fishing. The flies of Dave McNeese in the Steelhead section also show some wonderful examples of this type of fly. There is no doubt that flies of this type, slimly tied, are extremely effective for low, clear conditions in summer and should be much more widely used than they are.

he third major group of feather flies are the hackled flies. Here there is no winging at all; the fly normally consisting of a tail, a body and one or more collar hackles. Traditionally this type of fly is represented by the Grubs and Bugs which have been around since the early 1800s. More recent examples include the Black Pennell and flies of the spider-type. Flies of the spider-type have been used as trout flies for many years and have a collar hackle that is extremely long, often reaching well past the bend of the hook. The fly has a very mobile image in the water and the hackles reaching back and enclosing the body can present a very life-like and translucent body form. Depending upon the size of the fly they can represent bait fish or, in smaller sizes, various types of nymph. Flies

# Introduction

of this type seem to be more commonly used for steelhead than for salmon but examples such as the Spectral Spider (see page 86) show just how good they can look. Perhaps salmon anglers should look more closely at this construction, particularly for low water fishing.

Hackled flies such as the various Bumbles have remained popular for loch and lake fishing for salmon in both Ireland and Scotland but are not regularly used for river fishing. With the successes now being gained by the various types of surface-effect flies, particularly for grilse, this is again something that modern salmon anglers might like to have another look at. Steelhead fishermen in the USA and Canada have used such flies with great effect for many years, flies such as Skunk and Spade being amongst the most popular of all steelhead flies.

In conclusion we can see that, far from being relics of a bygone age, feather flies are alive and well and offer the modern angler a wide range of forms which are suited to a wide range of conditions. In the following pages we shall look at all these types of flies in more detail and present a huge range of patterns, all of which are effective today.

## ACKNOWLEDGMENTS

I wish to record here my thanks to all the fishermen and flytyers who have helped in many ways with the production of this book. Flytyers from many countries around the world have supplied me with superb examples of their art and have also shown patience and understanding as I bothered them to explain the how, when and why of the thoughts behind the patterns.

Particular thanks are due to the steelhead anglers from all over the USA and Canada who have responded to my requests for sample flies and information with great kindness. The unbounded enthusiasm that these fishermen have for all aspects of steelhead fishing and their great regard and respect for their quarry should be an example to us all.

Nearer home, special thanks are also due to Gordon McKenzie, Duncan Eagan, Peter O'Reilly and Stan Headley who have all allowed me to benefit from their wide knowledge.

As usual I also wish to express my thanks once more to Merlin Unwin and his team who, as always, are so easy to work with and have made my task as an author much easier than it might otherwise have been.

Finally I would like to make it clear that although I have had the privilege of receiving information from many sources, responsibility for any errors, omissions or misunderstandings, lies entirely with me.

Chris Mann
May 2006

# The History and Development of the Featherwing Fly

ne of the first things to say about this potted history of featherwing flies is that it is a simplified presentation of events and developments which, not surprisingly, did not always occur in an ordered manner so as to make the life of an author easy. History, and life itself, is always much more tangled than historians would like.

The simple story that follows may give the impression that there was a regular, logical progression from one type of fly to another along a linear time-line. This is simply not true, there are always exceptions to general rules and new developments in flytying very often proceed in tandem with the continued use of older fly patterns and styles.

I feel nevertheless that, despite the temptation to over-simplify, it is worthwhile to present the broad trends that certainly do exist, in order to give you some idea of the context in which featherwing flies evolved and were used.

There are four main families of featherwing flies:
  • Simple strip-wings, including two special sub-groups of the strip-wing flies: Spey flies and Dee flies
  • Whole featherwing flies, including herl-wing flies and topping wing flies
  • Hackle or grub flies
  • Complex mixed-wing flies

Of these groups the simple strip wings and the whole feather flies are undoubtedly the earliest, some of them dating back to the 17th century. The topping wing flies came into being at the end of the first quarter of the 19th century in Ireland. The most famous of these were flies such as the Golden Butterfly from Patrick McKay in 1810. The first of the Gaudy flies (George Bainbridge, 1816) was

# History and Development of the Featherwing

presented at about the same time and from then on development was mainly that of the complex mixed wing flies, combining the topping wings with the gaudy flies.

This process reached its first peak with the Spirit flies of William Blacker which were published in *Blacker's Art of Flymaking* in 1855.

The second half of the 19th century saw the arrival of the complex featherwings with which we are all so familiar. Patterns, ever more inventive and colourful are intimately connected with names such as Fitzgibbon, Rogan, Traherne, Maxwell, Francis Francis, Wright, Kelson, Hardy, Hale, Pryce-Tannatt and others. These anglers invented many of the exotic creations themselves but also, through their books, publicised a huge range of patterns made by anglers all over Great Britain and Ireland.

## Strip-wing & Whole Featherwing Flies

The earliest flies of which we have knowledge are simple flies with bodies of wool or fur, topped with wings consisting of simple strips of feather fibres or complete feathers. Complex ribbing, body and throat hackles and the other adornments so common in the second half of the 19th century play no part in the construction of these early flies. Many of the patterns have tags and ribs but it is almost certain that these were added at a later date by the authors of the 19th century. A fly with no tag, tail, rib or body hackle was considered so 'crude' that the Victorians could not leave it alone and simply felt compelled to embellish it, in order to 'improve' its fish-taking qualities. Exactly the same is true of the winging – flies such as the Dun Wing, Black & Teal and many others gained ever more complex winging. The addition of jungle cock eyes was regarded as a minimum requirement, even when the wing itself was left as a single feather strip.

This process of embellishment was not reversed until the first half of the 20th century when patterns were once again simplified to remove what were by then considered unnecessary complications. Ironically, the end result was to return many flies back to the form that they had had at the beginning of the 19th century.

One of the earliest known salmon patterns that we can find is that of the King's Fisher, also known as the Peacock Fly. This was presented by Richard Bowlker in 1774 in his book *The Art of Angling*. This fly was winged either with a whole piece of peacock eye feather or with a bunch of peacock herl and is thus a member of the 'whole feather' or 'herl-winged' flies, depending upon the variation used.

King's Fisher

A later version recorded by Francis Francis, and which was obtained from a Captain Hotchkiss, has a tag, tail and body hackle.

The Black Dog was described by Alexander Mackintosh in his book *The Driffield Angler*, published in 1808. In this book Mackintosh gave the patterns for seven salmon flies and also

Black Dog - Mackintosh

# History and Development of the Featherwing

described the method of tying in strip-wings. This fly of sombre appearance, relieved only by a flash of tinsel and tied in small sizes, is not very far removed from modern flies such as the Stoat's Tail and would almost certainly catch fish today.

The trend towards ever more complication was continued by Francis Francis, Kelson and Maxwell who offered a range of patterns for the Black Dog, all of which had additions: tags, tails, butts, multiple ribbing and complex mixed wings. These are certainly attractive flies but it is very doubtful if they are any more effective than the simple original.

One of the earliest recorded 'whole feather' flies is the Spring Fly which is described by George Bainbridge in *The Flyfisher's Guide* (1816) and, subsequently, by George Hansard in *Trout and Salmon Fishing in Wales* (1834).

Spring Fly

As we may have expected, later versions of this popular fly gained a tag, multi-feather tail and a body hackle. A typical example was the fly named the Bittern which is presented by Francis Francis in *A Book on Angling* in 1867. According to Francis this version of the fly was sent to him by Captain Hotchkiss and it originated in Wales.

Perhaps the most famous 'whole feather' fly of all, at least from a historical perspective, is the Gaudy Fly, first presented by George Bainbridge in *The Flyfisher's Guide*. The Gaudy Fly is one of the first truly colourful flies of which we have details and Bainbridge justifies its creation with the following quaint prose: '*So fastidious are the Salmon at times, that the more brilliant and extravagant the fly, the more certain is the Angler of diversion*'. True or not, this was a lesson that the later dressers of the classic flies took fully to heart.

Gaudy Fly - Bainbridge

The Toppy is a fly which has been documented by at least four of the early writers, but one of the very first references that can be found is that given by John Younger in 1840 in his book *River Angling*. The Toppy (although not initially named as such) is number two of six Tweed flies described by him. Whether he originated this pattern or not is a matter of debate. The Toppy was also described by Edward Fitzgibbon in *The Book of the Salmon* (1850), by Scrope in *Days and Nights of Salmon Fishing on the Tweed* (1843) and by John Kirkbridge in *The Northern Angler* (1837). Later writers to include the pattern in their books include Francis Francis, Sir Herbert Maxwell, Kelson and Pryce-Tannatt.

The Toppy has been very well-documented and recommended by a whole series of writers

Toppy

# History and Development of the Featherwing

over a long period of time. The version illustrated below is as described by John Younger, the later versions given by Kelson and Pryce-Tannatt are embellished with the normal improvements such as tags, complex tails and divided bodies.

The Teal and Black is a typical representative of a large group of flies that were based on the simple, old fashioned forms. By the middle of the 19th century these flies had been made more complex by the addition of jungle cock and golden pheasant feathers as well as tags and butts but they nevertheless retained a basic simplicity which ensured that they never totally went out of fashion. Many of the modern featherwings that are still in use, such as the Logie, derive from this group, the modern form of the wings using feather slips rather than whole feathers.

Black and Teal

 he focus for the next part of the story switches to Ireland, for it is there that the huge range of brilliant and showy flies that were to characterise the last half of the nineteenth century were to find their beginnings. The name that stands out in the early part of the century is that of Pat McKay. Apart from the flies that secured his fame, almost nothing is known about him, all we know is that he dressed salmon flies between 1810 and 1870. The story starts with an apocryphal visit to a milliner's shop in Ballyshannon where he was to discover the exotic feathers that became a signature of his flies. Who knows, the visit might have really happened, but whatever the reason, a range of patterns exploded onto the salmon angling scene that were to set the tone for salmon fly development for the next three-quarters of a century.

The Golden Butterfly was the first of this series of Irish flies and shows many of the features that were later to become the norm for almost all new flies.

The date of the Golden Butterfly is not certain but can probably be placed to around 1810 – it may

Golden Butterfly - McKay

not have been the first fly to make use of golden pheasant toppings, wood duck, kingfisher and cock-of-the-rock but it is the first for which we have proper documentation. As can be seen from the illustration, the golden pheasant topping for the wing was mounted curving upwards. In later times the downward curve became the standard but at first the upward curve was often used, presumably with the intention of providing the wing with more movement in the water.

Perhaps even more famous than the Golden Butterfly is the Parson series of flies, the first of which is credited to McKay in about 1836. This fly was the first to use golden pheasant tippet feathers as wings, a feature that formed the basis of many famous flies such as the Durham Ranger, which continues to be used in the present day.

The Parson type of fly soon proved to be extremely popular and the original was followed by a spate of similar patterns. All these flies shared the common wing construction of back-to-back

# History and Development of the Featherwing

Parson No. 1 - McKay

pairs of golden pheasant tippets. The Redwing from Dave McNeese (see page 110) and the Flag Wing Shrimp (*Shrimp & Spey Flies for Salmon*, page 89) are modern examples of this type of fly. They continue to be used because, in the correct circumstances, they remain extremely effective.

Incidentally, the front part of the body of the Redwing consists of bunches of red macaw feathers (or substitutes) tied in around the body in the same manner as chatterer feathers are used in the Chatterer fly developed by Major Traherne towards the end of the 19th century. This method of tying a fly body is now seen as a rather pointless exercise in overblown excess and, in terms of its use of rare and expensive feathers, this may well be correct. What is less well appreciated is that this construction works really well in quiet pools and tailouts, the body feathers providing a lot of movement in the slightest of currents. Tied using cheap, readily available hackle tips this idea may not be so overblown and useless as many may have imagined. In addition to many steelhead, Dave McNeese landed a 62lb Chinook salmon from the Trask river in 1989 using the Redwing.

The Black Ranger is thought to be the first of the Ranger flies and is usually attributed to James Wright in about 1840. The wing, more substantial than the Parson, is composed of two back-to-back pairs of tippet feathers, the outer pair being aligned with the black barring of the inner pair. Both these pairs of feathers enclose a pair of extremely long jungle cock feathers, also back to back. As well as the famous Durham Ranger, other members of this family include the Red, Blue and Silver Rangers.

Another hybrid fly using the same wing construction as the Black Ranger is the Dandy, which was also devised in the middle of the 19th century by James Wright. The Dandy differs from the Parson and the Ranger series in that the wings consist of whole golden pheasant tippet feathers enveloped by two whole summer duck feathers, a combination which makes this fly very striking – and also extremely expensive to tie!

The last of the flies which is illustrated in this section is the Red Sandy. This fly was devised

Dandy - James Wright

Black Ranger - James Wright

in about 1880 by a Mr Nicol McNicol and was included by George Kelson in his book *The Salmon Fly* in 1895 as well as being mentioned by Hardy, Hale and Pryce-Tannatt. The Red Sandy was highly regarded for use in Iceland and derivatives of it are still used successfully in Iceland and Scandinavia.

# History and Development of the Featherwing

Red Sandy - McNicol

The Indian Crow feathers used in the winging were difficult and expensive to obtain, even in the 19th century, and modern versions use dyed hackle tips as substitutes with no apparent lessening of the fly's effectiveness.

## Spey & Dee Flies

hilst the development of flashy new patterns went on throughout the middle decades of the 19th century, two early types of fly, which represented a completely different concept of fly design, continued to be used – the Spey and Dee flies.

These flies had their origins on the rivers of the same name and shared several important features. Firstly, the colours were very subdued, natural greens and browns predominating. Secondly, they were winged with simple strips of feather, although the 'set' of their respective wings was very different. Thirdly, the body was hackled with very long heron, or in the case of the Spey flies with Spey cock, a bird specially bred in the Spey valley for this purpose. The rationale behind these flies lay, not in garish colours, but in the movement in the water which the long hackling provided. Many of these flies are described in my earlier book *Shrimp and Spey Flies for Salmon* but I consider it worthwhile to include them here again because they represent an important and continuing theme in featherwing salmon fly design.

The main source of information about the early Spey flies is from a book called *Autumns on the Spey* (1872) by A.E. Knox in which he gives details of 16 patterns. Both Spey and Dee flies are mentioned by later authors such as Francis Francis, Kelson and Pryce-Tannatt although it should be noted that by this time the Spey and Dee flies were considered to be quirky, local designs, suitable for use on their home rivers but having little or no application on rivers elsewhere. This was a major misjudgment, although, considering the meagre knowledge about the natural history of the salmon at the time, one that is perhaps to be forgiven.

Many modern writers consider the Spey and Dee flies to be at their most effective when fished near the surface in fast water. However, there are steelhead fishermen on America's west coast, such as Trey Combs, who consider that they perform best when deeply sunk in smooth, moderate flows. Certainly the long hackle fibres will move to the merest whisper of a current, so it would seem logical to take advantage of this and to use them wherever there are light currents.

A really good discussion covering many aspects of fly selection for different water conditions was written by Dave Riding in an article in the magazine *Salmon, Trout & Seatrout* in April 1991.

The Gold Reeach, shown below, is one of the flies described by A.E. Knox in 1872 in his book *Autumns on the Spey*. This fly has a body hackle of natural red Spey cock (rather than heron which is often thought to be the norm for Spey flies). The hump-backed form, typical of these flies, together with the body hackles, gives the Reeach a shrimp-like appearance and the Spey and Dee flies are undoubtedly one of the major forerunners of modern shrimp flies. Variants of these forms continue to be used today and are particularly popular on the steelhead fisheries of the west coast of North America.

Gold Reeach

# History and Development of the Featherwing

The Grey Heron is another of the Spey flies presented by Knox. This fly, together with its close relative the Black Heron have extremely long heron hackles palmered along the body. At the turn of the 20th century other heron flies such as the Orange, Brown and Gold Herons were added to the range. These long-hackled flies are still extremely popular with the steelhead anglers of the west coast of America, primarily due to the influence of Syd Glasso who developed his own versions of Spey flies with hackle-tip winging.

We can now look at the first cousins of the Spey flies – the Dee flies. In modern times these two groups of flies have become inextricably interwoven, to the extent that they are most commonly referred to together. Superficially, the Dee flies are similar to Spey flies in many ways.

The hook style, hackled body, multiple ribbing and subdued colours all remain the same; the major difference lies in the set and form of the wings. Whereas the wings on a Spey fly are set 'keel fashion', closely cupping the body, the wing strips for a Dee fly are set apart in a scissor-like 'Vee' fashion. The body hackling for a Dee fly is invariably heron and it is extremely long (usually as long as the bird can provide). This feature therefore, so often perceived as an attribute of the Spey fly, is in fact much more typical of the Dee flies.

The pattern illustrated here is called the Gled Wing and is one of the oldest of the Dee flies, dating from the earliest years of the 19th century. The word Gled is an old Scottish word for a kite and the wings were originally strips of kite feathers. The Gled Wing is the forerunner of later flies such as the Glentana and the Dunt.

In the later part of the 19th century the Spey and Dee flies were relegated to a secondary role, seen as local oddities which, although they may have been useful on their own rivers, had little relevance to salmon fishing in the wider world.

Some Spey flies continued to be developed, but the new fashion was for complex built-wing

*Grey Heron*

Gled Wing

Glen Grant

# History and Development of the Featherwing

flies and the classical simplicity and purity of the original Speys was never repeated. The Glen Grant, illustrated below is typical of the later Spey and Dee flies. It was designed for the river Spey by the Grant family in the middle of the 19th century. As can been seen, the basic form was retained but the wing became much more complex, not to say expensive, by including three pairs of jungle cock feathers!

Black Dog - Kelson

The Black Dog, illustrated below, shows perhaps the ultimate development of the Spey fly. This pattern was described by George Kelson, who gave credit for its invention to his father, and recommended it as a high water pattern for the river Spey. Maxwell also has a version of the Black Dog but he claims that it is a modern version of an old Tay pattern. Whichever is true, it must be said that this pattern is one of the few to combine features of the older Spey flies with more complex winging methods. The result is a fly that is both harmonious and elegant.

The herl-winged flies are a small but important group of flies that include some of the earliest known salmon flies. The main feature of these flies is that the wing consists of a bunch of peacock herl, although strips of other feathers and toppings may also be added. Of these flies the best known is the Beauly Snow Fly which continues to be used in the present day. Apart from its use as a fly for Atlantic salmon it has also been used on the west coast of North America for steelhead (see page 105).

The fly illustrated is called the Laxford and dates from the middle of the 19th century and was described by Francis Francis in *A Book on Angling* in 1876. He obtained the pattern from Farlows, the tackle retailer, but whether Farlows originated the pattern is not certain.

## Mixed-wing Flies

The largest group of featherwing flies are the complex mixed-wing flies that came to the forefront of fly development in the middle of the 19th century and which maintained a dominance that lasted well into the 20th century. So dominant did this group become that almost all of the classic flies that are known today belong to this category. Flies such as the Jock Scott, the Baron, the Popham and the Doctor are well known to anglers who may have never consciously fished with 'mixed-wing' flies. These classic patterns are now tied as 'exhibition flies' by some of the most talented tyers who have ever lived.

We have seen in the earlier part of this chapter that George Bainbridge's Gaudy Fly was probably the first of the really complex flies, but the mantle of their development was taken up the great Irish tyers such as McKay and Rogan. A significant publication of this time was William Blacker's famous book *The Art of Fly Making* (1855). Of the fifteen patterns presented in this book the most famous, complex and colourful are the three Spirit flies.

This series of flies jumped, in one bound, straight into the complexities which we have since come to consider as the standard for classic salmon

Laxford

# History and Development of the Featherwing

flies. The flies are complete with tags, tails, butts, multi-segmented bodies, multiple hackles and wings which consisted of sheaths of married fibres taken from different feathers as well as golden pheasant toppings, cheeks and horns. The most important feature of these flies is the use of married fibres to build up a complex wing sheath. It is by no means certain that this technique was invented by Blacker but it is incontrovertible that he had a seminal influence both on the general form of the classic salmon fly and on the winging in particular. As we will see, winging techniques became ever more complex, culminating in Victorian times in the 'improved mixed wings' devised by George Kelson in which single fibres of several feathers were married together and the sequence repeated as many times as necessary to build up the complete wing. Secondary sheaths were also used outside the main sheaths, and this, together with sides and cheeks made the wing even more complex.

The Major (illustrated) was devised by the Rev. A. Williams in the first quarter of the 19th century and it represents a transitional form between the whole-wing flies and the complex mixed-wing flies. The core of the wing remains the two back-to-back golden pheasant tippet feathers, but over this on each side are sheaths of married fibres – in this case bustard, golden pheasant tail and three colours of swan. The wing is finished with a topping over all. Note that, although the body consists of various colours of pig's wool, there are no complex joints or butts and nor are there cheeks of jungle cock, chatterer or Indian crow – all very good indicators

The Lee Blue - after Kelson

that this is an early fly. The Major is detailed by Fredric Tolfrey in his book *Jones' Guide to Norway* published in 1848 and is also mentioned by Francis Francis and Kelson. Tolfrey maintains that this fly was known as the Namsen in Norway and it must be said that if the tippet underwing is removed, the fly is very similar indeed to the Namsen described by Francis Francis. It is likely that the Namsen is a derivative of the Major, adapted for use in Norway.

The Lee Blue is another of the early mixed wing patterns from Ireland which dates from the first quarter of the 19th century. The use of well picked-out seal's fur for the body is typical of many Irish flies, a style which has been retained to the present day. The underwings of golden pheasant tippet are another feature which typify

The Major - Rev. A. Williams

The Lemon Grey - after Kelson

# History and Development of the Featherwing

Plate 1 - Flies from William Blacker's *The Art of Flymaking*, 1855

Irish flies and can be found in many of the modern patterns. The Lee Blue has remained popular in Ireland and E. J. Malone gives four versions of the fly in his book *Irish Trout & Salmon Flies*.

The Lemon Grey is an early Irish fly that pre-dates 1833. Kelson attributes Jewhurst as the creator with a date of about 1830. The Lemon Grey is one of those flies which are much more effective in the water than a casual glance in the hand would have you believe and it has remained in use (in slightly varying forms) to the present day. Malone gives three versions of the fly in *Irish Trout & Salmon Flies*. Flies such as the Lemon & Yellow are really no more than derivatives of the original Lemon Grey.

William Blacker was an Irishman who lived in Belfast. But in the late 1830s, at the age of 45, he moved to London and opened a flyfishing shop. He published his first book on fishing, entitled *The Art of Angling* in 1842 but he became famous for his second book, *The Art of Flymaking*, which was published in 1855. This book included fifteen fly patterns, including the Ballyshannon and the famous Spirit fly series. All these flies were illustrated in the form of beautifully hand-coloured prints and the book has become one of the most desirable and difficult-to-obtain of the classic texts.

The Ballyshannon seems to have been of Blacker's own devising and is a most harmonious combination of colours, using a range of materials that must have been difficult and expensive to obtain, even in the 19th century. In modern times

# History and Development of the Featherwing

many of these materials are impossible to obtain and substitutes are used. The general form of the fly is that of a hybrid, the winging consisting of both whole feather and married fibre elements.

Three Spirit flies are described and illustrated in *The Art of Flymaking* and are deservedly seen as one of the pinnacles of classic salmon fly design. Wing design may have become even more complex as time passed by but there is no doubt that the Spirit flies remain a challenge to the best flytyers – even of today. Blacker was convinced that these flies imitated real insects (presumably butterflies), as the following passage from his book illustrates: *'Their lifelike and alluring appearance, when humoured attractively with the rod and line, will cause them to be very deceptive to the salmon, and they will rise out of the water at them with such greediness (the fun of it is) as to mistake them for living insects.'*

The first Spirit fly shown has a very complex body which is constructed with no less than five joints, each divided by turns of tinsel, ostrich herl and a hackle. The wing is a hybrid type, consisting of several golden pheasant crests, wood duck, cock-of-the-rock and kingfisher feathers, all surmounted by a Himalayan pheasant crest.

The second Spirit fly has a mixed wing, more in keeping with the newer style, consisting of married strips of various feathers.

The third Spirit fly is even more colourful than the first two and again features a complex body divided into four joints. The winging is a hybrid, combining both a whole tippet underwing with married elements at the sides. Blacker's descriptions of these flies date from a time before the modern conventions for describing a fly tying sequence had been settled. His descriptions are therefore sometimes very hard to follow, particularly with regard to the order in which the feathers were to be tied in. To produce the illustrations in Plate 1, I have followed the tying used by Mikael Frodin in his book *Classic Salmon Flies*.

Following on from the Spirit flies we enter the era in which the classic salmon flies blossomed into the plethora of colours and complexities which we know today. In the second half of the 19th century, anglers and flytyers such as Francis Francis, Traherne, Wright, Maxwell, Kelson, Hale and Pryce-Tannatt developed ever more colourful creations with ever more complex wings. These new flies were disseminated through the writings of Francis, Kelson and others and form the basis of the built-wing salmon fly style which did not change in any major way until well into the 20th century.

The original mixed-wing consisted of married strips of variously coloured feathers. This developed into the practice of repeating these feather pairings several times to make up the complete wing. The process came to its logical conclusion with the complex wings espoused by George M. Kelson, in which the strips of feather were reduced to single strands which were married together and then repeated several times until the ultimate height of the wing was reached. It was, and still is, a veritable tour-de-force of technique and patience but whether it improved the effectiveness of the flies in any significant way is very doubtful. It seems to me that the impact of the earlier versions, in which contrasting colours of wing feathers were juxtaposed, is to a large extent lost by the Kelson refinement of single-strands.

For those who are interested in tying wings in this manner, a very good explanation of the principles and procedures involved is to be found in the chapter by Marvin Nolte in Michael Radencich's book *Tying the Classic Salmon Fly*.

Kate - after Maxwell

Typical of the flies from the second half of the 20th century is The Kate which is ascribed by George Kelson to a Mrs Courtney and which is said to originate on the river Tweed. The Kate is also mentioned by Francis Francis, Maxwell, Kelson and Pryce-Tannatt, so it is one of the flies which has retained its popularity over a long period.

# History and Development of the Featherwing

The Bulldog, which is shown in the version put forward by Sir Herbert Maxwell, has a complex wing which is made up of multiple, repeated sections of black and yellow swan. This fly was

Bulldog - after Maxwell

said to be particularly successful on the river Eden in the county of Cumberland (now part of Cumbria) in northern England.

Beresford's Fancy is shown below as tied by George Kelson. It demonstrates clearly the effect gained by using multiple, repeated sequences of married fibres for the wings. The impact of the colour contrast in the wing is lost to a great extent but this may be compensated for by the banding effect that is gained. Kelson attributes this fly to General R. H. Beresford and recommends its use in Ireland. The fly was also known as the Half Blue & Orange.

Just to show, however, that development does not always progress in one single direction, the next fly is also a classic Irish fly dating to the second half of the 19th century. The Fiery Brown is one of the most famous of all the Irish salmon flies. Michael Rogan of Ballyshannon, was renowned for producing shades of this brown colour which no other fly tyer could reproduce. The fly illustrated, one of three different dressings given by E. J. Malone in *Irish Trout & Salmon Flies,* illustrates an important trait typical of many Irish flies in the later part of the 19th century, in that the winging has been much reduced and simplified so that it is merely an underwing of golden pheasant tippets with bronze mallard over. This style of of winging has continued to the present day and the so-called Irish wing is used on many other modern Irish featherwings.

Fiery Brown - after Malone

This winging style is easy to tie and has therefore given a new lease of life to many patterns that would not otherwise be used. In addition to the Fiery Brown, the Irish wing can be found on the Thunder & Lightning, the Doctor series of flies, the Lemon Grey, and many other featherwinged flies still in everyday use throughout Ireland.

## Wingless & Hackle Flies

Some of the earliest of all flies were wingless or hackled flies. For salmon fishing this style of fly first came to prominence in the middle part of the 19th century with the grub patterns recommended by Francis Francis, Kelson and Hale. Most of these early grub flies had divided bodies with two or three hackles, much in the manner of the later Irish shrimp flies, of which they were, without doubt,

Beresford's Fancy - after Kelson

# History and Development of the Featherwing

one of the main forerunners. These wingless flies were recommended for low-water fishing in the summer months and they were undoubtedly more suited to this role than the fully dressed flies with their rigid and complex winging. Kelson himself believed that grub versions of all the major salmon flies should be used throughout the summer months and in fact developed many of the patterns himself. Dressed slightly more simply and using less exotic materials, these types of fly would undoubtedly be effective today because of the inherent movement of the hackles.

The Wasp Grub was noted by Kelson as a simple but effective low-water pattern for use during the wasp (summer) season and he particularly recommended it for the river Usk. The Wasp Grub was certainly one of the earliest of the grub patterns probably dating back to around 1815, as can be seen from the fact that it has not been subject to the typical 'improvements' made to later versions such as the Ajax and Jungle Hornet.

The Wasp Grub was obviously meant to imitate a wasp at a time when anglers believed that salmon fed upon insects of various kinds. The fact that we now know that this is not so, does not stop the yellow and black body colours from being effective.

Wye Grub - after Kelson

The Black Pennell is another of the Victorian hackled patterns that has retained its popularity until the present day. Its inventor, who went under the splendid name of Mr. H. Cholmondley-Pennell, came up with one of those rare patterns which seems to have allure for all kinds of game fish. Since its inception the Black Pennell has been one of the standard patterns for brown trout, seatrout and salmon.

Black Pennell - Cholmondley-Pennell

Wasp Grub - after Kelson

Among the original Victorian wingless grubs the Wye Grub was one of the most successful, and was used on many rivers other than the Wye. This fly was very strongly recommended by Kelson and was also mentioned in the works of Hardy and Hale. It probably dates to around the middle of the 19th century.

The original dressing is quite simple, consisting of a tail of golden pheasant tippet (or sometimes topping), a body of black floss ribbed with oval silver tinsel and a collar hackle of black hen. There are, of course, many variations (Stan Headley lists six in his book *Trout & Salmon Flies of Scotland*), the main ones used for salmon include a dubbed body which is enhanced by a wound hackle. Other modern variants of the Black Pennell are listed in the chapter on European Featherwings (page 29). Simple but effective, the Black Pennell has remained one of the mainstays

## History and Development of the Featherwing

of loch fishing for salmon in Scotland. And, tied in small sizes, it is always worth a try on rivers during the difficult days of summer when water flows are low and clear.

Simple hackled flies continue to be used for all kinds of game fishing, but in Scotland their use for salmon is largely confined to stillwater fishing on the lochs. In Ireland this is also the case, except for the role played by shrimp flies. These can be considered as a special sub-set of the wingless fly and there are many variations widely used in Ireland. Details of the huge range of shrimp flies may be found in *Shrimp & Spey Flies for Salmon*, a companion volume to this book. New shrimp flies continue to appear and the pattern shown here is typical of the modern style, but with an unusual twist.

Known as the Pot Belly Pig, the fly was conceived by a gillie, Peter Whittingham, in 1997 but did not become widely known until it was publicised in an article in the October 2001 issue of *Trout & Salmon*. Since that time the Pot Belly has become one of the most successful flies of the last few years and is widely used throughout the United Kingdom and Ireland.

robust than hackle stalks and give a fly a distinctive kick or pulse in the water which seems to trigger the salmon into taking the fly.

In North America a small range of hackled flies are used on the East coast of Canada for Atlantic salmon fishing; and on the West coast of the USA a number of flies, such as the Spade, have been very successful and influential in steelhead fishing.

Pot Belly Pig - Whittingham

The version illustrated has a brown body and hackle (which has proved to be the most successful) but the fly can be tied in a wide variety of colours, all of which can be effective on their day. The fly was named because of the feelers which consist of curved boar's bristles which come from China. These feelers are stiffer than bucktail and more

# European Featherwing & Hackle Flies

 hilst there is no doubt that featherwing flies have been largely replaced with hairwings, a surprisingly large number of featherwing patterns continue to be used.

These flies are no longer the complex, built-wing flies of the 19th century, but a mixture of simple strip-winged flies, wingless hackled flies and newer types which use flexible hackle tips as wings. One area in which featherwings never lost their popularity is for use in high summer as low-water flies. This could well be due to the fact that hairwings, when tied very short, as is often the case for low-water flies, do not show the necessary mobility.

Featherwing flies and particularly hackled flies have always been preferred to hairwings for loch fishing for salmon. This is for a combination of reasons: firstly, the flies tend to be smaller than those used on the rivers and secondly the style of fishing is much more akin to trout fishing. It is interesting to speculate if the behaviour of the salmon changes once they have taken up residence in the loch, or whether the same kind of surface tactics would be equally effective on the rivers.

There are countless instances where small trout flies have been proven to be very effective for salmon, particularly for fresh-run fish in clear water conditions. I, like many other anglers, have caught salmon when actually targeting trout, using flies that, in the normal course of events, would not be considered at all suitable for salmon.

All of the following patterns are in current use and have all been proved to catch salmon over a long period of time.

# European Featherwing Flies

## GREAT BRITAIN & IRELAND

he first flies in this section come from Scotland and have been used since the 19th century. The fact that these flies have lasted so well is a good indication of their proven effectiveness.

The Logie is a pattern from the river Dee devised by W. Brown but has found regular use on rivers all over Scotland, particularly in low-water conditions in high summer. There is also a claret-bodied version of this fly which may well be better suited for use later in the season.

The Jeannie is another pattern devised by Brown, and used in similar circumstances to the Logie.

Logie - Brown

The Blue Charm is one of the most widely used salmon flies in the world. This pattern has found use in Scotland, Ireland, Canada and its derivatives are used on the West coast of the USA for steelhead. All in all it is a fly for all seasons.

Jeannie - Brown

The history of the Blue Charm is dominated by the name of A. H. Wood, the father of the floating line (greased line) technique. Fishing on the Cairnton beat of the river Dee, he caught 3,540 salmon between 1913 and 1943, the majority of them on the Blue Charm. With such a successful fly it is inevitable that a wide range of variants have appeared over the years. Most of the variations are in the details rather than the fundamentals of the fly.

The version shown here is that given by John Hardy and J.H. Hale, and the one below is a modern version from Scotland tied as a double.

Blue Charm

The Irish version of the Blue Charm has the typical 'Irish Wing' in which a bunch of tippet fibres are set as an underwing beneath mallard slips. It should also be noted that the Blue Charm and its variants have always been among the most popular and successful seatrout patterns.

The Doctor series of flies have been around since the Blue Doctor was devised by James Wright in about 1830.

The Blue Doctor was followed by the Black Doctor and the Silver Doctor. All of these flies have been in constant use since their inception and all remain, like the Blue Charm, effective today throughout the world for a wide variety of species.

# European Featherwing Flies

The first fly in this group that I have illustrated is the Silver Doctor. Rather than writing a great deal about this fly, I think its effectiveness can be best illustrated by quoting Peter O'Reilly from his book *Trout & Salmon Flies of Ireland*:

*'This is one of my favourite salmon flies for both fresh spring fish and later fresh grilse in June and July. .... I always use the featherwing dressing and would never consider the hairwing version. I find this fly extraordinarily effective for fresh grilse when fished on its own in small sizes'.*

When used in small sizes, the wing may be simplified to slips of bronze mallard with an underwing of tippet fibres.

The example shown here has a fully dressed wing but this could also be reduced to an underwing of tippet fibres with bronze mallard over.

The Blue Doctor is perhaps the least popular of the three Doctor flies illustrated. It was nevertheless widely used in Wales as it also had the virtue of being a good sewin (seatrout) fly. Patterns with a blue bias have always been popular in Wales (see also the Conway Blue on page 24)

The fly illustrated is taken from the pattern shown in Moc Morgan's book *Trout & Salmon Flies of Wales* and has a complex wing. This could also be simplified in line with previous recommendations to make a more usable, everyday fly.

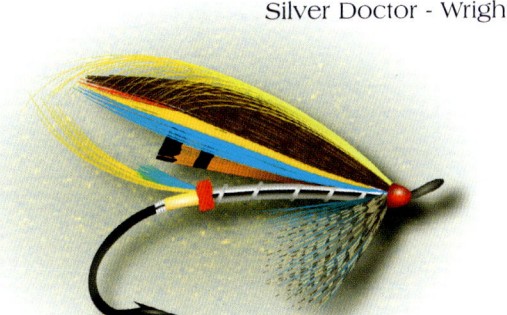

Silver Doctor - Wright

Blue Doctor

The Black Doctor is another pattern that still finds a place in modern fishing. Peter O'Reilly recommends the Black Doctor for overcast days and also thinks that it is worth a try towards the end of the season. In small sizes it is also a useful fly for loch use on dull days.

The Quack is a much more recent fly from Ireland but is very much in keeping with the 'Doctor' tradition and is closely related to the Black Doctor. Peter O'Reilly thinks that it was named, with typical Irish humour, by Owen Mullins of Newport House.

Black Doctor - Wright

Quack

# European Featherwing Flies

It has been generally used with some success for spring salmon on the Newport River and Lough Beltra and is recommended as an evening pattern.

The Whitewing (which is also known as the Hunter) was originally devised for use on the river Tay and is generally credited to James Wright. In more recent times it has become more closely associated with the river Tweed and is often used when the light starts to fade in the evening. There seems to be a general split in angler's opinions about white-coloured flies.

Whitewing

Many believe that dark is better at night (certainly many seatrout fishermen) but the majority of salmon anglers seem to consider white to be most effective. Both could be true: in the fading light of evening white may catch and concentrate the little light that is around.

Conversely, once night has fallen, a black fly shows up well against a lighter sky. Whichever is true, the river Tweed is one of the few rivers where flies containing a healthy amount of white are popular (see also the Junction Shrimp and White Shrimp in *Shrimp & Spey Flies for Salmon*).

Ghost

The Ghost is an all-white pattern which was supplied by David Mateer to Stan Headley for his book *Trout & Salmon Flies of Scotland*. It was highly recommended for seatrout fishing as well as salmon on the River Awe in Scotland.

Brown Turkey

The Brown Turkey is one of the very early flies dating back to the beginning of the 19th century. The Brown Turkey is still regularly used on the Ayr and Girvan rivers of Ayrshire, as well as on Loch Lomond for both salmon and seatrout.

The Mar Lodge is a pattern that originated in Scotland on the River Dee. It still finds occasional use in Scotland but it is in Ireland that it remains popular for spring fishing. The pattern illustrated is as given by Peter O'Reilly in *Trout & Salmon Flies of Ireland* and generally follows the tying as given by Kelson.

Mar Lodge

The Green Highlander is one of the classic flies that, in various guises, is probably more popular now than it was in the 19th century. The Green Highlander is widely used in Scandinavia

# European Featherwing Flies

and Canada as well as spawning versions that are used for steelhead fishing on the west coast of the USA. Whilst most of the modern versions are hairwings, there is still a place for the featherwing, particularly for spring fishing when water levels are high and a fly with impact is required.

Green Highlander

The version shown retains nearly all the features of the original dressing, apart from the outer wing sheaths of teal and summer duck. Jungle cock cheeks are optional.

Blue Elver - Ransome

The Blue Elver was devised by Arthur Ransome who was perhaps most famous as a writer of children's books. Less well known was the fact that he was an expert angler and also a writer of fishing books. It was designed to imitate the elver (young) of the common Atlantic eel which he thought might be a significant part of the diet of the salmon. This is now known to be unlikely but the fly is nevertheless still effective for fresh-run fish. The construction is very similar to the streamer flies of the east coast fisheries of North America which many anglers, including Joseph Bates, think are very much under-rated as salmon flies. The feathers of the vulturine guinea fowl which form the wings are extremely difficult to obtain and the saddle feathers of jungle cock are sometimes used as a substitute.

The Thunder & Lightning has to be one of the most popular and widely used salmon flies of all time. Its origin is not clear, some think that it was the brainchild of James Wright of Sprouston but others, equally firmly, give credit to Pat Hearns of Ireland.

Whichever is true, they gave us a great fly which has proved to effective in a wide range of conditions and at all times of year. The featherwing version is still in use in Scotland, particularly on large rivers such as the Tweed and Spey whilst in Ireland it is very popular and is used from north to south. Peter O'Reilly prefers a lightly-dressed version in small sizes for use at dusk.

Thunder & Lightning

The Thunder & Lightning also retains its popularity in Wales where its dark tones are well suited to peat-stained waters. The dressing given by Moc Morgan differs from the above in that the orange hackle is confined to the shoulder and not palmered along the front half of the body. Dressed in low-water style in small sizes, the Thunder & Lightning is also very effective towards dusk on a warm summer's day when the grilse are running. The Thunder & Lightning is also a pattern that can be tied in many different styles without losing its

# European Featherwing Flies

effectiveness and today it can be found dressed on treble or double hooks as well as tubes and Waddingtons.

Stuart's Killer

Stuart's Killer is an old fly from the River Spey which is recommended in small sizes for both salmon and seatrout on both rivers and lochs. When used for loch fishing it is often tied on a double hook. It is generally held to be most effective towards the end of the season which may be due to the red hackle and tail. Many effective end of season flies have a liberal dose of red.

Watson's Fancy

Watson's Fancy is another Scottish fly which seems to be equally popular in Ireland. In both countries it is used for both brown trout and salmon. In its salmon fly garb, the hackle may be tied in front of the wing. Watson's Fancy is mainly used for loch fishing for grilse but may be a useful river fly in larger sizes.

The home-grown salmon flies of Wales, as opposed to those which were used there by visiting anglers, were generally much more subdued than their Scottish and Irish cousins, using those materials which could be readily obtained from local sources. The construction of these flies also tended to be much more simple than the Scottish and Irish flies. Generally bodies were of dubbed seal's fur without the complexities of multiple joints. Wings were also simple, being mostly matched slips of bronze mallard or hen pheasant tail. Most of the following flies share these features.

Conway Blue - Jones

The Conway Blue is a Welsh fly that was devised by J.O. Jones for the river Conway during the 1930s or 40s. At the time that the fly was developed, most of the fishing was done immediately after a flood and the Conway Blue, with its strong colour, was well-suited to these conditions. The Conway Blue was also recommended for late season seatrout.

The Penybont is another Welsh fly which comes in various guises. A shrimp-like version was

Penybont

24

# European Featherwing Flies

illustrated in *Shrimp & Spey Flies for Salmon* but the version illustrated here is the standard pattern with a grey heron wing.

In *Trout & Salmon Flies of Wales,* Moc Morgan notes that this fly is sometimes fished using a Portland Hitch. In this method of fishing, the leader is looped back around the eye of the hook with a half hitch so that the fly rides cocked sideways. The fly is cast across the river and retrieved with some pace thus causing it to wake through the surface film. This method of fishing is very popular in Canada and on the West Coast of the USA but is rarely used in Europe. Surface-effect flies, either normal patterns fished in this manner or specially tied dry flies which wake in various ways, are especially effective for grilse and summer steelhead throughout North America but are generally held to be less effective in the United Kingdom. Whether this is actually true or if it is simply because this style of fishing is rarely used in the United Kingdom is very difficult to say.

The Red Turkey also originated from the river Conway in North Wales at about the same time as the Conway Blue. The Red Turkey had a good reputation as a grilse fly but as the grilse runs in Wales have diminished over the years, so has the appeal of this fly. Early versions of the fly tended to be heavily-dressed but in more recent times, a slimmer, more lightly-dressed form has become the norm.

The Black Turkey is a derivative of the Red Turkey and is considered by some to be more effective than the original. Black-bodied flies have always been effective for fishing clear water in summer and this fly is no exception.

The Haslam is one of the most popular and widely-used flies in Wales, particularly on the river Dovey. The history of this fly is long but its origin is not altogether clear. Moc Morgan attributes the pattern to Sam Haslam who founded the Rutland reservoir trout fishery. The spread of the pattern in Wales is largely attributed to Peter Vaughan, a tackle dealer on the river Dovey.

The Haslam is one of the very few modern flies which retains the horns so popular on the classic, complex winged flies of the Victorian era. It should be said that almost all the writers on this fly insist that the horns have function, rather than just being decorative. A version of this fly with a white body hackle has also become quite popular. For a fuller overview of the wide varieties of Haslam that have developed over the years, Moc Morgan wrote a very interesting article in the September 2002 issue of *Fly Fishing & Fly Tying* in which the history and range of Haslam is discussed in some detail.

# European Featherwing Flies

The Dwyryd Red & Yellow is another in the wide range of simple Welsh flies, in this case named after the river Dwyryd. The bright colours of this fly are ideally suited to fishing in brown stained water as a flood fines down; one of the most common and productive times to use the fly. The River Dwyryd is not large but good catches, sometimes exceeding five or six fish in an hour, have been made when the water is at the right height.

Dwyryd Red & Yellow

The Wil Harry was created by William Richards of Llandeilo for the River Towy in Wales. It is very colourful to ensure that it remains visible in difficult, coloured-water conditions. As Moc Morgan says, this fly is pleasingly simple but has the lethal appearance of a really good salmon fly.

Wil Harry - Richards

The Claret & Jay is an Irish fly that dates back to the early 19th century. Peter O'Reilly thinks that it probably comes from Donegal.

There is a series of Jay flies, all of which share subdued colours. The flies as detailed by Pennell, Kelson, Francis Francis and others generally had a more complex wing than the version illustrated which is a modern fly as given by Peter O'Reilly in *Trout & Salmon Flies of Ireland*.

Claret & Jay

The Connemara Black is a sombre-coloured pattern from the west of Ireland that is often used for spring salmon on the loughs of Ireland. It is also recommended in small sizes (10 singles) as a dropper fly, especially in a clearing spate. Jungle cock cheeks are optional.

Connemara Black

The Dusty Miller is one of the early classic featherwing flies that dates back to the beginning of the 19th century and is of a generally subdued colouring – mainly brown and silver. It is another

26

# European Featherwing Flies

of those flies that appear fairly nondescript in the hand but which, nevertheless, are more effective in the water than one may think. This fly has a long record of success and is documented by Kelson, Francis Francis, Hale, Maxwell and Pryce-Tannatt. On the loughs of the west and north-west of Ireland this fly has been a long-time favourite and remains in use to the present day.

Dusty Miller

The Goshawk has been around for some time, having its origins in the first quarter of the 19th century. In more modern times it has been closely associated with the River Moy in both hairwing and featherwing form. The fly illustrated below is a slightly simplified modern version which Peter O'Reilly recommends very highly, especially for the Ridge Pool.

Goshawk

Dressed on a low-water double it once took seven grilse for a friend of his on a difficult day.

The fly is very easy to tie, apart from the married wing elements, but even this can be simplified by simply tying in the red elements as slips over the sides of a wider, yellow wing. The form of the wing of this fly is very similar to that of the Parmachene Belle, a fancy pattern from the USA with a white, rather than yellow, base to the wing.

The Silver Grey in its original form was one of the flies detailed in William Blacker's book the *Art of Flymaking* which was published in 1855. It is another fly which, together with the Lemon Grey, the Mar Lodge and the Dusty Miller, form a group which share the subdued colouration of brown, yellow, grey and silver.

All of these flies have a certain look about them which speaks to any angler. Despite their lack of eye-catching colours they all say 'fish catcher' in loud tones. They all share a certain sparkle but are not so garish as to scare fish in clear water conditions; the colours seem 'natural' in a way that inspires confidence. The pattern as shown below is fully dressed with almost all of the elements of the original fly. It is widely used on Lough Beltra as a dropper for spring fishing and can also be effective on the river for bright days with clear water.

Silver Grey

The Silver Wilkinson continues the theme of silver-bodied flies and is another fly that has stood the test of time. Originally from Scotland where it may have been first tied by James Wright in about 1845, it is now regularly used in Ireland and, in its hairwing version, in Scotland as a small double for summer fishing. The dressing for the wing has varied over the years but the married slips of red, blue and yellow swan seem to be common to most

# European Featherwing Flies

patterns. The throat hackle of magenta is standard but may be combined with light blue or, as in the version illustrated, with widgeon. The Silver Wilkinson is effective in size 6 for spring fishing in clear water conditions. The Silver Wilkinson is also widely used in Ireland in its shrimp style version and in Scandinavia as a Spey-style fly (see *Shrimp & Spey Flies for Salmon*).

Silver Wilkinson

The Gosling is a trout fly which appears to have originated in the area of Lough Melvin and Lough Erne and which has become very popular throughout Ireland. Strictly speaking the Gosling is a style of tying rather than a particular pattern' as a whole range of Goslings have appeared since its inception. The diagnostic feature of all these patterns is the use of long-fibred mallard flank feather as a collar hackle. The Grey Winged Salmon Gosling is a very effective salmon fly of the same type, despite the somewhat cumbersome name. It is recommended as a good spring fly in either bright or dull weather and is equally effective for lough fishing.

Grey Salmon Gosling

The next fly is from Scotland and is a real rarity – a new, fully dressed fly that is designed for actual use rather than as a decorative wall hanging. The Macartair was designed by Nigel Griffiths for use on the River Thurso in Caithness. The colours of this fly, yellow, claret and orange, have proved be particularly effective on the Thurso and show up extremely well in its usually peat-stained water. First tied in 2002 the pattern has since proved to be a reliable taker of fish with scores of salmon to its credit. With 14 fish in one week in September it yet again proves how good claret can be at the end of the season. The fly is named the Macartair (gaelic for McCarthy) after Eddie McCarthy, the river superintendant.

Macartair - Griffiths

The Gold Sylph is a simple, sparkling little fly which is ideally suited for grilse fishing in thin water on summer days which alternate broken cloud with bright sunshine.

Gold Sylph

# European Featherwing Flies

The Assassin is an Irish fly with a long history which still remains popular on the River Bush in Northern Ireland. It is particularly effective when tied in small sizes and used as a dropper. The dressing illustrated is as given by E.J. Malone in *Irish Trout & Salmon Flies* and agrees with that given by John Todd in an article about the River Bush in the April 1999 issue of *Fly Fishing & Fly Tying*. The predominantly red and yellow colouration of this fly seem to be particularly successful on the River Bush. One of the most effective new flies of recent years, the Apache Shrimp, also shares this colouration.

Assassin

The next group of flies share a common theme: they are not salmon flies! That is to say, they are much better known as trout and seatrout flies. All of them are, however, extremely effective as salmon flies, even if they are not widely used in this role. Indeed, some of them are so consistently successful at catching salmon that it is perhaps surprising they are still considered to be trout flies. Most of them have been mainly used for salmon fishing in the still waters of the loughs of Ireland and the lochs of Scotland. It would, however, be foolish to think that they are restricted to this role; they can be very effective on rivers too. All of these flies are worthy of consideration by salmon fishers, particularly when fishing for grilse in the low, clear water conditions so common in summer.

The Bibio is an Irish pattern created by Major Charles Roberts of Burrishoole in County Mayo in the late 1950s. Originally designed as a seatrout fly for the loughs, it is equally effective for brown trout, rainbow trout, seatrout and salmon. Although it was designed for lough fishing it also works very well on the rivers of western Ireland when fished on the dropper.

Bibio - Roberts

We have already seen in the History Chapter the original Black Pennell but, as with all successful flies, a whole range of variants have been invented over the years. Many of these flies are more effective than the original. Brigg's Pennell was devised by Dr. Francis Briggs for use on the River Erriff in County Mayo in Ireland. It is at its best when fished in windy conditions when there is a good ripple on the water and if it is fished on the dropper of a two-fly cast. So successful is this pattern that Peter O'Reilly recommends it as an absolute must-have fly when fishing the spate rivers of western Ireland.

Brigg's Pennell

# European Featherwing Flies

Peterson's Pennell is one of Stan Headley's patterns which was designed for use on the lochs of the Highlands and Islands of Scotland. Originally conceived as a brown trout fly, it has proved to be even more effective for seatrout and salmon.

Peterson's Pennell - Headley

Peterson's Pennell has much in common with the Goat's Toe, another Irish fly that has also seen widespread use in Scotland. Stan Headley remarks that the Goat's Toe is probably the most popular and successful seatrout and salmon fly in use on the lochs of the Scottish west coast and islands. Peter O'Reilly notes that, although he lists it amongst the trout flies, it is more likely to take a salmon than a trout. The original fly was tied with a red wool body, ribbed with peacock herl but this was extremely fragile. The more modern form where these materials are reversed is much more robust.

Goat's Toe

The Zulu is regarded as a good fly in larger sizes (size 8) for salmon in the western lochs of Scotland. A version ribbed with pearl tinsel is also well regarded. Although it was originally regarded as a seatrout fly, the Blue Zulu is a very useful pattern for fresh run grilse on the rivers of the west coast of Ireland.

Zulu

Blue Zulu

The Dunkeld (opposite) is a Scottish fly that dates to about the middle of the 19th century. It has generally appeared in the form of both a salmon and a trout fly but it is not clear which was originally intended. I lean towards the view that it was a salmon fly which became simplified for trout fishing.

Whichever is true, it remains a very effective fly today. Apart from Scotland, the Dunkeld is widely used in Ireland and in many other trout fishing countries. It is normally recommended as a fly for use when the mid-summer doldrums are making life difficult. Peter O'Reilly recommends the fly for peat stained waters falling after a spate.

# European Featherwing Flies

He also recommends an underwing of red swan. As may be expected with a fly that has been around so long, there are many variations to the basic form. The loss of the palmered body hackle of orange cock and the jay over the orange hackle at the throat are the most common. The Golden Demon steelhead fly of the west coast of the USA is a very close derivative.

The Donegal Blue is used in both Ireland and Scotland. It is popular in the Western Isles for seatrout as well as salmon. In Ireland it is predominantly used in Donegal and on the loughs further south.

Dunkeld

Donegal Blue

The claret-bodied version of the Connemara Black (see page 26), known as the Connemara Claret, is of the same construction as the black-bodied fly and is ideally suited for end-of-season use. Claret based flies seem to come into their own at this time of year. For salmon fishing it is recommended in sizes 10 and 12 for use on deep pools on all spate rivers. Jungle cock eyes are optional.

The Bumbles are a series of Irish flies conceived by the great angler T.C. Kingsmill Moore. Since their inception they have increased in popularity and it is hard to imagine fishing for wild fish, whether brown trout, seatrout or salmon, on the loughs of Ireland without these flies. The Bumbles are also highly regarded in Scotland where they are widely used in the west and the islands. Of the flies illustrated overleaf the Golden Olive Bumble and the Claret Bumble are both original Kingsmill Moore tyings; the Leggy Claret Bumble is a Scottish derivative.

The Golden Olive Bumble is shown in its original form where the body hackle consists of a golden olive and a red game hackle wound together. Many now prefer to use a lighter, ginger shade of hackle instead of the red game.

The Claret Bumble is highly recommended towards the end of the season for both seatrout and salmon, the colour of the claret body being adjusted to suit conditions, a darker version being preferred for dull days.

Connemara Claret

 # European Featherwing Flies

The Leggy Claret Bumble comes from Scotland and is detailed in *Trout & Salmon Flies of Scotland* by Stan Headley. Stan notes that the Leggy Claret Bumble owes much to Stuart Leslie for its development over the years and that it is intended for use on wild, windswept days. Takes to this fly can be savage in these conditions.

Golden Olive Bumble

Claret Bumble

Leggy Claret Bumble

We have already seen the Grey Gosling and the next two patterns are variants of this fly. The Yellow Gosling is exactly the same in construction as the grey version and is used in very much the same circumstances. Goslings are extremely popular on Lough Melvin and are also used on loughs Conn and Mask for salmon.

The tying style of these flies can be altered by varying the amount of collar hackling. The more turns of hackle, the more the overhackle of mallard will stand out. Less turns of hackle will produce a much slimmer, nymph-like fly. Flies of this type can be seen as a kind of modified or exaggerated spider and are used throughout the world. The Spectral Spider, a steelhead fly from North America is a typical example.

Yellow Gosling

Gosling Variant - Rush

The second example illustrated is a variant from Cathal Rush which is particularly effective on loughs Melvin and Conn.

The Green Peter is the archetypal Irish lough fly for salmon and is particularly effective for grilse when fished as a bob fly. Peter O'Reilly considers the Green Peter to be the No. 1 lough fly and recommends a version without the body hackle as being the best for grilse.

Purcell's Peter is a derivative of the Green Peter which was devised by Eddie Purcell of

# European Featherwing Flies

Mullingar. Although it was primarily intended as a trout fly, it has had some real success with salmon, taking seven spring salmon one afternoon on Carrowmoor Lake in County Mayo. Any fly that will take seven salmon at any time, whatever the conditions that applied, is well worth taking seriously.

larger sizes for salmon fishing, both of these flies have the hackling in front of the wing, a practise that is extremely common on the east coast of Canada and which does seem to improve the performance of the fly, especially when tied in the larger sizes.

Despite its name, the Irishman's Claret is a Scottish fly that may be from the Mallard and Claret. Given that claret flies are extremely popular and effective in the west of Ireland and taking the name into account, it may well be however, that the Claret & Jay is the forerunner. The Irishman's Claret is recommended for the rivers of the west of Scotland.

The Dark Mackerel is another old, predominantly claret-coloured pattern. The fly was restored to modern use as a trout fly by David Leslie and then popularised by Bill Currie for use as a seatrout pattern. It now finds general use in the north and west of Scotland as a salmon fly. Hairwing versions of both these flies can be found in *Hairwing and Tube Flies for Salmon*. Tied in

The Lansdale Partridge (page 34) is a mayfly pattern which is regularly used on loughs Melvin and Arrow. Peter O'Reilly notes that it is usually fished as a point fly, where it is quite likely to take a salmon. The fly was a favourite of the late Canon Patrick Gargan who fished it with success for salmon on loughs Melvin, Furnace and Feeagh. It is unlikely that the salmon take it as a mayfly pattern as such; it is much more likely that the long, flowing hackles produce a lot of lively movement and transparency in the manner of other spider type flies (see Goslings on pages 28 and 32).

Canadian and steelhead fishermen from the USA seem much more inclined to use flies of this type than anglers in Europe. Maybe European

# European Featherwing Flies

anglers should try this type of fly more often for river fishing, rather than reserving their use solely for stillwater fishing on the lochs on Scotland and Ireland. It should be noted that the profile of these flies, with the collar hackling and long tails, is not a long way away from that of flies such as Ally's Shrimp, one of the world's most successful salmon flies over the last fifteen years.

body is little known in Scotland but is considered in Ireland to be a better fly than the silver bodied pattern, even if not so well-known. In Ireland it is generally used on the loughs rather than rivers. I think that either of these patterns could be well worth a try when low, clear water conditions make summer fishing difficult, particularly when there are fresh run grilse about.

Lansdale Partridge

Jungle Cock & Silver

Jacob's Ladder was originally a seatrout fly from Donegal but is now mainly used on the loughs of the west of Ireland. It is favoured for seatrout on the Delphi fishery but has also been effective for salmon on the Finlough. The general colouration is shared by many other successful flies, although the fact that the body is magenta rather than the more usual red may give it an edge.

The Kate McLaren was devised for use on Loch Hope in the north west of Scotland but has since spread widely and is now used all over Scotland and in the west of Ireland. The Kate McLaren is not a bright or impressive fly in the hand but is yet another example of a fly that, despite its nondescript appearance, succeeds for

Jacob's Ladder

Kate McLaren

The Jungle Cock & Silver is a general-purpose Scottish wet fly for seatrout and salmon. It makes a good summer fly when the water is low and clear. An Irish version with a black floss

all kinds of fish, from brown and rainbow trout to seatrout and salmon. A version with a tail of fluorescent yellow wool is also highly regarded when fished deep.

# European Featherwing Flies

The Kingsmill is another fly from the great Irish fisherman T.C. Kingsmill Moore. It is an all-round fly that will take brown trout, seatrout and salmon. The Kingsmill has general appeal at all times of the year but is at its best for salmon in low-water conditions.

Kingsmill

Whereas other flies from Kingsmill Moore, such as the Bumble series, were primarily designed for trout fishing, the Kingsmill was designed from the start to be a salmon and seatrout fly and still remains an extremely effective pattern which can be fished with confidence.

Red Arrow - Higgins

The Red Arrow was devised by Syl Higgins, a dentist from Longford in Ireland, as a lough trout fly. The body is tied in two halves, black seal's fur in front of red. When the rear body colour was changed from red to hot orange, the fly proved absolutely deadly for seatrout, and more than useful for salmon. The small jungle cock eyes were added by Peter O'Reilly. To me, this fly has all the hallmarks of a super little grilse pattern.

Burton

The Burton originated on the River Nith in Dumfriesshire as a salmon and seatrout fly. Today it is only used as a loch fly, particularly on Loch Lomond. Stan Headley notes that many of the patterns popular on Loch Lomond are particular to that loch and that many have an old fashioned look about them. This observation can certainly be applied to the Burton. Having said that, it still has the look of a fly that could be successful – the body colours are known to work and the dark hackle and wing offset the brighter body nicely. Maybe a fly that is worth giving a try more often?

Cinnamon & Gold

The Cinnamon & Gold is one of the really old flies that has never lost its effectiveness, even if it has not always been fashionable. Today it is still a must-have pattern for salmon on the Scottish lochs in the

# European Featherwing Flies

doldrum days of summer. Stan Headley notes that the fly is tied in an increasingly dark form the further north one goes. In larger sizes, the collar hackle tied in front of the wing is probably a better option.

The Grouse & Claret is one of a whole range of old grouse winged flies. The example shown is taken from *Trout & Salmon Flies of Scotland* by Stan Headley and again has the collar hackle in front of the wing. The wing in the example shown is of melanistic hen pheasant secondary feathers, rather than grouse. This is because of the difficulty of obtaining good quality, well marked grouse tail feathers and also because the hen pheasant is much more robust. The fly fits very well into the group of flies such as the Irishman's Claret and the Dark Mackerel (see page 33). The Grouse & Claret is a very good fly for the western lochs and is also recommended for Loch Lomond.

Stan Headley finds so appealing. Its resurgence is put down to the late Eddie Young's book *Fisher in the West*.

John Kennedy, the well-known angler from South Uist in the Western Isles, has devised several very well known and successful patterns for loch fishing. The Clan Chief is perhaps the best known of these flies and is very much in the tradition of Kingsmill Moore and the 'Bumble' series of flies. The Clan Chief is very often fished as the top dropper on a fly cast and is renowned for being very effective on wild and windy but grey days. Highly recommended, the Clan Chief is a fly that should always be in your fly box if you fish for salmon on the lochs of Scotland.

Grouse & Claret

Harold's Grouse & Claret

Clan Chief - Kennedy

Machair Claret - Kennedy

Harold's Grouse & Claret is a hackled fly that is another of the long-hackled, leggy patterns that

The Machair Claret is another John Kennedy pattern which shows a strong Irish influence. Palmered hackle flies have always been effective as bob flies when there is a good wave on the lochs and this fly maintains the tradition and also

# European Featherwing Flies

combines the dark claret and black colouration which seems so effective in the west of Scotland and Ireland.

The Ke-He is an Orkney Islands fly that was so named because it came about as a result of a collaboration between two anglers called Kemp and Heddle. The original fly had a hackle of ginger hen but for the Black Ke-He this is replaced by black. The Black Ke-He is generally considered to be a more effective pattern than the original and is a very effective pattern for both salmon and

The Loch Ordie is another fly which hails from the Orkney Isles. As well as being popular there, it is also well used in the west of Scotland. A darker variant which incorporates black hackles has now become more popular in Orkney itself. The Loch Ordie is a very simple fly consisting solely of wound hackles with no tail, body or wing.

The Gold Butcher (illustrated below) is a variant of the standard tying which has a black hackle. This variant comes from Ireland and is a useful fly for the Delphi and other western loughs.

Black Ke-He

Gold Butcher

Hardy's Gold Butcher

seatrout. The version with fluorescent wool and hot-orange dyed tippets for the tail is preferred for use in the late evening. Another variation with a hot orange collar hackle may also be preferred for a bright day when there is a peat stain to the water. Peacock herl bodies are quite common for loch flies in both Scotland and Ireland.

Loch Ordie

In Scotland the standard pattern is still found in occasional use for salmon on the western lochs.

Hardy's Gold Butcher is the pattern as delivered by the famous firm of Hardy. Whilst not as popular as it once was, it still has a reputation for finding bigger fish. Its use is normally confined to the lochs of the west of Scotland.

The Soldier Palmer has been known for many years as a consistently successful trout fly all over

# European Featherwing Flies

Fluorescent Soldier Palmer

The next group of flies are hackled shrimp flies that have all been publicized since Robert Gillespie and I published *Shrimp & Spey Flies for Salmon*. There are several shrimp flies that are called the Thunder Shrimp; the one shown below was described by Alexander Keachie in an article in the July/August

Thunder Shrimp

the United Kingdom. This fluorescent version is an extremely versatile fly and has a proven record for brown and rainbow trout as well as seatrout and is recommended as a good loch fly for salmon. Stan Headley recalls a day on Loch Fada, in South Uist, when a salmon took this fly with such savagery that he almost dropped the rod and ran.

The Delphi Silver is named after the Delphi fishery of south west Mayo in Ireland and is regarded as an excellent seatrout pattern. Although it is seen mainly as a seatrout fly it is in fact very

Delphi Silver

2001 issue of *Fly Fishing & Fly Tying*. The article in question dealt with the subject of fishing a two-fly cast with a top dropper, a technique which, whilst making the landing of a fish more difficult, certainly raises the odds of hooking one in the first place.

The Bladnoch Shrimp is another fly from Alexander Keachie and is named after the River Bladnoch where it was first used. The Bladnoch Shrimp shares a pearl tinsel body with the Thunder Shrimp, a feature also shared by Keachies's Krill, another most successful fly from the same

Bladnoch Shrimp - Keachie

similar to the Black & Silver Shrimp fly from Northern Ireland which is known to be a great fly for fresh-run grilse. The Delphi Silver, together with the Jungle Cock & Silver (see page 34) has the same kind of look about it and should be equally effective for summer grilse fishing. Well worth trying if water conditions are low and clear.

stable (see *Shrimp & Spey Flies for Salmon*). Alexander believes very strongly that a pearl body gives an iridescent sheen which closely imitates

# European Featherwing Flies

Black Boar - Walker

the appearance of living prey in the ocean. The Bladnoch Shrimp has been effective throughout the season but is at its best in water that has a slight peat tinge.

The Black Boar is a new shrimp pattern devised by Phill Walker in 2003. It uses Chinese boar bristles in the tail, a feature which was first introduced in the Pot Belly Pig fly (see page 18) and which has proved to be very effective. The Black Boar has since been used from spring to late autumn and has shown itself to be a good fly in all types of water conditions.

Nitro Shrimp - Moors

The Nitro Shrimp was devised by Frank Moors for use on the River Lune in northern England. Writing about this fly in the February 2005 issue of *Trout & Salmon*, he noted that the fly was specifically designed to be visible when the river ran with an odd kind of milky-coffee colour which occasionally occurred. The fly has indeed been successful in these conditions, but has also shown itself to be very effective in clear water as well. The tail of the fly is of golden pheasant breast feather dyed fluorescent red and in order not to lose the most colourful side of the feather, the fibres are not wound, as is usual with the Irish shrimp style, but are tied in around the fly in bunches with the best side outwards.

NessC - Sinclair

The River Ness that runs through the legendary Loch Ness is the home of the next fly. With its associations with the monster, it is no wonder that the name of the fly makes play of this. The fly is called the NessC (pronounced Nessie) and was the brainchild of John Sinclair who introduced the new fly in an article in the October 2003 issue of *Trout & Salmon*. The purple colour was chosen because of the fact that blood, when spilled underwater, appears to be purple. In the article, Sinclair noted the dearth of purple salmon flies in the UK, a fact that remains until the present day. This does not apply to steelhead flies – many successful purple patterns are to be found, not only in this book, but also in *Shrimp & Spey Flies for Salmon* and *Hairwing & Tube Flies for Salmon*. The NessC has

Silver Shrimp - Mackenzie

# European Featherwing Flies

been a prolific fly ever since its introduction and has proved to be the best fly for the last couple of seasons on the Ness Castle beat.

The Silver Shrimp is also a fly that comes from the River Ness. The fly is the work of local angler Graham Mackenzie. The Black Shrimp (see *Shrimp & Spey Flies for Salmon*) and the Silver Stoat have always been very popular on the Ness and this fly is a combination of the two. It is recommended for use from June onwards. A red-bodied version is probably a better bet towards the end of the season for resident fish.

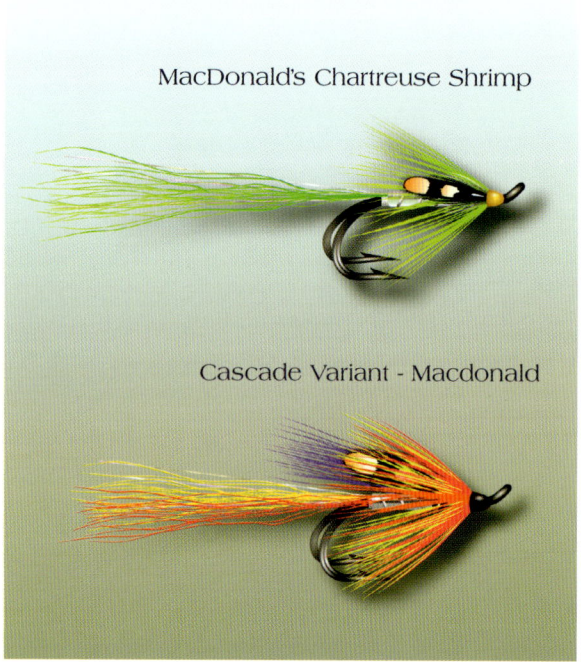

The next fly was also tied by Kenny MacDonald. The Chartreuse Shrimp is a bright little fly with a pearl body which is wound over an underbody of silver tinsel. The colour makes the fly suitable for low-water conditions, particularly when there is still a touch of colour remaining after a spate.

The Cascade Variant is a fly devised by Kenny Macdonald, Secretary of the Federation of Highland Angling Clubs who lives in Inverness and who has fished all over the highlands. The fly is a derivation of Alastair Gowan's Cascade (see *Shrimp & Spey Flies for Salmon*) and has proved to be particularly effective for fish that have settled into a pool. Hand lining the fly is also advised to help stimulate the fish. The jungle cock eyes, tied underneath the hackles are very important.

The Tailfire and Eany Tailfire are two flies from Michael Shortt from Ireland. Both these flies were based in part on Paddy Bonner's Shadow Shrimps (see *Shrimp & Spey Flies for Salmon*) in their design. The flies are tied on small trebles, sizes 10-14 and have proved equally at home in slower flows as well as streamy and heavier runs. The Tailfire (not to be confused with the fly from Michael Evans of the same name) was first tied in 1999 for summer fishing on the River Eany in Donegal. It was proved immediately successful, taking eight fish on its first day out, five to Michael and three for his father.

The lighter version, known as the Eany Tailfire was intended for fishing in falling spates still carrying a bit of colour. It has worked very well on the Lennon and Finn as well as proving itself on the Tay and Dee in Scotland.

# European Featherwing Flies

Black Snelda

German Snelda

Mike's Prawn - Evans

to kick the bucktail skirt into sinuous action. The German Snelda is a straightfoward colour variation, so named because it uses the colours of the German flag.

The next fly is from Michael Evans and is a variant of the Snelda, The fly is called Mike's Prawn and is a shrimp-style derivative of the Snelda which incorporates elements of the Francis fly which is also a standard for Icelandic waters.

Red Demon - Eadie

Copper King - Eadie

The next flies are all based on the Snelda an Icelandic fly which is very popular on the East Ranga river, as well as being successful in Russia and Scotland. The original Snelda is a plain black fly that relies very much on its shape for its success. The word Snelda is Icelandic for a dancing girl and that is what characterises these flies. The Snelda is designed to drift tail down, allowing the current

Glasgow Rangers - MacAffer

The isle of Islay is perhaps more famous for its whisky than for its fishing – its seven distilleries produce some of the best, and certainly most distinctive, malt whiskys in the world. The River Laggan is a small spate river that runs through the middle of the island and is the home water of Calum MacAffer. Glasgow Rangers is one of his fly patterns, specially devised for the peaty water and named after his favourite football team.

The next two flies come from the River Thurso in the north of Scotland and are the work of John Eadie, a gillie on the Thurso in the 1960s and 70s. Flies for the Thurso have always tended to be colourful and these two patterns are no exception.

# European Featherwing Flies

Black Gorbenmac Ranger - Mackenzie

Black & Gold Gorbenmac Ranger - Mackenzie

Green Gorbenmac Ranger - Mackenzie

he next group of flies are the work of that excellent fly dresser and all-round gentleman, Gordon Mackenzie of Redcastle. The flies started life as trout flies and the salmon flies were a development of them.

The precursor, known as the Gorbenmac, was devised in 1954 for fishing the streams of the Amatola mountains in South Africa. Another fly which also had a great influence on the development of the salmon patterns was the Durham Ranger which, in a trout version, was very popular in South Africa in the 1950s and 60s. Gordon has always been very keen on flies with peacock herl in their bodies, a tendency he puts down to the fact that the very first of his own flies that he caught a trout with was an Alder.

In the case of the Gorbenmac salmon flies, the herl is used as a ribbing, although more recently Gordon has been experimenting with peacock Lite Brite dubbing. Gordon believes the sheen and iridescence of peacock herl is attractive to all migratory fish and that it is therefore worth accepting that the ribbing itself is not the most robust.

The Gorbenmac salmon flies have developed into two groups: the Gorbenmacs, which are conventionally winged; and the Gorbenmac Rangers which are derived from the Durham Ranger and use the winging style typical of this fly.

There are five flies in the Gorbenmac range – The Red, Green, Black, Orange and Purple. All these flies share the same construction: a tail of golden pheasant tippet and topping which is dyed to match the body, a tag which is colour-matched to the body, a rib of peacock herl, a dyed or natural black peacock wing with a topping dyed to match the body over and a blue jay throat hackle.

The Gobenmac Rangers share many features of the Gorbenmac flies, particularly the dyed components but the winging follows that of the classic Durham Ranger. Winging of this style is in no way lacking mobility, the only drawback lies in the not-inconsiderable cost of the jungle cock, four feathers per fly. There are three flies in this series – Black, Black & Gold, and Green.

In both series of flies, the colour-coded dyeing adds considerably to the look of the flies, producing an overall sense of oneness and well thought-out design. All these flies are tied on Bartleet or Salar single or low-water double hooks.

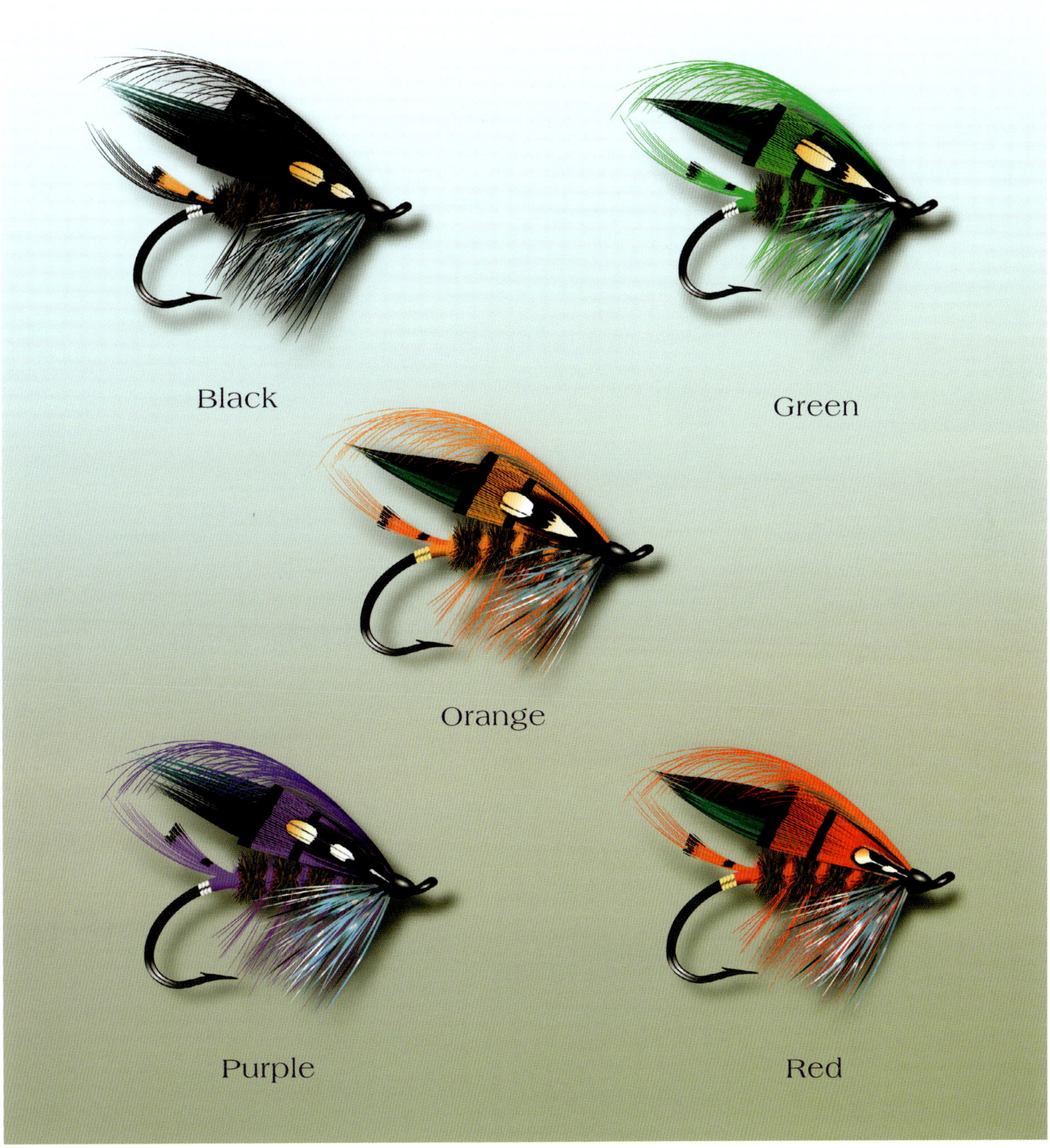

# European Featherwing Flies

Black

Green

Orange

Purple

Red

Plate 2. Gorbenmac Salmon Flies - Gordon Mackenzie of Redcastle

# European Featherwing Flies

## ICELAND & SCANDINAVIA

Modern Scandinavian fly design is dominated by the fatback tube flies, such as the Templedog, which were first introduced in the 1970s by tyers such as Haken Norling and Mikael Frodin. So heavy has this emphasis been that one can be forgiven for thinking that all Scandinavian flies are six inches long and of eye-catching colours. There is, however, much more subtlety to Scandinavian fly design. Tyers such as Ismo Saastamoinen, the Russian Jurij Shumakov, Nestor Dupo and others demonstrate that superb flies in a more traditional vein are still devised and produced and are still very effective indeed.

Silver Wilkinson Spey

The Silver Wilkinson Spey is a good example of a modern form of an old fly. Apart from the extra long Spey hackles, the general appearance of the original fly has been maintained. The simple Spey-style winging is of bronze Mallard. This fly is very similar to a wingless Spey that I was given at the British Fly Fair and may in fact be the winged version of that fly.

The Crosfield is an old Icelandic fly which was devised by Ernest Crosfield in the early part of the 20th century. There seems to be a couple of variations to the dressing, the most common of which is that the wing may be changed from teal to darker mallard. Another variant has a wing of bronze mallard veiled with teal. Low-water tyings have the hackle behind the wing as a beard.

By any other name this fly could also be the Silver Blue, a classic seatrout fly, a fact that leads one to believe that the Crosfield might well be worth a try for steelhead

Crosfield

The Blue Sapphire is said by Bates to be one of the few Icelandic flies that is not derived from a British classic. The fly illustrated below is taken from *Atlantic Salmon Flies & Fishing*. Bates also notes that this fly was the favourite of the crooner Bing Crosby when he fished in Iceland. In slightly simplified form, perhaps with a blue underwing veiled by a mallard overwing, this fly could still be highly effective today

The next flies in this section (opposite) are from Ismo Saastamoinen, a professional fly tyer from Sweden. The Dawn series of flies were documented in *Hairwing & Tube Flies for Salmon* but, because the wings are a hybrid of both hair and featherwing, they are equally at home here.

There are seven flies in this beautifully elegant series to cover a wide range of water colour conditions. All of these flies have an underwing

Blue Sapphire

 # European Featherwing Flies

Dawn

Black Dawn

Yellow Dawn

Thunder Dawn

Green Dawn

Blue Dawn

Red Dawn

Plate 3. The Dawn Series of flies from Iso Saastamoinen

# European Featherwing Flies

consisting of two hackles set back to back with a fox hair overwing. This combination of hair and feather is not all that common but further examples can be found amongst the steelhead flies of north-western U.S.A. The idea of winging with hackle tips actually has much to recommend it – it provides a veil of colour with no bulk, keeps the head small and in no way reduces the mobility of the fly, indeed it may well enhance it. Many further examples of hackle tip winging are to be found amongst the flies of Sydney Glasso and others.

favourite pattern in Scotland. The fly has been around a long time, at least since the beginning of the 20th century, but never seems to appear on the lists of the most successful flies. It might just be that, being small and dark, it was one of those flies which always had its share of success without ever being seen as a killer. Exactly those characteristics noted above, mean that it will still perform well in the right conditions today. Try it in low, clear water in summer for fresh-run grilse.

Dream - Saastamoinen

Heggeli - Caspari

The Dream is another fly from Ismo Saastamoinen in the same vein as the Dawn series. Hackle tip underwinging is again a feature of this fly which has certainly been proved to be effective, having taken fish in Norway, Finland and Scotland as well as Sweden.

The Heggeli is a Norwegian fly with salmon, sea-trout and brown trout to its credit. It was originally devised in the 1960s by Bernhard Caspari for use on the Heggeli lakes and river in the Nordmark, north of Oslo but has since caught many thousands of fish all over Norway.

Sweep

Tana

The Sweep was originally a British fly, although Bates notes, incorrectly as far as I can tell, that it was a

The Tana is another Norwegian fly, named after the River Tana in northern Norway which forms the border with Finland. The subdued brown, yellow and white colours of this fly are a marked contrast to many

# European Featherwing Flies

of the flies from Norway which tend to have very bright colours indeed. The Tana is bright but in a different way and it is highly recommended for summer fishing in the far north when there is no night at all in high summer. The overall impression of this fly is very reminiscent of the Dusty Miller, Mar Lodge and the Silver Grey – all have a sparkling, light touch to them, without being garish – ideally suited to gin-clear water.

The Laerdal was devised by the famous Norwegian fly tyer Olaf Olsen and is named after the River Laerdal. The overall effect of this fly is also fairly subdued

Laerdal - Olsen

but it is slightly darker than the Tana. The Laerdal is recommended for use on days of changeable light and also for the evening in fading light.

Peer Gynt - Sand

Peer Gynt was devised in 1963 by John Sand of Norway and was included by Bates in *Atlantic Salmon Flies & Fishing* and by John Veniard in *A Further Guide to Fly Dressing*, together with a wide range of other Sand patterns.

Many of these featherwing patterns, including the Peer Gynt, look fairly subdued compared to the eye-catching fatback hairwings that we have come to associate with modern Scandinavian fishing. They should not be ignored however – these flies formed the backbone of the patterns that enabled anglers such as Sand, Børre Pettersen, Olaf Olsen and others to make huge catches of salmon over the years. Whilst the new style flies certainly have advantages in certain conditions, neither they, nor any other fly style, are a panacea for all conditions and the older style flies still have their place in the fly box.

Valdum - Pettersen

Valdum is a Børre Pettersen pattern dating from 1984 which is named after a beat on the River Gaula. Since its introduction it has become a general purpose pattern which has proved effective at all times of the year and in all kinds of water conditions. Apart from salmon it has also been effective for seatrout – not

Sheriff - Sand

47

# European Featherwing Flies

surprising when you look at the colours – black and silver have always been popular for seatrout flies, particularly in Wales.

The Sheriff (previous page) is another pattern from John Sand. The predominantly dark wing and forebody contrast nicely with the gold rear body and yellow hackle. This pretty pattern has just enough sparkle to make it noticeable without being too garish. It looks to me as if it could be a good summer grilse pattern when tied in small sizes.

Gullnøkk - Steen

The Gullnøkk is a pattern from Torgeir Steen which is very similar indeed to the Sheriff from John Sand. Indeed it is so similar that it is surely a variant of the Sheriff. However it was arrived at, it is noted in *A Guide to Salmon Flies* by Buckland and Oglesby as being Børre Pettersen's favourite fly for peat stained water conditions.

The Golden Mallard is another of John Sand's patterns and again one cannot help but note more than a passing resemblance to both Gullnøkk and the Sheriff.

Golden Mallard - Sand

It would seem that the golden rear body combined with a black front body is obviously a most effective combination for Norwegian rivers. It surely can't be coincidence that the colour theme and also the general construction is repeated on all three flies.

The following two patterns are both called Namsen after the Norwegian river of that name, but they are so different that it is clear that at some time in the past two or more patterns were confused.

The first pattern, with the white wing, is illustrated by Bates although he does not give a tying recipe – I have taken the details from John Veniard's *Further Guide to Fly Dressing* which has the pattern as given by John Sand.

The second fly is also shown by Bates but in this case he does give a dressing. The fly is illustrated as per the details given to Bates by Yngvar Kaldal of Oslo who says that it is the most popular version. There is also a third dressing given by Bates which he has taken from Jones' *Guide to Norway & Salmon Fishers Pocket Companion* which was first published in London in 1848.

Of the two flies, I prefer the white winged version. It is simpler but seems better balanced and I think it would be effective at dusk – maybe one for the Tweed

Namsen #1

Namsen #2

48

# European Featherwing Flies

fishers, many of whom, like a bit of white in a fly for evening use (see Whitewing, page 22).

The Ola and the Otteson are two Norwegian flies that are to be found in John Veniard's book as well as Bates' *The Art of the Atlantic Salmon Fly*. According to Veniard these patterns, amongst others, were passed to him by John Sand. This does not, however, confirm that they originated with Sands, although it seems highly probable.

The colouring is subdued, but this simply means that this fly joins a large group of very effective flies that do not rely on bright colours for their success. There is no doubt that the modern trend in salmon flies is for more and brighter colours, Despite this, there are so many flies that seem to be effective, despite the fact that they have very nondescript colours – one can only draw the conclusion that some of the more natural colours have an appeal for salmon in a way that we simply do not understand.

Ola

Spitfire

Ottesen

Vi Menn Flua is a Norwegian fly named after a weekly magazine. The fly was designed by Olaf Olsen in 1977 and since then it has become a widely-used fly. It has the reputation of being at its

Vi Menn Flua - Olsen

The Spitfire is a Norwegian hackle fly which is to be found in John Veniard's book. Hackle flies do not seem to be very common in Scandinavia but this is one of the few exceptions. The general look of the fly is very reminiscent of a large number of Irish hackled flies.

# European Featherwing Flies

best when there is a bit of colour in the water. The construction of the fly should be familiar by now with the hackling restricted to the front half of the body.

Pålsbu

The Pålsbu is an old Norwegian trout pattern that has been successfully adapted for salmon. It is particularly effective for cock fish when the rivers are low and warm in summer. For the fly to be at its most effective, the body should be bulky, using at least five strands of bronze peacock herl.

Em-Te-Flugor

The Em-Te-Flugor is a hybrid winged fly which is to be found in John Veniard's *A Further Guide to Fly Dressing*. The body is of peacock herl in a similar vein to the Pålsbu and the hackle tip wings are of furnace cock. The whole fly gives quite a sombre impression but it has been around for a long time so has proved its effectiveness.

Børre Flua - Pettersen

The Børre Flua is a fly from Børre Pettersen. The colours were said to have been developed during some experiments to establish how salmon see colours. Whatever the reasons, the end effect is a dark fly, relieved by just a splash of colour at the back as an aiming point. Flies such as this have been consistently successful over the years and this fly would surely be no exception. This is a fly which is perhaps well suited for use in ultra-clear water conditions.

# North American Featherwing & Hackle Flies

he history of native featherwing flies in North America contrasts strongly with that of the United Kingdom and Ireland. Until the beginning of the 20th century, the flies in use on the east coast of the USA and Canada were basically a sub-set of the classic patterns used in the United Kingdom.

Whilst there are many examples of native North American patterns emerging, very few of these were of the complex, mixed and built-wing types which were the norm in Europe.

Instead, the flies developed were much more of the simple strip-winged types that later became the norm in Europe. Another example of the difference in the emphasis of fly design is illustrated by the widespread use of streamer flies. These flies were very popular indeed all along the east coast and are still used to this day. Some of this development may have had to do with the fact that a lot of fishing was done for so called 'black fish' – that is what in Europe would be called well mended kelts. These fish are extremely vulnerable to long-bodied lures, possibly because their feeding habits are returning strongly as they make their way back out to sea. Land-locked salmon, common on the lakes of the eastern USA, were also susceptible to these lures and thus was built up a tradition that continues to this day.

An extensive overview of many of the early North American featherwing patterns is to be found in *Atlantic Salmon Flies & Fishing* by Joseph D. Bates. There a few flydressers who had a considerable influence on the development of the North American patterns: among them the name of Ira Gruber stands out. He was

51

responsible for many of the patterns that are known today and his influence on the style of North American flies continues. His preference for small, simply constructed flies, particularly for low water summer fishing, was extremely influential and still has echoes today.

The general conformation of the typical eastern fly with its cigar-shaped body and short, body-hugging wing owes much to Gruber. Most of Gruber's flies were developed in the period from 1925 to 1945. Bert Miner of Doaktown, New Brunswick, was another flydresser who also a had a major influence. Flies such as the Blackville and the Down-Easter are still widely known and have spawned a wide range of derivatives.

On the west coast, the steelhead fisheries have a lot shorter history and the story there begins with simple strip-winged flies. In the USA anglers such as Jim Prey and Van Zandt designed patterns for the Eel and Rogue Rivers whilst north in British Columbia the names of General Noel Money, Roderick Haig-Brown, Tom Brayshaw and others were associated with the development of the steelhead fly. Many of the flies that were devised by these anglers are still in use today.

In more modern times the mantle of development was taken on by the legendary Syd Glasso who re-invented the Spey fly and ensured its continuing part in steelhead fishing history. The Glasso legacy is still extremely strong and the tradition is carried on by flydressers such as Harry Lemire, Bob Ververka, Dave McNeese and Bill McMillan.

Among the steelhead anglers of the east coast, hairwing flies have never assumed the dominance over featherwings that is so typical of the Atlantic salmon fisheries of the east coast of America and Europe. Much of this is due to the influence of Syd Glasso and his successors. Whilst he certainly didn't invent the use of hackle tips for winging, he was undoubtedly responsible for its widespread use among steelhead flydressers.

Hackle flies have always had a strong following among the steelhead anglers and this continues today. Spider-type flies, with long flowing hackles, are popular and patterns such as the Spade and Skunk ensure that the trend continues.

## ATLANTIC SALMON FLIES

The first flies illustrated are taken from the streamer flies that we mentioned earlier. The fact that at least ten featherwing streamers are shown in *Flies: The Best One Thousand* published in 1992 by Randle Stetzer shows that there are still a small band of enthusiasts keeping these flies alive.

The Cains River Streamers are a group of over a dozen flies which first appeared in the 1920s. Many of them are no longer used but the following two patterns are listed in *Flies for Atlantic Salmon* by Stewart & Allen and still find a use today.

The Cains River Silver Doctor is a derivation of the classic Silver Doctor fly but would be much more reminiscent of the original if the head was red. It remains, however, a most attractive-looking pattern.

Cains River Scotch Lassie

Cains River Silver Doctor

# North American Featherwing Flies

The Cascapedia is a much more modern fly which was designed by Marc Leblanc. The fly was devised to counteract the high water conditions often found on the Petite Cascapedia in the spring. It is usually fished in large sizes up to a 2/0.

Cascapedia - Leblanc

The Grey Ghost is probably the most famous of all streamer patterns. First tied by Carrie Stevens of Maine in 1924 as a smelt imitation, the Grey Ghost was primarily designed for land-locked salmon but it has always had its fans as an Atlantic salmon fly. Stevens was formerly a milliner and he did not tie flies in the conventional sense; the feathers were glued together in groups and then finally all mounted together on the hook.

Grey Ghost - Stevens

The Chaleur Bay Smelt is another Marc Leblanc pattern which was devised in 1983. It is intended to imitate the smelt of the Bay of Chaleur which run the south coast rivers of the Gaspé in early summer. It is not dissimilar to Carrie Stevens' Grey Ghost shown above.

Chaleur Bay Smelt - Leblanc

The Northeast Smelt was created in 1997 by Jack Ripley to imitate the smelts that enter the rivers flowing into the Northumberland Straight. It was effective right from the start and in its first year accounted for nineteen fish. Many of the most effective fish imitations use grizzle hackles as winging. Streamer flies have never been very popular for salmon fishing in the United Kingdom, although there is a steady following for this type of fly for seatrout. There is no doubt that they can be very effective and it may be that some patterns are beginning to stage a comeback (see the Sandeel Streamer on page 62 of *Hairwing and Tube Flies for Salmon*).

Northeast Smelt - Ripley

The Fiery Brown Streamer (overleaf) is another pattern included in the *Best One Thousand Flies*. It provides an interesting contrast to the more conventional Fiery Brown illustrated on page 16 of the History chapter. The original Fiery Brown was generally considered to be an autumn pattern,

53

# North American Featherwing Flies

although Peter O'Reilly thinks that it is just as likely to take fish in the spring in Ireland.

Fiery Brown Streamer

The Green Beauty is another old Carrie Stevens pattern, again primarily a landlocked salmon fly but one that has had some success with Atlantic salmon on the east coast rivers.

Green Beauty - Stevens

The next flies are some of the earliest named patterns from the east coast. One or two of these flies date to around 1900 but most were devised between 1920 and 1950. Whilst it is true that many of these patterns see only the occasional outing at the present time, there is no doubt that they would all catch fish, given a try at the right time.

Abe Munn was a guide on the Miramichi river in the early 1920s and the Abe Munn Killer dates from this period. According to Bates, the fly became famous after it was described in an article in *Fortune* in June 1948. There is also a little known variant of this pattern called the Abe Munn Upriver – this is an identical fly except for the wing which is changed from oak turkey to birch partridge. Bates thinks that this was probably due to the fact that Munn could not always obtain oak turkey feathers. The variation would seem to make little difference to the fly.

Abe Munn Killer

The Night Hawk is even earlier than the Abe Munn Killer, dating back to around 1900. The fly was devised by the architect Stanford White for use on the Restigouche. The red butt and head, together with the silver body, make this pattern a close relative of the Silver Doctor on which it was very possibly modelled. It is one of the patterns that has stood the test of time and is still in use nearly 100 years after its conception.

Night Hawk - White

The Black Hawk is an Ira Gruber pattern which was specifically designed for the Big Hole Brook Pool, near Doaktown, on the Miramichi River. This pool was famous for the large number

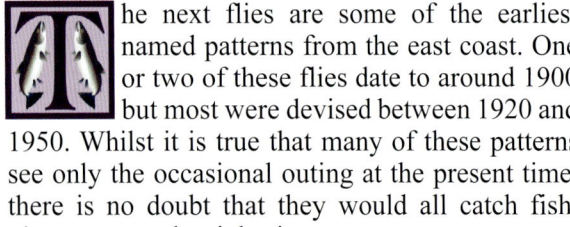

# North American Featherwing Flies

of fish that took up residence there in the summer months. The fly is a typical summer pattern that is not too startling for the fish. It is recommended in small sizes down to a size 12.

*Black Hawk - Gruber*

The Nipisiguit Grey was conceived for the river of the same name in about 1927 according to Joseph Bates. He also gives the originator as probably being D. A. Lapointe of New Brunswick. The dressing given by Bates is fairly simple, although he notes that in the larger sizes the wing may be dressed in a more complex manner. Poul Jorgensen gives a fully dressed version of the fly in *Salmon Flies: Their Character Style & Dressing*. In its hairwing form the Nipisiguit Grey is rather like the Grey Rat.

*Nipisiguit Grey - Lapointe*

The Oriole, devised around 1930 by Ira Gruber, is probably his best known pattern. It is still widely used, particularly on the Miramichi system and is still effective. The wing of the Oriole is dyed yellow and it does seem that yellow and green flies are especially popular on the Miramichi. The Oriole, in common with many of these early patterns, has a cleanness and economy of design about it. In *The Art of the Atlantic Salmon Fly* by Judith Dunham, published in 1991, Jerry Doak bemoans the fact that modern flies have lost this economy and have become, in his words 'flamboyant, overhackled and overdressed'.

*Oriole - Gruber*

The Baron is another of Gruber's patterns and was based on the old British classic fly of the same name. The silver, black and red colours of this fly represent one of the classic combinations that have proved to be extremely effective over the years. This is a pretty little fly which I am sure would find favour on a few Scottish rivers.

*Baron - Gruber*

The Reliable (overleaf) is probably second only to the Oriole as one of Ira Gruber's best known and most widely used flies. The Reliable is one of a long line of black bodied flies with a yellow butt, a combination that has always been successful. It

# North American Featherwing Flies

Reliable - Gruber

was named the Reliable because it was of proven effectiveness throughout the season.

The Blackville was created in about 1945 by Bert Miner of Doaktown, New Brunswick. Bates considers the Blackville to be a very important fly in Canadian fly development. Certainly a wide range of variants seem to trace their ancestry back to this fly. Bates also thought that the Blackville itself was an adaptation of the classic Dusty Miller and there is no doubt that, apart from the simple wing, it shares the same general colouration.

Blackville - Miner

Professor

The Professor is another early pattern that bears a close resemblance to the Abe Munn Killer. The fly was adapted from an old trout pattern which is no longer in use. The salmon fly remains a useful pattern. Bates notes that red feather sections are occasionally used for the tail instead of golden pheasant topping.

The next couple of flies are more like classics in the sense that they have many of the attributes of the fully dressed flies of the 19th century.

The Lady Amherst is a handsome American classic that was devised by George Bonbright in 1925. It has always been seen as an early season pattern and whilst it is more commonly used as a hairwing today, the featherwing version still sees the occasional outing. In heavy water conditions, after a spate, the featherwing with its stiffer, vertically aligned wing, is probably more effective than the hairwing. The tippet feathers of the Amherst pheasant, from which the fly takes its name, are not nearly so often used as the ubiquitous golden pheasant.

Lady Amherst - Bonbright

The Bastard Dose is a simplified version of the classic Black Dose. The fly is similar in just about every respect apart from the wing that is reduced to teal strips over a pair of golden pheasant tippet feathers mounted back-to-back. Bates says that this pattern is also a simplified version of the Canadian Black Dose which he then describes as have a black tag and a black seal's fur body with a black throat hackle. Bates also lists a reduced Black

# North American Featherwing Flies

Dose which again has a black throat hackle and a completely black body with a black wing. I have to say that these all black flies don't sound much like the classic Black Dose to me – if there are any bastards around, I think it is these. Whatever the antecedents, however, the Black Dose and its variants have always been popular throughout Canada and remain so to this day.

Bastard Dose

The Durham Ranger is one of the classic British flies dating to around the middle of the 19th century. Although the fly is British I have included it in the North American section because it is still popular. Kelson attributes the Durham Ranger to James Wright but a Mr William Henderson who lived in the city of Durham seems a more likely candidate. The winging style of the Durham Ranger with its golden pheasant tippet has remained popular and is still used for new fly designs

Durham Ranger

The next flies are very similar to the foregoing patterns in that they are very much in the classic mould although they are in fact quite recent designs.

Lamqui is a new design in the classic vein from Daniel Dufour which was named after his hometown. It has proved to be very successful having taken many fish on the Matane and Matepedia rivers.

Lamqui - Dufour

The Blue Sandy is a modified Spey-style fly designed by Marc Leblanc. It should be noted that many of the flies that are now known generically as Spey flies are in fact more like the Dee flies rather than their cousins. The extremely long hackles, formerly made of heron, are much more diagnostic of Dee flies than Spey flies which were often hackled with Spey cock. All these flies are extremely effective in light flows where the long hackles respond to every whisper of water movement.

Blue Sandy - Leblanc

# North American Featherwing Flies

Denise is another Marc Leblanc pattern. Very much in the style of the Durham Ranger and Lady Amherst, it is intended for use on the Gaspé rivers for the large salmon that run in the early part of the season.

Denise - Leblanc

The Crimson Glory is another fly which uses golden pheasant tippet feathers as a wing. In this case they are dyed crimson. The fly was designed by a New York angler named Herbert Howard in 1925. According to Bates the fly was successful in Quebec and Newfoundland as well as in Norway.

Crimson Glory - Howard

The Lanctôt is a simpler fly which was devised in 1920 by Ivers Adams of the Moisie Salmon Club. It is named after Charles Lanctôt who was a club member. There are various versions of this fly but the one illustrated shows the most popular variation on the Moisie river.

Lanctôt - Adams

The Black Fairy is one of the very simple old classic salmon flies from Scotland. It has certainly been around for a long time because both Hale and Hardy have it in their books. Such a simple pattern in black with just a touch of colour at the rear, cannot help but be effective. In Canada it is still seen on the rivers although it has been overshadowed to some extent by the Black Bear with a yellow butt which shares the same basic colouration.

Black Fairy

Closely related to the Black Fairy, the Brown Fairy is another old Scottish pattern that is far more widely used in North America than it is in its home country. Bates notes that it is very popular on the Miramichi and that the Brown Bomber from Joe Aucoin is very similar, but with a hairwing of red squirrel hair. A black ostrich herl butt is sometimes added to the fly.

As we saw in the History chapter, the herl-winged flies form a small group. The Alexandra is probably the most famous herl-winged fly and, over

# North American Featherwing Flies

Brown Fairy

the years, has been used for brown trout, rainbow trout, steelhead, seatrout and salmon fishing. Its reputation has see-sawed over the years – at one time it was banned in Scotland because it was held to be too effective. In more recent times in Europe its use as a trout fly has declined but, curiously, it has gained a larger following for seatrout fishing. Peacock sword fibres seem so attractive to anglers that it doesn't seem hard to believe that they have the same fascination for fish.

Alexandra

Darbee's Spate Fly was devised in 1946 by Harry Darbee of Livingston Manor, New York. As the name suggests it was designed for the high water conditions that often occur in the autumn on the Magaree River in Nova Scotia. The fly actually has a hybrid wing as there is an underwing of brown bucktail. However it is the barred wood duck flank that forms the most important feature and gives the fly the high visibility necessary for the conditions.

The Neptune was created in 1982 by Yvon Gendon of Neptune Flies in Quebec. The Neptune is a fly for all seasons: it is effective at all times of the year and in all water conditions. The Neptune,

Darbee's Spate Fly

together with its hairwinged brother, have been responsible for some remarkable catches in Quebec and New Brunswick. The full, guinea fowl hackle seems to be important to the success of this fly, a feature that has been noted on other occasions and other flies.

Neptune - Gendon

The March Brown (overleaf) is one of the oldest of all the flies presented in this book. Its origins are lost in history but it, or something very similar, has been around since the 18th century. The original fly was probably first used for trout fishing but with its nondescript, natural colours it would be effective for all freshwater game fish. According to Stewart and Allen it was one of the flies favoured

# North American Featherwing Flies

by Harry Darbee for use on the Margaree River. Bates has a copper-bodied variant in his book which I have also illustrated below. Bates suggests that it was the forerunner of the Copper Killer which became very widely used. Silver and gold bodied versions also exist and are useful flies for salmon fishing on the lochs of Scotland. As the name suggests, the original fly was an imitation of an early hatching ephemerid. The fact that the March Brown imitates an actual fly probably has no bearing at all on its success with salmon. Far more likely, the natural colours do not frighten fish and thus the fly is taken with confidence.

ne of the success stories of the featherwing flies over the last thirty years has been that of the Spey and Dee type flies. When the use of most other types of featherwings has been steadily decreasing, the Speys have shown a marked resurgence in their popularity. In North America much of this is due to the influence of the steelhead fisheries of the west coast and to that of flydressers such as Syd Glasso, Dave McNeese and others.

March Brown

Copper March Brown

Mitchell

If the March Brown is one of the oldest patterns from the United Kingdom, then the Mitchell is one of the oldest from North America. The fly was conceived by Archibald Mitchell of Connecticut in 1887 for use on the Penobscot River in Maine USA. The most unusual feature of this fly is the second tag and butt in front of the usual tag, tail and butt. The colours of this fly, predominantly yellow and black with a touch of red, have always been effective and the long lifetime of this fly only serves to prove the point.

The following flies are a mixture of traditional with modern patterns. The modern flies are perhaps not quite the same as the traditional flies from Scotland but they retain many of the most important features, particularly the long, flowing body hackles. Most importantly, whatever the differences in detail, they retain the overall feel and philosophy of the original flies. Whilst some of the more modern patterns feature bright colours, the Spey flies rely on the movement and mobility of the hackles for their effectiveness. Although it is said that they were originally intended for fishing fast flowing waters, they are also killers in light currents.

The Catch-A-Me-Lodge is the work of Dave Goulet, owner of the Classic & Custom Fly Shop in New Hartford, Connecticut. Although the fly is tied in the Spey style, the set of the wings which are splayed, scissor fashion, is much more in the Dee fly tradition. The colours used are very much in the modern idiom, the fluorescent green tag being one of the most common features of recent fly designs.

# North American Featherwing Flies

Catch-A-Me-Lodge - Goulet

The Heron series of Spey flies are among the original Scottish patterns which date from the early part of the 19th century. Both the Black and Grey Herons are listed by Knox in his book *Autumns on the Spey* published in 1872, although it should be said that they were old flies even then.

Black Heron

Grey Heron

The Mickey Spey was devised by Joel Sampson of Halifax to retain the colours of the Mickey Finn whilst adding the mobility of the long Spey hackle. The Mickey Finn has been around a long time and is still a most useful pattern. In addition to the Atlantic salmon fisheries of the east coast, the Mickey Finn has also travelled to the steelhead fisheries of the west coast.

Mickey Spey - Sampson

The Lady Caroline is one of the most widely used of the classic Spey flies. It has general currency throughout the east coast fisheries and is also popular in Scandinavia. Steelhead anglers also rate the Lady Caroline very highly and it is one of Trey Combes' favourite flies for smooth, gently flowing water.

Lady Caroline

The next flies (overleaf) are all Syd Glasso patterns that were originally intended for steelhead. All of these flies have all the attributes necessary to make them very effective for Atlantic salmon. Any east coast angler who wishes to try a Spey-style fly could do worse than turn to these patterns.

# North American Featherwing Flies

| | |
|---|---|
| Brown Heron | Sol Duc Spey |
| Orange Heron | Courtesan |
| Gold Heron | Silver Heron |

Plate 4 - Sydney Glasso Spey Flies

As can be seen from the illustration above, several of the Glasso Speys use hackle tips as winging. This technique, which was pioneered by Glasso, gives a degree of mobility much greater than that offered by normal feather slip-wings. Whilst the effect in the hand is slightly different to the normal wing set using feather slips, once the fly is in the water the hackle tips slick back down over the body. As the pull on the fly varies with the current, so the wings flex attractively.

# North American Featherwing Flies

Black Skagit Spey

Orange Skagit Spey

White Skagit Spey

Yellow Skagit Spey

Yellow Eagle

Grey Eagle

Plate 5 - Skagit Speys and Eagles

The Black Eagle belongs to a select group of specialised flies that had their origin on the River Dee in Scotland. These flies were the original Marabou flies although the feather came from the lower legs of eagles, a material that was hard to obtain even in those less-enlightened times. Ironically the modern turkey marabou, one of the most easily-obtained and cheapest feathers

# North American Featherwing Flies

available today is a perfect substitute. The original Yellow and Grey Eagles are illustrated in Plate 5.

The Skagit Spey flies were devised by John Farrar during the years that he guided on the Skagit River on the west coast of the USA. Although these flies were designed with steelhead in mind, they fit perfectly into the Eagle series. With the long marabou hackle providing movement in even the merest whisper of current, these flies are sure to be extremely effective when fished in smooth water and light currents.

Black Eagle

The Black Eagle is not one of the original flies but is a modern variant that is given in Poul Jorgensen's book. The teal throat is not part of the details given by Jorgensen but it is diagnostic of the early eagle flies and I consider that it improves the pattern.

Matepedia Spey

The Matepedia Spey is another fly which utilises the fluorescent chartreuse tag that has become so common on modern flies from the east coast. It is highly regarded on the Matepedia River.

The last two flies in this section are slightly modernized versions of two classic old Scottish flies from Steve Gobin.

The Tartan is a fly from the River Dee which dates back to the first half of the 19th century. The wings are tied in typical Dee style – set low and splayed out scissor fashion. The hackling over the front third of the body is of grey heron but blue-grey schlappen would make an acceptable substitute if heron cannot be obtained.

The Purple King is from the River Spey and is one of the original Spey flies that was hackled with Spey cock, rather than heron. In this version black schlappen is used although silver badger dyed to a slate blue-grey colour would be true to the original. The wing of bronze mallard is set in the traditional Spey manner, the feathers hooded over the body like the keel of an upturned boat.

Tartan

Purple King

# North American Featherwing Flies

pider-style patterns have never been the most popular flies for salmon fishing which is rather curious because the few that are used are very effective indeed. They provide a tremendous amount of mobility in the water and are ideally suited to low water conditions. When working in the current, the long hackles are slicked back over the body giving a veiled effect that provides a translucent look to the fly that is very appealing to the fish.

The Chartreuse Spider is a design from Brian Sturrock that has been very successful on the Matepedia River. The fly was included by Paul Marriner in *Modern Atlantic Salmon Flies*.

Chartreuse Spider

The Green Spey is very similar to the fly shown above. The major difference is that the body is of green Mylar tinsel rather than floss. Although the fly is called a Spey it actually isn't a proper Spey because there is no body hackle at all. The effect is gained by tying the mallard flank feather as an extremely long, full collar.

Green Spey

The Gaby is a Michel Boivin pattern which was inspired by an article by Alec Jackson about pseudo-Spey patterns. The colours, black and chartreuse, are very well-proven for the Gaspé and the fly was an immediate success, taking two fish on its first outing on the Madelaine River. Since then it has been effective on many other rivers, particularly in clear water and bright conditions.

Gaby - Boivin

The Purple Spey is a Marc Leblanc pattern from 1989 that copies many of the features of the modern steelhead Spey flies. Again, it is better described as a quasi-Spey fly as the long hackling is confined to the collar. Purple is a popular colour for steelhead flies but has never really caught on for Atlantic salmon patterns.

Purple Spey - Leblanc

# North American Featherwing Flies

The Dragon series of flies was devised by Fran Stuart of New Hampshire in 1988 during a long, hot summer on the Penobscot River in Maine. Apart from the fluorescent green version illustrated there are also versions with yellow, red and orange fluorescent floss bodies. In all cases the floss is underwound with a tinsel underbody to maintain the brightness of the colour when it is wet. The Dragons are normally tied on low-water double hooks. The unusual ribbing is of peacock herl which is not very durable but seems to add something to the pattern.

Dragon

The Black Labrador is a 'buggy' little pattern that was taken from Len Rich's book *Newfoundland Salmon Flies*. It is typical of many very simple flies from the early days of salmon angling in North America, constructed from materials that were easy to find. All black is as good a colour as be found for fishing in the gloaming as night begins to fall.

Black Labrador

The next couple of flies are just about as simple as a salmon fly can be. The Corneille is another all-black fly, this time with a crow wing. The Corneille is at its most effective in small sizes – 10 down to 14 – and in the last 15 minutes of dusk before darkness falls.

Corneille

The Loch Lomond is a pattern from Ian Wood who lived near Loch Lomond in Scotland. He used only one fly when fishing the loch for salmon – the pattern illustrated with a gold tinsel body and a wing of black and white turkey. His reasoning for the gold body was that he thought silver too bright except in broken water and that gold gave a gentler gleam. This fly could be just the thing to fish in slow water where a bit of judicious handlining might provide the necessary movement.

Loch Lomond - Wood

Winter's Hope from Bill McMillan is a west coast steelhead fly that has made a successful transition to Atlantic salmon on the east coast. Originally, it proved to be particularly effective in large sizes for high water conditions but since

# North American Featherwing Flies

### Winter's Hope - McMillan

then it has taken many fish in a wide variety of water conditions. The hackle tip winging allows a prismatic mixing of colours.

The Marigold also has hackle tip winging. The pattern was created by Mike Martinek of Massachusetts, an extremely able flydresser (see *The Atlantic Salmon Fly – The Tyers & Their Art* by Judith Dunham), and the influence of his love of streamer flies is clear to see. Marigold is especially effective early in the season and apart from Quebec and Labrador, has also taken fish in Iceland and Great Britain.

### Marigold - Martinek

The classic Red Sandy has already been mentioned in the History chapter, but this is a modern version from North America that also uses hackle tip winging. Many of the features of the original fly have been retained but the wing has lost the jungle cock which was such a feature of the original. In this version it has been replaced by an underwing of red dyed tippet feathers. The Indian crow feathers originally used for the rear body veilings have been replaced by red dyed hackle tips. The Red Sandy was highly regarded for use in Iceland and Scandinavia and versions are still in use there, particularly for early season fishing when the water is carrying some colour.

### Red Sandy Variant

Campbell's Fancy is an old trout pattern that has converted well to salmon fishing. This bright little fly looks absolutely ideal for grilse fishing in the bright days of summer. The gold tinsel body is probably less flashy than silver in very clear, low water conditions and less likely to scare fish.

### Campbell's Fancy

The Green Drake (overleaf) was originally designed in the 1930s by the LaPointe brothers from the Gaspé. The version illustrated here is a slightly simplified version which was developed by Ira Gruber in the 1940s. Although the Green Drake was formerly very popular on the Miramichi, the Matepedia and the Restigouche Rivers, in more recent times its use seems to be restricted to the Miramichi.

# North American Featherwing Flies

Green has always been a popular colour for the flies used on the East Coast fisheries, but the modern hairwings seem to have superceded this pattern to a great extent.

Green Drake

Madame Hazel is a pattern devised by John Cuco in 1978 and named after Hazel Maltais, a flydresser and angler from Montreal. The fly is very well regarded on the Gaspé and on northern rivers such as the George and the Whale.

Madame Hazel - Cuco

The Aguanus is a pattern with a most unusual construction. The winging consists mainly of two bunches of golden pheasant tippet fibres. After the first bunch is tied in, it is veiled with a pair of yellow hackle tips and followed by a bright blue collar hackle. A second bunch of tippet fibres are then tied in as an overwing and this is followed by a final collar hackle of natural black cock. The fly was created by Francois Barnard and was named after a river on the north shore. The Aguanus is effective in small sizes.

Aguanus - Barnard

The Branchu is a prawn-style fly which was devised by Jean-Guy Côté, the owner of Uni-Products, in 1978. The fly is used mostly in the early part of the season in the lower part of the river near the estuary – as an alternative to the General Practitioner.

Branchu - Côté

Queen of Waters

# North American Featherwing Flies

The Queen of Waters is another variation of an old trout fly. It is reputed to work very well on the rivers of Quebec's north shore which often run with a tea-stained colour. The fly is usually fished with a greased line technique, allowing a drag free drift.

The following fly is a hackle tip winged variant of a Marc Leblanc fly called the Gageure (bet or wager). The fly is so called because Leblanc

Gageure - Leblanc

bet a friend that it would catch a salmon over 20 lbs for him. Of course it did – the salmon weighed 24 lbs! Jungle cock and silver strikes again.

The Hornberg is another trout fly that has made the transition to salmon fishing. Because of the natural buoyancy of the featherwing the fly tends to float when it first hits the water. Bates suggests that it is fished 'dry' like this until it gradually absorbs the water and eventually sinks. It is then fished on the swing like a normal wet fly.

Nuptiale - Gendron

The Nuptiale is a fly from Yvon Gendron, created in 1988. It is usually tied on either a low-water single or small double hook. It is held to be a very effective fly when fished in small sizes in low, clear water conditions.

The Traffic Ticket is the creation of David Ledlie from Maine in the USA. The fly has been very effective on the Gaspé, the north shore of Quebec and rivers in Newfoundland. A size 10 Traffic Ticket was responsible for Ledlie's largest ever salmon, a fish of nearly 30 lbs. This is a very simple, very nondescript kind of fly. Just the kind

Hornberg

Traffic Ticket - Ledlie

# North American Featherwing Flies

of thing which we have seen time and time again being absolutely deadly for no apparent reason! Ledlie describes the fly as *'a sure-fire, guaranteed, banned in Boston fly'*.

The last two flies in this section are two versions of the same pattern. The Mörrum is a Swedish pattern named after the Swedish river of the same name. Although the fly is still sometimes used in Sweden, and other Scandinavian countries, I was given the name by at least two separate anglers as a fly which has enjoyed considerable success on the rivers of Canada's East Coast. The second version, illustrated above, is a Spey-style derivative tied by Nestor Dupo.

The Spey version has all the characteristics to suggest to me that it will be even more successful than the standard version.

# North American Featherwing Flies

## STEELHEAD FLIES

One of the most striking features for a European researching steelhead flies, is the number of featherwinged patterns that are in everyday use. The variety of pattern types is also very wide, ranging from Spey-type flies with feather slip wings, through spider and quasi-Spey flies which rely on extremely long collar hackles, to standard strip winged flies.

Although hairwings were first developed in North America into the widespread patterns that we see throughout the world today, North American anglers never did stop using featherwinged flies, unlike European anglers who, in their enthusiasm for the easier-to-tie hairwings, very nearly threw the baby out with the bath water, forgetting every featherwinged pattern, including the ones that had always been really effective flies.

When European anglers study the huge range of featherwing patterns on offer in the following pages they may be inspired to rediscover the virtues of featherwings once again. The disadvantages of the complex, classic mixed and built-wing flies, the lack of mobility and translucence, certainly do not apply to the long-hackled Spey and Dee-type flies or use of hackle tips for other flies. All in all, there is still a place for featherwinged flies in the modern angler's armoury. It is simply that many of us have forgotten just how good they can be.

The following pages will demonstrate the wide range of superb featherwinged flies that the anglers of North America have developed for steelhead fishing. Many of them will be of great interest to open-minded Atlantic salmon anglers and there is no doubt that many of them would be at least as successful in this role as they are for steelhead.

The first group of flies in this section are Spey and quasi-Spey patterns. The widespread use and almost mystical reverence given to Spey flies by steelhead anglers is one of the most remarkable features to any European studying steelhead fly the patterns.

The difference between true Spey flies and what have become known as quasi-Speys, lies in the way that the hackling is applied. In a true Spey fly, the hackling is palmered along the body, following the ribbing. In quasi-Speys, the hackling is restricted, either to the front one-third of the body or to a full and long collar hackle.

It is also worth examining the way that modern Spey flies are winged. The traditional wing for a Spey fly was a pair of featherwing slips, usually bronze mallard, which were tied short and low, cupped over the body, rather like the keel of an upturned boat. In contrast, the wing of a Dee fly consisted of two long, thin feather slips which were tied low, but in a splayed fashion, rather like a pair of scissors. Some purists would also say that the slips should curve round and come back together at the rear of the fly.

As will be seen in the pages that follow, modern Spey flies use wings of both of these types, in addition to paired hackle tip wings which were pioneered by Syd Glasso. They could therefore be considered hybrids which mix features of both Spey and Dee flies. The Spey flies of North America are therefore flies which vary from their classic forerunners in detail but which, much more importantly, maintain the ideals of mobility and form inherent in the old patterns.

The name of Sydney Glasso is already famous as one of the pioneers of Spey flies for steelhead fishing. His flies inspired a whole generation of new flydressers to emulate the elegant patterns that he created.

It is fitting therefore that the first fly illustrated (overleaf) should be named after him. Mr Glasso is a pattern from Dick Wentworth who was taught both to fish and to tie flies by Syd Glasso and the Mr Glasso fly is his tribute to his teacher. Mr Glasso is based on the Orange Heron and obviously works well because it caught a 21 lb 8oz steelhead in March 1981 on the Sol Duc River. Any fly-caught steelhead over 20 lbs is a real specimen.

Purple Prince - McNeese

# North American Featherwing Flies

Mr Glasso - Wentworth

The Quillayute is also a Dick Wentworth pattern named for the rivers in the Quillayute chain on the Olympic peninsular. It is primarily a fly for winter-run fish.

Quillayute - Wentworth

The next two flies are purple Speys, one from Keith Mootry and one from Dave McNeese.

The Purple Spey from Dave Mootry is also much in the tradition of the Orange Heron but in this case the winging is of hackle tips dyed purple. The version from Dave McNeese is very similar except that the wing is changed to golden pheasant flank dyed purple with purple dyed golden pheasant toppings over.

Both versions of the Purple Spey are especially effective on the North Santiam River in Oregon. One evening in October 1978, Mootry and McNeese, fishing together, took ten steelhead using this fly.

Purple Spey - Mootry

Purple Spey - McNeese

The next fly also continues the purple theme. This time the fly is the Deep Purple Spey from Walt Johnson which was also inspired by his experiences when fishing together with Syd Glasso. According to Johnson this is his most consistently successful fly for summer-run steelhead for the last 30 years and is particularly effective for rivers with a light bottom such as the North Fork of the Stillaguamish.

Deep Purple Spey - Johnson

# North American Featherwing Flies

The Golden Spey is another Walt Johnson pattern which has been effective over many years. The deep yellow seal's fur dubbing is laid over an underbody of fluorescent yellow floss in order to maintain the brightness of the colour when the fly is wet.

Golden Spey - Johnson

We have already seen one fly from Dave McNeese and the following pattern is another of his striking creations. The Spawning Spey is one of McNeese's favourite winter patterns and has been tremendously effective ever since its conception.

Spawning Spey - McNeese

The Purple Hilton is a quasi-Spey type derivative of the classic Silver Hilton. The fly was first created in 1985 and has been consistently successful ever since. McNeese considers this variant to be better than the original.

Purple Hilton - McNeese

The Polar Bear Spey is also a Dave McNeese pattern that again uses his favourite purple/hot orange colour combination. The brilliant effect that he achieves with these flies is due to the fact that he dyes his own materials with acid dyes. The hackling along the front body portion is of polar bear hair, hence the name of the fly.

Polar Bear Spey - McNeese

The next fly, the Purple Goose Spey (overleaf) from Deke Meyer, is another fly with a good portion of purple in its make-up. In this case the hackling is of purple goose, although the wings are of bright pink hackle tips. The colour combination is quite stunning and is surely at its best when there is a bit of colour to the water.

# North American Featherwing Flies

*Purple Goose Spey - Meyer*

The Halloween Spey is another Deke Meyer pattern. The Spey hackling for this fly consists of burnt goose flank feathers. This produces a hackle which is somewhat stiffer than heron or pheasant rump and thus produces a fly which is more effective in heavier flows which would make the softer hackles collapse.

*Halloween Spey - Meyer*

Incidentally, for tyers who wish to try Spey flies for the first time, Deke Meyer gives a really good overview of the differing styles, together with tying tips and instructions in his book *Advanced Fly Fishing for Steelhead*. The reasoning behind the various styles, their strengths and weaknesses, all get a really good airing.

The Soft Hackle Spey or Spey Spider is Meyer's term for a Spey-style fly that is tied without any winging. The Spey hackle is palmered along the body and the fly is finished with a long front hackle. This allows more movement of the hackles, particularly along the top of the fly, usually masked by the wing, and also shows off the body and ribbing to maximum advantage in terms of colour and translucent sparkle. The example shown combines orange and purple but many alternative colour schemes are possible.

*Soft Hackle Spey - Meyer*

The next three flies are the creations of Gary Alger. The first fly depicted, the Golden Purple Spey, is a combination of a dubbed purple body, reddish-brown Spey hackle and a wing of golden pheasant red breast feathers. It is a pleasing combination of colours that are bright without being too overwhelming. It has been noticed by many anglers over a long period of time that the brick-red breast feathers of the golden pheasant exhibit a most eye-catching effect when in the water; they are much more visible than one might suppose and seem to have a kind of glow about them.

The second fly, the Trophy Hunter, is a combination of red and black, again with red pheasant breast feather wings.

The last fly illustrated is the October Caddis Spey. This is named after the caddis flies that hatch in October and has the yellow-brown colouration that you would expect from a caddis imitation. Whether the steelhead actually take this fly for a caddis is difficult to know.

# North American Featherwing Flies

Golden Purple Spey - Alger

Trophy Hunter - Alger

October Caddis Spey - Alger

One can only remark that many steelhead anglers are convinced that this is the case and many, therefore, fish caddis imitations that undoubtedly take many autumn fish.

The Red Guinea Spey is an Alec Jackson pattern tied in the pseudo-Spey style that he has developed. This style of fly presents the same profile from all angles. The pattern illustrated is in red and claret but many other colour combinations are possible.

Red Guinea - Jackson

The Cerise-Claret Spey is a another pseudo-Spey pattern from John Newbury of Chewelah, Washington. The fly is included amongst the recommended flies in the *Flies of the Northwest* by the Inland Empire Fly Fishing Club. The combination of cerise and claret is certainly eye-catching and should make this fly effective if there is colour in the water.

Cerise-Claret Spey - Newbury

# North American Featherwing Flies

Another pattern in the same book is the Heavy Breather Orange designed by Harry Dritz, also of Washington. The fly is recommended as being a good winter fly which works particularly well on the Kalama River. The body is underwound with tinsel in order to maintain the brightness of the body colour when the fly is wet. This causes extra work when tying the fly but so many of the best anglers and flytyers think it worthwhile that it behoves us to take notice and invest a little more time ourselves.

Black Reeach - Shewey

Heavy Breather Orange - Dritz

Midnight Canyon - Shewey

The following three flies are from John Shewey, co-author with Forrest Maxwell of *Fly Fishing for Summer Steelhead*. Although the book is nominally about summer fishing, the three flies shown here are in fact recommended winter patterns.

Shewey's Black Reeach is a derivative of the Gold Reeach, one of the very oldest of the Spey flies from Scotland (see page 10). The original Reeach was hackled with Spey cock; this version uses a much longer hackle of black-dyed blue-eared pheasant.

Midnight Canyon is a dark fly relieved only by a sliver of orange in the wing and jungle cock eyes. As an option, the Spey hackle over the very front of the body may be changed to orange with black-dyed tips.

The last of the trio, the Orange Angel, is a much brighter fly which is substantially orange with white wings. The orange marabou Spey hackle has the tips dyed black.

Orange Angel - Shewey

# North American Featherwing Flies

The General Money #1 Spey is based upon the fly which was developed by General Noel Money in the 1930s. The fly remained extremely popular until the 1970s when it seemed to fall out of favour. The colour combination of silver, black, burgundy red and orange certainly remains effective and I think it well worth preserving this splendid pattern. The Spey-style undoubtedly makes the fly more appealing to modern anglers.

General Money #1 Spey

General Money #2 was also developed in the 1930s for use on the Stamp River and, like the #1, has fallen out of regular use. It is quite clear however, that it would still be an effective fly today and the Spey treatment may encourage modern anglers to give it a try.

General Money #2 Spey

The Summer Frontier Spey is one of a series of five summer Spey flies which are sold by Troy Bachmann's Frontier Fly company and are to be found in his book *Frontier Flies*. The Summer Midnight Express, the Summer Sunrise, the Summer Deep Purple and the Summer Lady Caroline are also part of the same series.

Summer Frontier

Summer Lady Caroline

Summer Deep Purple

# North American Featherwing Flies

### Summer Midnight Express

### Winter Punch

### Winter Candlelight

### Summer Sunrise

The next six flies are also Frontier flies but this time they are part of the Winter Spey series.

The Winter Punch Spey is a bright concoction with an eye-catching combination of pink and lime green. This fly should be visible, even in highly-coloured water and, for the Atlantic salmon angler, may make a good back-end fly, especially if there are a lot of leaves in the water. The salmon certainly won't have seen anything similar!

The Winter Candlelight Spey utilises the yellow, black and orange colour combination that has proved to be so effective over the years and is closely related to the Sol Duc from Syd Glasso. A Spey version of the Sol Duc from Bob Ververka is shown on page 62.

The Winter Green Butt Skunk is a derivation from the well-known Skunk but with a fluorescent green body. Because of the way that the fly is tied, the only part of the body that is visible is the rear, thus giving the effect of a green butt. Black flies with green butts (usually fluorescent) can be found all over the world. From the east coast of Canada to Europe and Scandinavia you can find Atlantic salmon flies of this colour, so it is no surprise that they have also proved to be effective for steelhead.

### Winter Green Butt Skunk

# North American Featherwing Flies

The Winter Jack O'Lantern is also a traditional colour combination, this time gold, black and orange. Although this fly is also called a Spey, the winging of long, thin slips tied in a splayed configuration is in fact typical of the Dee flies. I love the way the body glows beneath the hackle veiling on this fly. For the salmon anglers, why not try this one as an alternative to the Willie Gunn or Munro Killer?

Winter Jack O'Lantern

The Winter Expression Spey returns to the very familiar purple theme, this time with a white wing and a two-part body consisting of fuchsia floss and purple dubbing.

Winter Expression

The last in the Winter series is the Winter Sunkist which, as the name suggests, is a hot orange colour combined with a touch of red and a white wing. This is a highly visible pattern, ideal for off-coloured water.

Winter Sunkist

The next three flies in this section are Spey patterns from Bill Chinn. The Steelhead Spey is predominantly red and is primarily intended for winter-run fish. The style is classic Spey with a wing of bronze mallard mounted in the traditional manner.

Steelhead Spey - Chinn

There are two version of Bill Chinn's Pink Spey, a dark and a light. The lighter version of the two is both brighter and usually tied in smaller sizes than the dark version. For the darker version, the Spey hackle is grey heron, dyed hot pink. This produces a dark, pinkish-red colour. The Spey hackle on the light version is also dyed hot pink but this time on white heron breast feather, giving a much brighter, lighter colour. The hackles are also dressed much shorter. The rear half of the body on the darker fly is of pink seal's fur while the front half is of claret seal's fur. The lighter fly has a body completely of pink seal's fur.

# North American Featherwing Flies

Dark Pink Shrimp - Chinn

Light Pink Shrimp - Chinn

The next three flies are also shrimp patterns, in this case new Spey versions of the old classic Polar shrimp. The Polar Shrimp has been around since about 1936 and the number of variants seem to increase every year, a tribute to the lasting appeal of this fly. Most of the new versions have the aim of increasing the mobility and transparency of the original.

The first version is from Bob Blumreich and is very much in the red end of the spectrum. The wing retains the original white colouring.

Polar Shrimp Spey - Blumreich

The next two flies are variants from Steve Gobin, one dark and one light. Two versions of patterns have developed over the years. This undoubtedly widens the range of conditions in which they are effective whilst still maintaining the elements of what is known to be a successful fly.

Light Polar Shrimp - Gobin

Dark Polar Shrimp - Gobin

Mike Brooks is an angler from Oregon and his home waters are the lower McKenzie and the Middle Fork of the Willamette. The following two flies are his own creations. The RVI is named after steelhead guide Ron Van Iderstine from Springfield Oregon. The RVI has been Brooks' most consistently successful pattern from mid to late summer in the evenings. The best result, to a light orange version, was ten fish risen and seven landed in one evening. The RVI can be tied with various coloured bodies – light orange, green and purple have all been effective. Both these flies are presented using a classic wet fly swing on a ten foot sink tip line. At the end of the swing Brooks always strips a little line back in before letting it out again on the dangle. He may repeat this up to

80

# North American Featherwing Flies

thirty times per cast. I have met other anglers who swear by this hand lining before the line is lifted off the water so there may well be something to it.

We have already seen that the Heron series of flies, both classic old patterns from the Spey and newer versions from the USA, have been tremendously successful. Here then, are another group of modern variants for your consideration.

The first three flies illustrated are from Bob Ververka and have hackle tip winging in the style of Syd Glasso. The Black & Orange Heron has the look about it of a fly that would do very well in clear water conditions. The orange gives the fly a touch of brightness without being too garish.

Green and Blue flies are not that common in steelheading but these two Herons offer a good 'change of pace' when the fish have seen all the orange, red, pink and purple flies and remained unimpressed.

The following two flies (overleaf) are from Dave McNeese and are typical McNeese patterns – elegant, colourful and a masterful combination of materials. The Golden Heron is mainly used in riffles on the North Umpqua and North Santiam Rivers, particularly if there is sun on the water.

# North American Featherwing Flies

Another fly in the series, the Red Heron, is identical to the Golden Heron except that the wing is changed to a red macaw feather or red hackle tip substitute. The red-winged version is particularly effective in the autumn.

of complementary colours brings added brightness and impact to each colour separately and that the resulting mixing by the eye produces a richness of colour unobtainable by simply mixing the pigments together.

The next two flies from Scott Noble are unusual in that they both have wings of married fibres, something that is very rare in a new pattern in the last twenty years. These are, however, every-day flies that produce highly-visible images in both clear and coloured water conditions. The Prismatic Spey is considered strictly a winter fly whereas the Midnight Spey is effective throughout the year.

The idea of prismatic mixing of colours in flies is not new. Certainly in North America, flies such as the Lord Iris and Lady Iris from Preston Jennings have had a lasting influence and it may not be coincidence that many flytyers over the years have come to the conclusion that colours produced by the conjunction of different shades are more effective than a solid colour. In the world of painting it has been well understood for years that the juxtaposition

The Winter's Hope Spey from Bob Blumreich is a sparkling new take on the standard fly from Bill McMillan (see page 67). The colours in this version are lighter than the original but it has retained its effectiveness on the rivers of the Great Lakes area.

# North American Featherwing Flies

The Skykomish Light and the Skykomish Dark from Steve Gobin are based on the classic steelhead hairwing fly, the Skykomish Sunrise. The bodies on both the new flies retain the original colours with a combination of orange and red with yellow Spey hackling. The original wing of white bucktail has been replaced here by a Spey wing of bronze mallard. The difference between the Light and Dark versions resides solely in the throat hackle which may not sound much but, as the illustration shows, is sufficient to alter the look of the fly quite markedly.

The first two flies are patterns from Rick Kustich who runs the Oak Orchard Fly Shop near the Niagra in New York State. As the name suggests, the Purple & Orange Marabou Spey is a combination of these colours which Kustich has found to be very effective. The Purple October is a darker fly, combining black and purple, another combination that has become a steelhead standard.

Purple & Orange Marabou Spey - Kustich

Skykomish Dark - Gobin

Skykomish Light - Gobin

Purple October - Kustich

The next group of Spey flies all originate in the Great Lakes area of the USA. Many of the flies from this area are atypical of the normal range of steelhead flies. Much of this is to do with the fact that the steelhead use the lakes as their equivalent of the ocean, feeding there just as the west coast steelhead go to sea. The major difference is that the transition from fresh to saltwater does not occur. The feeding patterns in rivers therefore tend to be quite different, prompting, until recently, a totally different approach to fly design.

The Reverse Akroyd (overleaf) is a pattern from Larry Halyk of Ontario. Quite why it is called the Reverse I don't know as the tying is very much in line with the original Akroyd. The only parts missing are the yellow hackle over the orange part of the body and the jungle cock cheeks set below the hook shank. These two features could always be added if a

# North American Featherwing Flies

fuller dressing was required but I don't think that the lack damages the fly in any way. Another version of the Akroyd from Mike Yarnot can be found below.

*Reverse Akroyd - Halyk*

The October Spey is another pattern from Larry Halyk. It is called the October Spey but I am not quite sure whether it is so-named because of the brown-orange colours of the fly or because it is at its most effective in the autumn. It should be said that there are a range of October patterns from Walt Johnson and others which also share these general rusty orange tones.

*October Spey - Halyk*

Yarnot's Steelhead Akroyd is yet another variant of the classic Akroyd. This version has a good dash of claret in it, a colour that I believe is very effective towards autumn for a Atlantic salmon. The originator, Mike Yarnot, lives in Wisconsin and is regarded as one of the best tyers of Spey flies in the Great Lakes area. He has a passion for traditional flies and this version of the Akroyd shows this very well as it has all the attributes of the original pattern.

It might well be that these small touches, such as the ostrich herl butt between the body sections, do not add much to the performance of the fly. Nevertheless they do add to the enjoyment of using such patterns. To many anglers it somehow seems right that the prince of fish deserves a real investment in the flies used to capture him.

*Steelhead Akroyd - Yarnot*

Mike Yarnot is also the creator of the Wild Turkey Orange, a really elegant fly that combines natural wild turkey marabou plumes with an orange wing, body and throat hackle. This fly, like Halyk's October Spey, has all the look of a really good back-end pattern.

*Wild Turkey Orange - Yarnot*

The Emerald Eagle is a fly that would fit very well into the classic Eagle series (see pages 63 & 64). It is also a very unusual colour combination for a Spey fly. Many flies have a chartreuse or green butt or rear body but it is very unusual to see the colour employed for the hackling. The shade of the hackle colour is also unusual in that it is emerald green.

# North American Featherwing Flies

This combines beautifully with the black to produce a glowing effect which really is rather reminiscent of the gemstone. The tips of the green hackle are dyed black but a trick developed by Bob Blumreich might help here. Use a felt tip pen with spirit-based ink to colour the tips as desired. Let the feather dry out and then comb out. Not only will you have the colour that you want but the spirit-based ink will have burnt the feather slightly, removing the flue and producing the fine tips which are so desirable.

the inheritors of Syd Glasso's mantle. He is also regarded as one of the finest tyers of the classic, complex-winged flies in the world. All of these flies are superb examples of prismatic mixing of colours. Each has a combination of two hackle colours which produce an effect that is quite different to that produced by a hackle of one mixed colour.

Emerald Eagle - Yarnot

Orange Sunset - Veverka

The Purple Guinea Spey is illustrated in *Steelhead Dreams* by Mat Supinski; no attribution is given for it so it may be one of his own patterns.

Blue & Bronze Sunset - Veverka

Purple Guinea Spey

Steelhead Sunset - Veverka

The Sunset series of flies are from Bob Ververka, one of the most famous fly dressers working in the USA today. Ververka is justly renowned for his Spey flies and is seen as one of

# North American Featherwing Flies

Spider type flies have a very long history. They started life in the 18th century on the upland streams of northern England as trout fly nymph imitations and have been around ever since. The spider design is very simple: a short body is veiled by a long and sparse collar hackle normally fashioned out of a webby, soft hen hackle. The hackle is very long compared to normal flies, the idea being that in the water the current would slick back the hackle forming a translucent shell around the body of the fly thus producing a convincing imitation of the transparent body of the nymph.

This idea spread to salmon flies and at various times over the last two hundred years, spider flies have briefly come into fashion and then disappeared again. For salmon flies the concept of a nymph imitation was not taken seriously. Firstly the flies were of a size that no real nymph could ever reach and secondly, as the feeding habits of salmon became clearer, there was convincing evidence that salmon did not feed at all when they returned to their natal rivers. This in itself did not mean that the flies were not successful: the reasons why spider-type flies are attractive are much more to do with the movement and mobility of the hackles and the veiling effect they have on the body colours, allowing sparkling glimpses of ribbing and body materials.

Spider flies have become very successful for steelhead fishing and a small but selective group of anglers and flydressers have developed a range of patterns that are not only beautiful to look at but are also extremely effective flies.

The first fly in this group is the Wet Spider from Al Knudson devised about 1940. This is probably the first Spider pattern tied specifically for steelhead and is very simple: a yellow chenille body and a grey mallard flank hackle. Trey Combes recommends spider flies for fishing soft-water flats and tailouts when rivers are low and clear and believes that they are the finest flies for these conditions.

Spectral Spider - Johnson

The Spectral Spider is a pattern from Walt Johnson. The name of the fly is derived from the prismatic effects which were discussed by Preston Jennings in his *A Book of Trout Flies*. Johnson believes that the subtle flash of the stacked wing, together with the veiling of the barred mallard, produces a very lifelike baitfish imitation. It has become one of Johnson's favourite flies for summer-run steelhead.

Wet Spider - Knudson

Low & Clear Spider - Canfield

# North American Featherwing Flies

As the name would suggest, the Low & Clear Spider from Mark Canfield (see opposite page) is designed for use in exactly those conditions. The fly is quite complex with a tail, tag, butt and two-part body. The underwing of long jungle cock feathers back-to-back is unusual today but follows a very old tradition. The front hackle is of lemon wood duck but dyed mallard flank would be an acceptable substitute.

The San Juan Spider from Bob Bettzig is a brighter example of a spider. The body is of fluorescent orange sparkle chenille. The front hackles are a fluorescent yellow-dyed hackle followed by yellow-dyed mallard flank. The red topping is of red hackle fibres or bucktail.

Gold Hilton Spider

San Juan Spider - Bettzig

The next two flies are from Karl Hauffler and were devised for use on the Kispiox. Originally they had no names but Trey Combes, in *Steelhead Fly Fishing*, named them the Gold and Purple Spiders.

Gold Spider - Hauffler

The Gold Hilton Spider is given by Deke Meyer in *Advanced Fly Fishing for Steelhead*. The Gold Hilton is a variant of the Silver Hilton and both of them date to around 1950. They were originally designed for use on the Klamath and Trinity Rivers. The Hiltons are further examples of flies that are generally muted in colour and yet which seem to have a special kind of fascination for the fish. Adding a long collar hackle to give more mobility can only improve the efficiency of the fly, particularly in light currents. The Silver Hilton, which is identical apart from the tag and ribbing of silver rather than gold tinsel, could obviously be treated in the same manner. Dave McNeese also uses a Green Butt Silver Hilton Spider in which the rear third of the body is of fluorescent green floss or sparkle chenille.

Purple Spider - Hauffler

# North American Featherwing Flies

The Sandy Spider is a pattern from Bachmann's *Frontier Flies*. The rear part of the body has a construction which consists of Edge Bright wrapped over an underbody of silver tinsel. Edge Bright is a plastic material which collects light and transmits it from its edges. Dr. Art Cohen discovered that if Edge Bright is wound over silver tinsel, it becomes translucent and emits a lantern-like glow.

Sandy Spider

The next fly is the well known Paint Brush from Bill McMillan. The Paint Brush was developed in 1973 as a winter pattern to be effective fished on a floating line with a dead drift technique. The first February it was tried it proved to be a superb pattern taking no less than twenty steelhead in its first month. The hackles used at the shoulder of the fly should be as soft and webby as can be found. The Steelhead Carey and the Green Butt Spider are two flies from

Paint Brush - McMillan

Sean Gallagher which were developed for use on the Green and Skykomish rivers. The Steelhead Carey has proved to be extremely effective for fishing in the late summer and early autumn during periods of low water. It is usually fished using the traditional greased line method. A variant is tied with a purple seal's fur body.

The Green Butt Spider is a superb general fly for summer steelhead, also fished with the greased line method.

Steelhead Carey - Gallagher

Green Butt Spider - Gallagher

The next group of flies are hackle flies, that is, flies that have no wing at all. They are different from the foregoing spider patterns in that the hackles are shorter. Hackled flies were very popular in the early days of steelheading and although only a

# North American Featherwing Flies

few patterns survived, there are now many new ones which keep the tradition alive. Many of these flies eschew bright colours and extravagant construction: in fact they are often designed to be totally innocuous. This is Bob Arnold, creator of the Spade which we shall see later, on the thought process involved in its creation. *'... a drab fly that looked like something found in the river and would ride along, whatever the speed of the current, in an upright position..... I wanted it to look so natural, so lifelike, that a steelhead might open its mouth to sample it, thinking it food.'*

The Burlap is one of the oldest hackle flies, created in 1945 by Arnold Arana for use on the Klamath. This is one of the few early hackle flies that is still in regular use and was one of the inspirations for the Spade.

Burlap - Arana

The Brindle Bug was created in about 1960 by Lloyd Silvius, a professional fly tyer from Eureka. It was very popular amongst anglers on the Klamath and Trinity rivers. The body consists of black and yellow variegated chenille.

Brindle Bug - Silvius

The Prawn Fly is a pattern from General Noel Money which dates back to the mid-1920s. According to Arthur Lingren in *Fly Patterns of British Columbia*, the Prawn Fly was one of the most popular flies in British Columbia for many years and was also very successful on the Rogue River. With the introduction of the General Practitioner, the Prawn Fly fell into disuse but Lingren relates that when he tried this fly on the Dean River when the water had a bit of colour, he landed three steelhead in the day. Perhaps a pattern that was discarded too soon!

Prawn Fly - Money

The Quinsam Hackle is a pattern from Roderick Haig-Brown, named after the Quinsam River, which dates to the late 1940s. According to Haig-Brown, the fly was also intended to be a prawn imitation.

Quinsam Hackle - Haig-Brown

# North American Featherwing Flies

The Trinity Brown and Grey are two simple hackle flies which originate on the Trinity River. They date to the mid-1960s and were in common use on the Klamath and Trinity rivers until the end of the 1980s. These flies present a nymph-like profile and could be any kind of natural food item found in the river.

Woolly Worm

Trinity Brown

Trinity Grey

The Woolly Worm is another old fly that has been a long-time favourite of western steelhead anglers. The basic pattern calls for a black chenille body palmered with a grizzly hackle, tied on a long shank hook. It should be said however, that almost any fly which has a chenille body and a palmered hackle qualifies as a Woolly Worm. There are variants with grey, brown and green bodies and hackles in almost every shade of brown, green, black, badger or furnace as well as grizzly. The Woolly Worm is generally used as a summer pattern for low and clear water conditions. Trey Combes gives the originator as Don Martinez.

The next series of flies featured in Plates 6 and 7 are current flies in use on a range of rivers all over the west coast. They are all based on the Spade which was devised by Bob Arnold in 1964. Since then the pattern has proved so popular for summer fishing that a whole family of Spade derivatives have come into use. It is probably a moot point as to when a variant becomes another fly – some of these variants change the tail, the body colour and the hackle colour as well as altering the shape. I leave you to make your own judgement! The original Spade was first fished on the North Fork of the Stillaguamish below Deer Creek at the Elbow Hole when the water was extremely low and clear. Arnold's original pattern consists of a tail of grey-brown deer body hair, a body of black chenille and a soft grizzly shoulder hackle.

One of the best-known variants has a body where the last third is of orange seal, thus giving the fly the look of a caddis pupa imitation. Many anglers believe that this variation is more effective than the original. Apart from the orange butt version, Bob Arnold also ties a range of variants that have a fluorescent green butt or a body of red dubbing or an equally divided body of orange and black seal's fur. The grizzly shoulder hackle may also be replaced with a brown hackle or a mixture of red and yellow hackles.

John Farrar ties a Spade variant in which the body is of black seal's fur and the tail is of fine brown bucktail. The hackle is more swept back in this version making the whole fly appear much more elegant.

 # North American Featherwing Flies

Original Spade

Orange Butt Spade

Spade (Farrar)

Green Butt Spade

Blue Spade - Hunnicutt

Polar Spade - Hunnicutt

Plate 6 - Spade variants

 # North American Featherwing Flies

Fancy Spade

Fancy Red Spade

Red Guinea Spade

Yellow Guinea Spade

Whaka Blonde

Jacob's Coat

Plate 7 - Spade variants - Alec Jackson

# North American Featherwing Flies

The Blue Spade is a variant from Jimmy Hunnicutt which has a very well picked-out body of orange and iron blue dun seal's fur. The second of his variants is the Polar Spade which has a butt of greenish blue followed by black seal's fur. The short grizzly hackle is over-wrapped with teal flank.

Alec Jackson has at least six Spade variants to his credit which are illustrated in Plate 7. The Claret Guinea Spade and the Yellow Guinea Spade share the same construction. The tail is of extra-fine deer body hair, the body itself is of black ostrich and at the shoulder a couple of turns of stiff genetic quality hackle is wound before the final collar of dyed guinea fowl. The effect is a three dimensional fly that is normally fished on a sink-tip line. The Fancy Spade has a rear body of thin peacock herl; the front body is plump and of black ostrich herl rope. The Fancy Red Spade replaces the black ostrich with red. Jacob's Coat is yet another Spade variant, this time with a variegated body consisting of six ostrich strands of varying colours. The collar hackle is of hen grizzly hackle of a colour to match the body. The last of Jackson's Spade flies is called the Whaka Blonde, an ironic name because the fly is in fact all purple.

The following group of four flies shown in Plate 8 are all soft-hackle patterns from Jim Garrett.

Candy Montana     Dana Montana

Denise Montana     Libby's Black

Plate 8 - Montanas - Jim Garrett

 North American Featherwing Flies

The flies illustrated are all tied on gold-plated Alec Jackson hooks. This colour shines through the floss when it is wet and gives a translucent look to the fly. The flies are designed for use on summer run steelhead when the rivers are low and clear. Garrett believes that the brighter-coloured flies are more effective for fresh run fish, while the darker flies work better later in the season. Libby's Black is designed for use at the end of the season when fish are well into their spawning run.

The Sundowner series of flies were devised by Bob Wagoner in 1986 to utilise the then brand new Krystal Flash material. The flies are simple in their construction but have a great deal of flash.

They have been used mainly on the Clearwater and Grande Ronde rivers. In the tying details the Krystal Flash, although it cannot be considered a normal wing, is noted as a wing simply because it is tied in the position usually occupied by a conventional wing.

The Sweet Loretta (opposite) is another pattern from Jimmy Hunnicutt. The name was given because the fly reminded him of a certain lady with bright red lips and raven black hair – seems a good reason to me! The fly once took a 41-inch hen fish on the Thomson River which took over 40 minutes to land using a sixteen-foot rod. The fly is designed to work in the surface film, more damp than wet.

Black Sundowner    Orange Sundowner    Pink Sundowner

Purple Sundowner    Red Sundowner

Plate 9 - Sundowner Series - Bob Wagoner

# North American Featherwing Flies

Sweet Loretta - Hunnicutt

John Valk, owner of Grindstone Angling Outfitters of Watertown, Ontario is the creator of the Steelhead Petite series of flies. As the waters of the Great Lakes clear dramatically due to the filtering effects of zebra mussels, small flies are bound to becoming increasingly important.

The Steelhead Petite series is Valk's answer to this problem and are tied in a series of effective colours in sizes 6 to 12. There is a kind of wing to these flies but it is tied very short and is secondary to the front hackle so that they can certainly be considered as hackled rather than winged flies. Although they were designed for the Great Lakes, these pretty little patterns would surely be effective for low and clear water conditions anywhere.

The next group of flies shown on Plate 11 (overleaf) share a special body construction which consists of a strip of Edge Bright wrapped over an underbody of silver tinsel.

Edge Bright is a plastic material which has the property of collecting light and transmitting it from its edges, rather in the fashion of an optic fibre, giving an intense glow.

The Dean River Lanterns were first developed by Dr. Art Cohen of San Francisco who discovered that if Edge Bright is wound over an underbody of silver tinsel it becomes translucent and emits a lantern-like glow, thus giving the name to this series of flies.

Plate 10 - Steelhead Petite Series - John Valk

# North American Featherwing Flies

Plate 11 - Dean River Lanterns - Cohen

The next group of flies are from the United Kingdom, but I think they may well be of use to steelhead anglers. The flies are seatrout patterns (sea-run brown trout) from Tony King, one of the most knowledgeable seatrout fishermen in Britain. The flies were described in an article in the February 2003 issue of *Fly Fishing & Fly Tying* magazine. There are obvious parallels between seatrout and steelhead fishing and many seatrout flies have been successful for steelhead. Hopefully the following flies will be of interest to steelhead fishermen – they continue the tradition of English north country wet spiders (à la Stewart) and have proved to be hugely successful.

The flies are tied on silver (sometimes gold) Salar hooks from Partridge. This obviates the need for tying in a silver body but if more weight is required, silver fuse wire (10 and 13 amp) can be tied in at the head, wound backwards down the body in touching turns and then over-wound back to the head in open ribbing turns – neat and effective! The patterns themselves have some very traditional names but they are radically simplified – tying silk for a body, a couple of turns of hackle at the head and a few wisps of mallard or teal for a wing. Apart from the patterns shown, it is clear that this technique can be applied to any of your favourite flies. 'Simplificate and add lightness,' as the founder of Boeing once said!

It is fairly clear that to fish flies like these you need to have confidence in them. Many anglers find it hard to believe that fish can see such inconspicuous scraps, but see them they do and what's more, they take them with total confidence. They also have other advantages. Being quick and simple to tie (not to say cheap) they are flies that can be lost without causing too much heartache. You can afford get down to where the fish are lying, even at the cost of some flies. The weighted versions, being unencumbered by lots of dressing materials, cut through the water very quickly and reach the required depth without the need for frequent mends. Tony King normally uses interchangeable sink-tip lines rather than sinkers.

# North American Featherwing Flies

Peter Ross

Teal, Blue & Silver

Mallard & Claret

Blue Charm

Plate 12 - Seatrout Spiders - King

Steelhead Stick - Butorac

The Steelhead Stick is a pattern from Joe Butorac which uses the same colours as the Flatcar from Randall Kaufmann. The Stick is a greased line fly for fast water and is suggested as an imitation of an emerging October caddis, the long black hackle representing the folded wings.

The Woolly Bugger (overleaf) is reckoned by many anglers to be the most all-round effective fly for trout fishing anywhere in the world. It looks like a leech, or a nymph or a crayfish or just about anything else that the trout might find edible – not exactly like anything in particular but something like almost everything. It should come as no surprise to know therefore that there are literally hundreds of variants of this pattern.

# North American Featherwing Flies

Red Woolly Bugger

Orange Woolly Bugger

Black Woolly Bugger

Purple Woolly Bugger

Plate 13 - Crystal Chenille Woolly Buggers - Wagoner

The four Woolly Buggers shown in Plate 13 are from Bob Wagoner and are tied with bodies of Crystal Chenille. The tails consist of two matched marabou blood hackle tips and as an option some strands of Krystal Flash of a matching colour can be included. The use of complete blood hackles means that the stalks offer some extra stiffness which helps to keep the tail from wrapping around the hook. The colours of these flies are such that it is unlikely that they are taken for natural food items: the mobility of the tail is probably the most important feature.

The next variant is the Peacock Woolly Bugger from Mark Bachmann. The name comes from the fact that the body is of peacock herl.

Peacock Woolly Bugger - Bachmann

# North American Featherwing Flies

The Black and Red Steelhead Woollys are patterns from Joe Butorac which are like a cross between a Comet and a Woolly Bugger. The tails, which are about one-and-a-half times the hook length are of bucktail and the body is of braided silver tinsel.

Red Steel Woolly - Butorac

Black Steel Woolly - Butorac

The Comet seems to have its origins in the late 1940s or early 1950s and was, by the account of Bill Schaadt, first created by a young amateur fly tyer who could not really tie properly. The fly however was picked up by Joe Paul who was connected to the Golden Gate Angling and Casting Club and it became very successful, particularly on the lower water of the Gualala where Paul and Alan Curtis landed at least ten fish between them on one occasion.

The Comet remains to this day one of the most popular Californian wet flies for winter steelhead. The large bead-chain eyes were not always included in the original tyings but they have become diagnostic of modern versions, helping to get the fly down in the water and, because of its nose-heavy construction, offering a very enticing rise-and-fall diving motion when subject to the current and pull on the line. The original Comet is now known as the Orange Comet and a wide range of variants have followed. These include the Black, Gold and Silver Comets as well as the Howard Norton Special, the Boss and the Salmon Fly. It isn't surprising that the Comet flies have remained popular as they have a lot of advantages – they sink quickly and have a lot of flash as well as mobility provided by the long tail. They are also cheap and easy to tie.

Comet

Orange Comet

Boss

# North American Featherwing Flies

There are fashions in fly patterns just as in other walks of life, and, as with other fashions, logic has little to do with it. The following flies are no longer in fashion – this certainly doesn't mean that they are ineffective: indeed most of them were created by the leading anglers of their day and have accounted for many hundreds if not thousands of fish. Most of them would catch fish today if they were used and they combine beauty with functionality.

The first flies are the creations of three of the pioneering fishermen of the west coast steelheading and of British Columbia in particular. Oddly enough, all three were born Englishmen

Black, Orange & Jungle Cock       Black, Tippet & Yellow

Golden Red       Dick's Fly

Rainbow       Grey Fly

Plate 14 - Steelhead Flies from General Noel Money

100

# North American Featherwing Flies

but became Canadian. The three are General Noel Money, Tommy Brayshaw and Roderick Haig-Brown. These three fishermen of differing ages were all friends during their lives and the baton of building a tradition of steelhead fishing and fly design was handed down to each in turn.

Brigadier General Noel Money first settled with his family in Vancouver Island shortly before the World War I, intending to open a hotel for travelling salmon anglers at Qualicum Beach. This plan was interrupted by the war in which he served in the Middle East.

After the war he returned to Vancouver Island and his hotel was finally opened. General Money created many steelhead flies but, as his fishing experience was firmly learnt in the pursuit of Atlantic salmon, it is no wonder that he saw no reason to change the techniques that he had formerly used. Accordingly, many of his flies are direct descendants of classic Atlantic salmon flies. His flies have had a lasting influence on succeeding generations of steelhead fishermen and, although they are no longer widely used, they topped the best-selling list of the Harkley & Haywood sporting goods store in Vancouver until the 1970s.

We have already seen the General Money patterns numbers 1 and 2 (see page 77) in a slightly modernised Spey style. The six flies illustrated in Plate 14 (opposite page) were designed for use on the Stamp and Somass rivers and are presented in a normal hackled form which is much closer to the originals as tied by General Money.

The next flies illustrated were all created by Tommy Brayshaw, an English emigrant who eventually settled down in the small town of Hope in British Columbia in 1946. Apart from angling and fly tying, Brayshaw was also a brilliant artist whose illustrations were later used by Roderick Haig-Brown in his book *The Western Angler*.

The flies are named for the Coquihalla River which became Brayshaw's home water until 1959. The first of these flies, the Orange Dark was christened in 1949, the last being the Red in 1959. The Coquihalla Orange Light has the distinction of being the fly that led to the very first fly-caught steelhead from the Thomson River in 1953.

This momentous event occurred during a trip to the Thompson in the company of Roderick Haig-Brown. The Black & Silver dates to 1946

Coquihalla Orange Dark - Brayshaw

Coquihalla Orange Light - Brayshaw

Coquihalla Red - Brayshaw

Black & Silver - Brayshaw

# North American Featherwing Flies

and it is with this fly that Brayshaw caught his first summer-run steelhead on the Coquihalla. Because it was so reliable, the Black & Silver soon became Brayshaw's fall-back fly whenever a fish refused another fly or when he fished down a pool for the second time.

Brayshaw sometimes embellished these flies further with golden pheasant toppings in the tail and over the wings and also often added jungle cock cheeks.

Roderick Haig-Brown is probably best-known for his monumental book on all types of angling in British Columbia, *The Western Angler*, published in 1939. The connection between the three men was made clear in this book – the illustrations were done by Tommy Brayshaw, 20 years Haig-Brown's senior, and the dedication of the book was to General Noel Money, from whom Haig-Brown had learnt much of his steelhead knowledge and who died in 1941.

The Silver Brown dates to the 1930s and was originally intended for sea-run cutthroats before becoming a reliable pattern for summer-run steelhead. The Silver Brown is very similar to the Haslam (see page 25), a Welsh fly that is not only effective for salmon but has a very good record for taking seatrout (sea-run brown trout) as well.

The Silver Lady is from the same era and was also created for the summer-run steelhead on the Vancouver Island streams. It was also effective for cutthroats. There are two versions of this fly, each with different winging on the same body. The version with the blue hackle tips looks really good for use in low, clear water conditions.

The Golden Girl is basically a reduced Durham Ranger which was tied for winter fishing on the Campbell River on Vancouver Island in about 1940. Lest it be thought that this type of construction is no longer relevant to modern fishing, the Redwing from Dave McNeese (see page 110) is very much in the same mould.

Other recent flies which use the golden pheasant tippet winging include the Macartair (see page 28) and the Gorbenmac series of salmon flies from Gordon McKenzie (see pages 42-43). An overwing of golden pheasant topping is optional.

Silver Brown - Haig-Brown

Silver Lady 1 - Haig-Brown

Silver Lady 2 - Haig-Brown

Golden Girl - Haig-Brown

# North American Featherwing Flies

The Chappie is a hackle-winged pattern devised in 1940 by C. L. 'Outdoor' Franklin. The Chappie became one of the classic steelhead flies and was used from the Skeena to the Sacramento but was most popular on the Klamath, Franklin's home waters, for over thirty years. According to Trey Combs, the Chappie still sees occasional use.

Chappie - Franklin

Very much in the same style, with its distinctive hackle tip winging, is the Silver Hilton which was created in about 1950, also for the Klamath and Trinity rivers. It remained one of the most popular and effective patterns on these rivers until the late 1970s and still has its adherents. A gold variant has a rib of gold rather than silver tinsel, and a mallard flank wing. A spider-style derivative of this fly is shown on page 87.

Silver Hilton

The next fly is a modern variant of the Silver Hilton from Dave McNeese. The Green Butt Silver Hilton is, as its name suggests, a variant with the addition of the ubiquitous green butt. Another Silver Hilton derivative from McNeese, the Purple Hilton, can be found on page 73.

Green Butt Silver Hilton - McNeese

The Black & Blue is a modern fly from British Columbia developed in the early 1970s by Van Egan. For summer-run fish the body is of black floss; for winter fishing, a heavier body of dubbed black seal's fur is recommended. The pattern took three fish on its first outing and since then has proved to be effective on many rivers including the Campbell, Gold, Nimpkish and Dean. A slight variation replaces the yellow tag with light blue.

Black & Blue - Van Egan

# North American Featherwing Flies

The Doc Spratley was an old lake trout pattern that has, in slightly modified form, made the transition to a river fly for steelhead. The inventor of the original fly is lost in history but Art Lingren gives credit for the introduction of this modified pattern to the Thompson River to Dave Winters in the late 1960s. The original lake pattern was tied short and stubby to give a buggy look to the fly; the steelhead version is much more slimly dressed. Because of the success of anglers such as Dave Winters, Jerry Wintle and others the Spratley has become a regular Thompson River pattern.

Doc Spratley

Harry Lemire is one of the best-known and widely-respected steelhead fishermen of modern times. The Black Diamond is a pattern that was first devised in 1963 and is named after his coal mining home town in Washington state. The Black Diamond answers the need for a small, dark fly and was originally intended for use in slightly coloured water. Since then, however, it has proved to be successful in all kinds of water conditions and at all times of year. Trey Combs favours the Black Diamond for fishing shallow tailouts in low light conditions.

Black Diamond - Lemire

The Squirrel & Teal is a Lemire pattern for low, clear water conditions, its muted colours designed so that fish are not frightened.

Squirrel & Teal - Lemire

The Golden Edge Yellow and Orange flies were devised in 1970 and 1971 respectively. These flies are the backbone of Lemire's wet fly fishing and are used throughout the year. Small sizes are for the summer and much larger for winter fishing with sink-tip lines or fast-sinking heads.

104

# North American Featherwing Flies

The Beauly Snow Fly is one of the really old flies from the River Beauly in Scotland, dating back to the first half of the 19th century. The name has nothing to do with the weather but comes from the originator, a Mr Snowie of Inverness. The reason that the pattern is included here is that it is one of the recommended patterns from Mike Brooks for use on the Lower McKenzie, the Willamette and the North Fork of the Umpqua. Brooks regards the Snow Fly as his fall-back pattern which he uses when all else has failed.

Beauly Snow Fly

The next two flies are from Arthur Lingren, author of *Fly Patterns of British Columbia*. The Black Spey is very much in the classic Spey mould and according to Lingren was inspired by the Black Spey listed by Knox. The Black Spey has proved to be successful on the Thompson River, and why not? The mobility of the long hackles, combined with black, relieved by a touch of red at the tail, and teal at the throat makes a winning combination.

As Specified #1 was created in 1982 and is one of Lingren's favourite flies for floating line work. It has been used with success on the Morice, Dean, Campbell and Thomson Rivers for summer-run fish. The As Specified, together with the Black Spey, has a sleek, streamlined look which is characteristic of many Lingren flies and which I find most attractive.

As Specified #1 - Lingren

The Claret & Black is another Lingren pattern, usually tied with a hair wing of black squirrel. The version shown below, is my conversion of this fly to a featherwing. I am a great believer in claret as a colour to be used towards the end of the summer and into autumn as well as being very effective at dusk. This fly has all the hallmarks of a successful fly and I don't think that the featherwing will in any way spoil its usefulness.

Claret & Black Featherwing

Black Spey - Lingren

Mike Kinney has spent most of his life guiding fishermen on the Olympic Peninsular

# North American Featherwing Flies

| Car Body | Turkey Tracker |
| Dragons Tooth | Boulder Creek |

Plate 15 - Mike Kinney Spey Flies

and has gained an encyclopedic knowledge of the Stillaguamish and Skagit Rivers.

His Spey flies are practical fishing flies, mostly dark in hue which combine a striking silhouette with vivid splashes of colour. Four of his flies are illustrated in Plate 15. The chartreuse Mylar ribbing used on many of his flies is unusual, as are some of the colour combinations. The green wing of the Turkey Tracker is a good example of this.

The next two flies are from Bob Veverka: the Purple Heart and the Purple Heart Spey. The two flies are closely related and the wing structure is identical. The technique of overlaying hackle tip wings of differing colours is one of the trade marks of Ververka's Spey flies and the combination colours produced are very striking indeed.

Purple Heart Spey - Veverka

106

# North American Featherwing Flies

We have already seen instances of the prismatic mixing of colours and these flies are further superb examples of the effects that can be achieved. The end result is certainly more than the sum of the parts! The Sunset series of flies shown on page 85 are further examples of this technique but they combine different coloured throat hackles rather than wing feathers.

Purple Heart - Veverka

The last fly in this series from Ververka is a variant of Syd Glasso's famous Sol Duc fly. This pattern uses the dark purple which has become so popular for steelhead flies.

Purple Sol Duc Spey - Veverka

Following on from the theme of prismatic mixing, the next fly from Preston Jennings is the fly that started it, at least by design. The Lord Iris was devised in the 1930s in accordance with the theories that Preston Jennings developed about the prismatic splitting effect that water has on sunlight. Jennings devised a series of flies which were designed to match the seasons from spring through until winter. Of these flies (Lady Iris, Lord Iris, Murky Iris and Dark Iris) only the Lord Iris has remained in use among steelhead anglers able to master the married wing technique employed in its construction.

Although Jennings' theories never quite took hold of the imagination of his fellow anglers at the time, his ideas have found much more resonance in modern times. Much of this may have to do with the difficulty of tying married wings and the fact that in more recent times similar results are obtained using translucent hackle tips.

Lord Iris - Jennings

Taylor's Golden Spey (overleaf) is a pattern designed by Robert Taylor in 1978. It was inspired by the Orange Heron from Syd Glasso but differs in the way that the wings are mounted. The Orange Heron has wings of hackle tips which always proved difficult to set correctly, a problem that even Glasso himself had. Taylor's answer was to use the red breast feathers from a golden pheasant and to set a pair of them flat, cupped over the body. The fly was first tried in the spring of 1978 on a trip to the Bella Coola river and proved immediately successful. Since then it has taken many fish on the Thompson, Dean, Skeena and other rivers. The throat as shown on the illustration is of lemon wood duck flank but a slightly different effect may be achieved by changing this to a golden pheasant red breast feather.

# North American Featherwing Flies

Golden Spey - Taylor

Blue Sky - Young

Black Sky - Young

Rusty Sky - Young

The Sky series of flies is the creation of Stan Young of Bellvue, Washington. Young retired from the National Park service in 1982 and spent the time afterwards fishing rivers from the North Umpqua to the Kispiox.

The Blue Sky is a fly for all water conditions and all times of the season. The set of the wings and hackle look rather odd when the fly is dry but both the soft hackles and the hackle tip wings are very mobile, sleeking back over the body when the fly is in use, giving a Spey-like appearance. The hook sizes used can vary from a 1/0 in winter to a 10 in summer and the flies are fished on either a floating line or a short sink-tip.

If you are a fan of black flies then the Black Sky is for you. It is as black as they come, unrelieved by any other colours apart from a flash of tinsel. The Black Sky is normally used during winter and spring in all water conditions, from low and clear to high and discoloured.

The Rusty Sky is recommended as an excellent fly for high, coloured water conditions.

Forrest Maxwell, co-author with John Shewey of *Fly Fishing for Summer Steelhead,* is the creator of the next two patterns. The Deschutes Skunk is a variant of the Skunk, one of the classic steelhead flies which has been around since the 1940s and which is probably one of the most popular steelhead flies of all time. The red tail and black body of the original has been retained but the wing has been changed from white bucktail to bronze mallard or dark turkey. The second version illustrated has a long body hackle of Chinese pheasant rump, turning the fly into the Deschutes Skunk Spey.

# North American Featherwing Flies

atuka-style flies originated in New Zealand and, over the years, have had a small but dedicated band of followers in the United Kingdom as lake flies for stillwater trout fishing. For salmon angling they have never really caught on but for steelheading it has been a different matter and in recent years they have become quite popular.

Matuka-style flies have much to recommend them – due to the keel-like construction of the wing they are stable, even in fast, heavy water conditions. They have presence without bulk and cut through the water, sinking quickly.

The three flies illustrated are matuka patterns from Forrest Maxwell and Deke Meyer and are shown in *Advanced Fly Fishing for Steelhead*.

The first two are two different versions of the Purple Matuka from Forrest Maxwell, one with a dubbed black body and one with a silver tinsel body. The third fly is the Halloween Matuka from Deke Meyer which he has found to be particularly effective for winter-run steelhead.

A further version which is also highly recommended for both summer and winter fishing is called the Surgeon Gerneral (or Del Cooper) which has a red body and purple hackle.

# North American Featherwing Flies

olden Demon II from Dave McNeese has echoes of an earlier era – the use of multiple (six to eight) golden pheasant toppings harks back to the early Irish flies such as the Golden Butterfly and the Parson series. McNeese uses this pattern in bright sunlight, so making maximum use of the effect gained by the crests. The fly literally glows in the water. Modern anglers tend to use new flashy products such as Krystal Flash when they need a bit of extra sparkle in a fly, but golden pheasant crests have been doing the same job effectively for years.

Golden Demon II - McNeese

The Redwing is an exceptional fly in its construction, appearance and in its use. The front part of the body consists of bunches of red feathers tied in around the hook, completely enclosing it. Four to six clumps of feathers are needed to make a complete body. The only other fly that I can find that shares this feature is the Chatterer, one of the flies devised by Traherne in the 19th century.

The Redwing is used by McNeese as the fly that will produce a fish when nothing else will – when he has fished through a pool with no success, but knows that a fish is there – on will go the Golden Demon and many times it has delivered.

When the fly is fished in moderate-to-low flows, the small feathers packed around the body can produce a lot of movement. As the fly drifts they tend to stand out at right angles, pulsing and flattening as the water flow increases when the fly comes under tension. Multiple golden pheasant toppings are also a feature of the Redwing. The fly is often tied on double hooks, usually in quite small sizes – sixes and eights. Just to show how effective the Redwing can be, it also caught a sixty-two pound chinook salmon for McNeese after a $1^{3/4}$-hour struggle on the River Trask in Oregon in 1989.

Redwing - McNeese

The Spawning Purple was first tied in 1977 for winter steelhead in clear water conditions. The body is of seal's fur spun on a loop to produce a ragged, ball-shaped body. As you may have noticed from this and many other flies illustrated, the combination of hot orange and hot purple is one that McNeese finds very effective and which he uses for many of his patterns.

Spawning Purple - McNeese

The last of the McNeese flies is the Knouse. This pattern was named after Stan Knouse who was a regular on the North Umpqua for many years and after whom Knouse's pool on the Umpqua is also named. The Knouse is used for both summer and winter steelhead and is particularly effective in British Columbia in large sizes.

# North American Featherwing Flies

Knouse - McNeese

Teresa's Tease - Garrett

D'Ana Marie - Garrett

Sara Teen - Garrett

Bobbie Jean - Garrett

he next, large group of flies are all the work of one man, Jim Garrett of the Sol Duc on the Olympic Peninsular. Trey Combs considers Garrett's featherwing flies to be among the most beautiful in steelheading. Garrett himself finds them not only aesthetically pleasing but practical as well. In *Steelhead Fly Fishing* by Trey Combs he is quoted as saying: *'Today's anglers are enamoured of hairwings'*. How true, and how much more true of European anglers!

Garrett uses these flies in late summer and early autumn, as well as in low water periods in spring. They are particularly effective when fish have taken up lies in broad, shallow tailouts. He sums up the advantages of featherwings as follows:

*'The flies have a translucency that only certain feathers possess, producing an effective blending of colours that could not exist in a hairwing fly. Study the Kate underwater in bright sunlight, and observe the radiance that occurs when the colours blend. The effect is unobtainable with any other materials'.* Exactly!

The following 17 flies demonstrate the point even more clearly – elegance combined with utility. The colour combinations used for these flies offer a wide range of options for different conditions and yet again show how effective the prismatic mixing effect can be.

It should be noted that most of these flies have teal flank wings which have a natural translucence. All of these flies are tied on gold Spey-style hooks to give added sparkle.

# North American Featherwing Flies

QE3

Kate

TC3

Helen's Fancy

Night Train

Mac Garrett

Father Bill

Soul Duck

Plate 16 - Steelhead Flies from Jim Garrett

# North American Featherwing Flies

Peterson M.D.

Johnson M.D.

Septober Candy

Septober Pheasant

Septober Orange

Plate 17 - Low-Water Flies from Jim Garrett

These last five flies are Garrett's answer to low-water conditions. Garrett uses these flies on extremely long leaders (as much as 14 feet) thus enabling him to present the flies repeatedly to a reluctant fish without scaring it. The colours range from straightforward attractors, to more insect-like combinations.

# North American Featherwing Flies

# Catalogue of Dressings

he following pages contain a full catalogue of all the flies which are illustrated within the main text. Dressing details for each fly are given, together with an illustration. The flies are organised in alphabetical order. The page numbers for each of the dressings may be found within the index.

We have not given hook details for these dressings; this is not an oversight but simply because hook types vary so widely and the rules governing what is and is not allowable in each area and country vary enormously. The typical hook sizes also vary according to the geographical area and the type of fish.

Dressings have been shown on a variety of hook types – singles, doubles and trebles. Most of the dressings given here will translate quite easily from one type of hook to another.

Another important point concerns materials from rare or protected species. Some of the dressings given in the following pages mention feathers from birds such as macaws, toucans etc. in order to maintain historical accuracy. On no account do we wish to encourage the illegal use of plumage from protected species: in any case perfectly acceptable substitutes are readily available. Even if the use of such plumage is not illegal we can see no reason why rare species should be further endangered by flytyers. The fish certainly can't tell the difference when a substitute is used!

# Catalogue of Dressings

### ABE MUNN KILLER
**TAG:** Silver gold tinsel
**TAIL:** Two narrow sections of mottled turkey
**BODY:** Buttercup yellow floss or wool
**RIB:** Oval gold tinsel
**THROAT:** Sparse bunch of mottled turkey with several turns of brown hackle tied as collar then pulled down
**WING:** Mottled turkey slips tied low to body
**HEAD:** Black

### AGUANUS
**TAG:** Flat silver tinsel & yellow floss
**TAIL:** Two narrow sections of mottled turkey
**BUTT:** Black ostrich herl
**BODY:** Burnt orange floss
**RIB:** Oval gold tinsel
**WING (1):** Small bunch of GP tippet fibres with yellow hackles each side.
**COLLAR (1):** Bright blue hackle
**WING (2):** Small bunch of GP tippet fibres
**COLLAR (2):** Natural black hackle
**HEAD:** Black

### AKROYD, HALYK'S REVERSE
**TAG:** Silver tinsel
**BODY:** Orange seal's fur
**RIB:** Oval gold tinsel
**THORAX:** Black seal's fur
**BODY HACKLE:** Black schlappen over thorax
**COLLAR HACKLE:** Teal
**WING:** Mottled turkey quill
**HEAD:** Black

### AKROYD, STEELHEAD
**TAG:** Silver tinsel
**TAIL:** GP crest dyed claret
**BUTT:** Black ostrich herl
**REAR BODY:** Claret seal's fur
**RIB:** Flat gold tinsel
**CENTRE BUTT:** Black ostrich herl
**FRONT BODY:** Black floss
**RIB:** Oval silver tinsel
**BODY HACKLE:** Claret over rear body, black heron over front body
**COLLAR:** Teal
**WING:** Claret goose
**CHEEKS:** Jungle cock
**HEAD:** Black

### ALEXANDRA
**TAIL:** Two matched slips of red feather
**BODY:** Flat silver tinsel
**RIB:** Oval silver tinsel
**THROAT:** Black or badger hackle
**WING:** Full bunch of peacock sword fibres
**HEAD:** Black

### ALL NIGHT SPEY
**BODY:** Purple floss underbody with purple and black Lite-Brite dubbing over
**RIB:** Flat silver tinsel and oval silver tinsel
**BODY HACKLE:** Black marabou, long
**COLLAR HACKLE:** Natural guinea fowl
**WING:** Black goose with married strands of purple goose over
**CHEEKS (optional):** Jungle cock, drooping
**HEAD:** Black

### AS SPECIFIED #1
**TAG:** Oval gold tinsel & purple floss
**TAIL:** Purple hackle fibres
**RIB:** Oval gold tinsel
**BODY:** Rear 1/3rd purple floss, front 2/3rds purple seal's fur
**BODY HACKLE:** Long black hackle from 2nd turn of tinsel
**THROAT:** Two turns of widgeon or teal
**WING:** Bronze mallard slips
**HEAD:** Black

### ASSASSIN
**TAG:** Silver tinsel & yellow floss
**TAIL:** GP crest with GP tippet & kingfisher
**BODY:** Scarlet seal's fur
**RIB:** Oval silver tinsel
**BODY HACKLE:** Dyed red cock
**SHOULDER HACKLE:** Yellow cock
**WING:** GP tippet; married red, yellow & blue swan, teal; bronze mallard; GP topping over
**CHEEKS:** Jungle cock
**HEAD:** Red

### BALLYSHANNON
**TAG:** Puce floss
**TAIL:** GP crest with scarlet Ibis
**BODY:** Yellow brown seal's fur
**RIB:** Oval silver tinsel
**BODY HACKLE:** Yellow cock
**WING:** Four GP toppings with barred summer duck back to back; married strips of pheasant tail, white tipped turkey tail, guinea fowl, Himalayan pheasant; red Himalayan pheasant crest over all.
**CHEEKS:** Blue kingfisher
**HEAD HACKLE:** Scarlet cock
**HEAD:** Black ostrich herl

 # Catalogue of Dressings

**ABE MUNN KILLER**     **AGUANUS**     **AKROYD, HALYK'S REVERSE**

**AKROYD, STEELHEAD**     **ALEXANDRA**     **ALL NIGHT SPEY**

**AS SPECIFIED #1**     **ASSASSIN**     **BALLYSHANNON**

# Catalogue of Dressings

### BARON
**TAG:** Oval silver tinsel & dark red floss
**TAIL:** GP crest and red hackle fibres
**REAR BODY:** Flat silver tinsel veiled with red hackle fibres underneath orange seal's fur
**RIB:** Flat silver tinsel
**CENTRE BUTT:** Black ostrich herl
**FRONT BODY:** Black floss
**RIB:** Oval silver tinsel
**THROAT:** Bright red hackle fibres with black hackle tied as collar and pulled down
**WING:** Bronze mallard
**HEAD:** Black

### BASTARD DOSE
**TAG:** Oval silver tinsel & golden yellow floss
**TAIL:** GP crest
**REAR BODY (1/3rd):** Light blue seal's fur
**FRONT BODY (2/3rds):** Black seal's fur
**RIB:** Oval silver tinsel
**THROAT:** Claret hackle
**WING:** Pair of GP tippet feathers back to back, dark barred teal flank over. GP crest overall
**HEAD:** Black

### BEAULY SNOW FLY
**RIB:** Medium flat silver tinsel followed by oval gold tinsel
**BODY:** Kingfisher blue seal's fur
**BODY HACKLE:** Black heron, counter wrap with fine oval silver tinsel
**WING:** Bunch of bronze peacock herl
**COLLAR HACKLE:** Two or three turns of black heron, reaching at least bend of hook
**HEAD:** Collar of spun orange rabbit guard hair

### BERESFORD'S FANCY
**TAG:** Silver tinsel & magenta floss
**TAIL:** GP topping
**REAR BODY:** Blue floss
**FRONT BODY:** Orange floss
**RIB:** Oval silver tinsel
**BODY HACKLE:** Black cock from 2nd turn of ribbing
**THROAT:** Claret-magenta cock with blue jay over
**WING:** GP tippet; married strands bustard, swan dyed claret-magenta, blue & orange; bronze mallard
**HORNS:** Blue macaw
**HEAD:** Black ostrich herl

### BIBIO
**TAG:** Silver tinsel
**BODY:** In three parts – black, red, black – seal's fur
**RIB:** Oval silver tinsel
**BODY HACKLE:** Black cock
**FRONT HACKLE:** Black cock, longer than body hackle
**HEAD:** Black

### BLACK & BLUE
**TAG:** Fine oval gold tinsel & yellow or blue floss
**TAIL:** Golden pheasant crest
**BODY:** Black seal's fur or floss
**RIB:** Oval silver tinsel
**THROAT:** Bright blue cock
**WING:** Married strips of blue, yellow & red goose; bronze mallard; golden pheasant crest over
**CHEEKS:** Jungle cock
**HEAD:** Black

### BLACK & SILVER
**TAIL:** Golden pheasant crest
**RIB:** Oval silver tinsel
**REAR BODY:** Flat silver tinsel
**FRONT BODY:** Black floss
**THROAT:** Natural guinea fowl
**WING:** Red golden pheasant breast feather with bronze mallard strips over; golden pheasant crest
**CHEEKS:** Jungle cock
**HEAD:** Black

### BLACK & TEAL
**TAG:** Silver tinsel & gold floss
**TAIL:** GP crest
**BUTT:** Black ostrich or chenille
**REAR BODY (1/3rd):** Orange floss
**FRONT BODY (2/3rds):** Black floss or seal's fur
**RIB:** Flat silver tinsel
**BODY HACKLE:** Black cock over front body
**THROAT:** Guinea fowl
**WING:** Two long and two short jungle cock feathers, back to back, enveloped by two teal or pintail whole feathers: GP topping over
**HEAD:** Black

# Catalogue of Dressings

**BARON**  **BASTARD DOSE**  **BEAULY SNOW FLY**

**BERESFORD'S FANCY**  **BIBIO**  **BLACK & BLUE**

**BLACK & SILVER**  **BLACK & TEAL**

# Catalogue of Dressings

### BLACK BOAR
**TAG:** Silver tinsel
**TAIL:** Three Chinese boar bristles dyed ruby red. A few strands black bucktail & two strands orange Crystal Hair
**BODY:** Flat silver tinsel
**RIB:** Oval silver tinsel
**THROAT:** Black squirrel
**WING:** Black squirrel with ruby red dyed GP tippet feathers
**FRONT HACKLE:** Soft fibred black hen
**HEAD:** Red

### BLACK DIAMOND
**TAG:** Silver tinsel
**BODY:** Black floss
**RIB:** Oval silver tinsel
**THROAT:** Guinea fowl
**WING:** Four peacock sword fibres with grey squirrel over
Overwing: Guinea fowl
**CHEEKS:** Jungle cock
**HEAD:** Black

### BLACK DOCTOR
**TAG:** Silver tinsel & yellow floss
**TAIL:** GP crest with topping of red hackle fibres
**BUTT:** Scarlet wool
**RIB:** Oval silver tinsel
**BODY:** Black floss
**RIB:** Flat silver tinsel
**BODY HACKLE:** Black cock from 2nd turn of tinsel
**THROAT:** Guinea fowl dyed blue
**WING:** Underwing of tippets in strands; red, blue & yellow swan, golden pheasant tail; bronze mallard over; strips of wood duck & teal; GP topping over
**HEAD:** Red

### BLACK DOG (MACKINTOSH)
**BODY:** Lead coloured pigs wool
**RIB:** Fine oval gold
**THROAT:** Black cock
**WING:** Blueish-grey heron wing over brown turkey tail
**HEAD:** Black

### BLACK DOG (KELSON)
**TAG:** Silver tinsel & canary yellow floss
**TAIL:** a topping and red ibis
**BUTT:** Black ostrich
**RIB:** Yellow silk with oval silver tinsel each side
**BODY:** Black floss
**BODY HACKLE:** Black heron from 3rd turn of rib
**THROAT:** Turns of body hackle
**WING:** Underwing of two red-orange hackles back to back; unbarred summer duck, light bustard, Amherst pheasant, scarlet & yellow dyed swan; two toppings
**HEAD:** Black

### BLACK EAGLE
**TAG:** Silver tinsel
**TAIL:** GP crest & Indian crow
**BODY:** Black seal's fur
**RIB:** Oval silver tinsel
**BODY HACKLE:** Black marabou
**THROAT:** Teal flank
**WING:** Two strips white tipped dark turkey tail
**HEAD:** Black

### BLACK FAIRY
**TAG:** Oval gold tinsel & yellow floss
**TAIL:** GP crest
**BUTT:** Black ostrich herl
**BODY:** Black seal's fur
**RIB:** Oval gold tinsel
**THROAT:** Black hackle
**WING:** Bronze mallard set low
**HEAD:** Black

### BLACK HAWK
**TAIL:** Summer duck fibres
**BODY:** Light slate grey floss
**RIB:** Black floss
**BODY/THROAT HACKLE:** Black hackle from mid-point of body. Extra turns at throat, tied as collar then pulled down
**WING:** Slate grey duck slips
**HEAD:** Black

# Catalogue of Dressings

**BLACK BOAR**  **BLACK DIAMOND**

**BLACK DOCTOR**  **BLACK DOG (MACKINTOSH)**  **BLACK DOG (KELSON)**

**BLACK EAGLE**  **BLACK FAIRY**  **BLACK HAWK**

# Catalogue of Dressings

### BLACK KEHE
**TAG:** Silver tinsel
**TAIL:** Tuft of fluorescent red wool under GP tippet fibres
**BODY:** Bronze peacock herl
**RIB:** Oval silver tinsel
**HEAD HACKLE:** Black hen, straggly & long
**HEAD:** Black

### BLACK LABRADOR
**TAIL:** Black bear hair or calf tail
**BODY:** Cigar shaped wool or dubbing
**COLLAR HACKLE:** Long black cock or hen
**HEAD:** Black

### BLACK ORANGE & JUNGLE COCK
**TAG:** Oval silver tinsel
**BODY:** Black floss
**RIB:** Oval silver tinsel
**THROAT:** Purple cock
**WING:** Orange dyed goose
**CHEEKS:** Jungle cock
**HEAD:** Black

### BLACK PENNELL
**TAG:** Silver tinsel
**TAIL:** GP crest
**BODY:** Black floss
**RIB:** Oval silver tinsel
**BODY HACKLE:** Black cock
**HACKLE:** Long black cock
**HEAD:** Black

### BLACK RANGER
**TAG:** Silver tinsel & yellow floss
**TAIL:** GP crest with Indian crow
**BUTT:** Black ostrich herl
**BODY:** Black floss
**RIB:** Oval silver tinsel
**BODY HACKLE:** Natural black from 2nd turn of ribbing
**THROAT:** Light blue hackle
**WING:** Two long jungle cock eye feathers, back to back enveloped by two pairs GP tippets (outer pair shorter). GP topping over
**CHEEKS:** Chatterer (blue hackle)
**HORNS:** Blue macaw
**HEAD:** Black

### BLACK REEACH (SHEWEY)
**TAG:** Hot orange dubbing or wool
**BODY:** Black orange seal's fur
**RIB:** Flat gold tinsel followed by oval gold tinsel
**BODY HACKLE:** Pheasant rump dyed black, counter rib with fine oval gold tinsel
**COLLAR:** Teal flank
**WING:** Bronze mallard
**HEAD:** Black

### BLACK SKY
**TAG:** Silver tinsel
**TAIL:** Black hackle fibres
**BODY:** Black floss or yarn
**RIB:** Oval gold tinsel
**HACKLE:** Black hen, wrapped full on both sides of wing
**WING:** Black hackle tips
**HEAD:** Black

For Blue Sky: replace all black with blue

For Rusty Sky: replace all black with rusty orange

### BLACK SPEY
**TAG:** Oval gold tinsel & black floss
**TAIL:** Red-orange
**BODY:** Black floss
**RIB:** Medium oval gold tinsel
**BODY HACKLE:** Black heron or substitute
**THROAT:** Two turns of teal flank
**WING:** Bronze mallard
**HEAD:** Black

### BLACK TIPPET & YELLOW
**TAG:** Oval silver tinsel
**TAIL:** Golden pheasant crest
**BODY:** Black floss
**RIB:** Oval silver tinsel
**THROAT:** Red cock
**WING:** Underwing of golden pheasant tippet, overwing of yellow dyed goose
**CHEEKS:** Jungle cock
**HEAD:** Black

# Catalogue of Dressings

| BLACK KEHE | BLACK LABRADOR | BLACK ORANGE & JUNGLE COCK |

| BLACK PENNELL | BLACK RANGER | BLACK REEACH (SHEWEY) |

| BLACK SKY | BLACK SPEY | BLACK TIPPET & YELLOW |

# Catalogue of Dressings

### BLACK TURKEY
**TAG:** Silver tinsel & yellow floss
**TAIL:** GP crest & red feather
**BODY:** Black seal's fur
**RIB:** Oval gold tinsel
**THROAT:** Ginger cock with blue jay over
**WING:** Brown mottled turkey tail strips
**HEAD:** Black

### BLACKVILLE
**TAG:** Silver tinsel & yellow floss
**TAIL:** GP crest
**BUTT:** Peacock herl
**BODY:** Flat silver tinsel
**RIB:** Oval silver tinsel
**THROAT:** Orange hackle applied as collar then pulled down, guinea fowl over
**WING:** Two matched pairs grey mallard flank
**HEAD:** Black

### BLADNOCH SHRIMP
**TAG:** Silver tinsel
**TAIL:** Red bucktail with three strands pearl Crystal Hair. Twice length of body
**BODY:** Flat pearl tinsel
**FRONT HACKLE:** Three or four turns of red cock
**CHEEKS:** Jungle cock
**HEAD:** Red

### BLUE CHARM
**TAG:** Silver tinsel & golden yellow floss
**TAIL:** GP crest
**BODY:** Black floss
**RIB:** Oval silver tinsel
**THROAT:** Blue hackle
**WING:** Strips of mottled brown turkey or bronze mallard with strips of barred teal flank over. GP crest over all
**HEAD:** Black

### BLUE CHARM, DOUBLE
**TAG:** Silver tinsel & golden yellow floss
**TAIL:** GP crest
**BODY:** Black floss
**RIB:** Oval silver tinsel
**THROAT:** Blue hackle
**WING:** Strips of mottled brown turkey or bronze mallard with strips of barred teal flank over. GP crest over all
**HEAD:** Black

### BLUE CHARM SPIDER
**HOOK:** Salar silver
**COLLAR HACKLES:** Long light blue under long black
**WING:** Bronze mallard fibres
**HEAD:** Black

### BLUE DOCTOR
**TAG:** Silver tinsel & yellow floss
**TAIL:** GP crest & tippet fibres
**BUTT:** Red wool
**REAR BODY:** Light blue floss
**FRONT BODY:** Light blue seal's fur
**RIB:** Oval silver tinsel
**BODY HACKLE:** Light blue cock over seal's fur
**THROAT:** Kingfisher blue with widgeon over
**WING:** GP tippet; married red, yellow & blue swan; Bronze mallard; Barred wood duck; GP topping over
**HEAD:** Red

124

# Catalogue of Dressings

### BLACK TURKEY
### BLACKVILLE

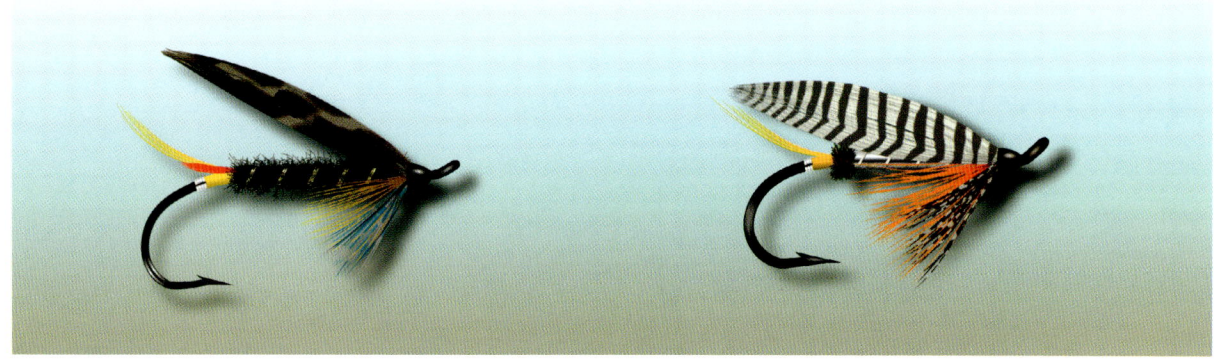

### BLADNOCH SHRIMP
### BLUE CHARM

### BLUE CHARM, DOUBLE
### BLUE CHARM SPIDER
### BLUE DOCTOR

# Catalogue of Dressings

### BLUE ELVER
**TAG:** Silver tinsel
**BODY:** Black floss
**RIB:** Oval silver tinsel
**WING:** Two long striped vulturine guinea fowl neck feathers back to back, tied streamer fashion
**COLLAR HACKLE:** Cobalt blue vulturine guinea fowl
**CHEEKS (optional):** Jungle cock
**HEAD:** Black

### BLUE SANDY
**TAG:** Silver tinsel & light blue floss
**TAIL:** GP crest with barred wood duck over
**BUTT:** Black ostrich herl
**REAR BODY:** Flat silver tinsel veiled top & bottom with kingfisher
**RIB:** Oval silver tinsel
**CENTRE BUTT:** Black ostrich herl
**FRONT BODY:** Blue seal's fur
**RIB:** Flat silver tinsel & oval silver tinsel
**BODY HACKLE:** Black hackle over blue fur
**THROAT:** Teal
**WING:** Paired black & white silver pheasant neck feathers, tied flat with black edges outward
**CHEEKS:** Jungle cock, drooping

### BLUE SAPPHIRE
**TAG:** Oval gold tinsel & yellow floss
**TAIL:** GP crest with red and blue hackle fibres over
**RIB:** Oval gold tinsel
**BODY:** Black floss
**BODY HACKLE:** Black & blue hackle wound together from 2nd turn ribbing.
**THROAT:** Extra turns of blue body hackle
**WING:** Underwing of white tipped brown turkey tail. Outer wing: married strips of blue goose & mottled turkey; bronze mallard; GP topping over
**CHEEKS (optional):** Jungle cock
**HEAD:** Black

### BOBBIE JEAN
**BODY:** Hot orange floss
**RIB:** Oval silver tinsel
**BODY HACKLE:** Black hackle
**WING:** Bronze mallard with Amherst pheasant crest dyed claret over
**CHEEKS:** Jungle cock
**HEAD:** Claret

### BØRRE FLUA
**TAG:** Oval silver tinsel, yellow floss followed by red floss
**TAIL:** Dyed red hackle fibres
**BUTT:** Black ostrich herl
**RIB:** Oval silver tinsel
**BODY:** Black floss
**THROAT:** Blue dyed guinea fowl
**WING:** Black goose
**CHEEKS (optional):** Jungle cock
**HEAD:** Black

### BOSS
**TAIL:** Black bucktail at least as long as body
**RIB:** Flat silver tinsel
**BODY:** Black chenille
**COLLAR HACKLE:** Red cock
**HEAD:** Silver bead chain eyes

### BOULDER CREEK
**BODY:** Black floss
**RIB:** Chartreuse Mylar tinsel
**BODY HACKLE:** Black saddle
**THROAT:** Kingfisher blue hackle with guinea fowl over
**WING:** Two red GP flank feathers back to back. GP topping over
**HEAD:** Black

### BRANCHU
**TAIL:** Golden pheasant tippet
**BODY:** Hot orange seal's fur, very full & picked out
**RIB:** Oval silver tinsel
**WING:** Single symmetrical wood duck flank feather tied flat
**CHEEKS:** Half a jungle cock eye feather each side
**COLLAR HACKLE:** Cree
**HEAD:** Red

### BRIGG'S PENNELL
**TAG:** Silver tinsel
**TAIL:** GP tippet
**BODY:** Black seal's fur
**RIB:** Oval silver tinsel
**HACKLE:** Long black hen
**HEAD:** Black

# Catalogue of Dressings

| BLUE ELVER | BLUE SANDY | BLUE SAPPHIRE |

| BOBBIE JEAN | BØRRE FLUA | BOSS |

| BOULDER CREEK | BRANCHU | BRIGG'S PENNELL |

# Catalogue of Dressings

### BRINDLE BUG
**TAIL:** Natural brown hackle fibres
**BODY:** Black & yellow variegated chenille. First turn wound under tail
**FRONT HACKLE:** Natural brown
**HEAD:** Black

### BROWN FAIRY
**TAG:** Oval gold tinsel
**TAIL:** GP crest
**BODY:** Fiery brown seal's fur
**RIB:** Oval gold tinsel
**BODY HACKLE:** Brown cock over front half of body
**THROAT:** Brown cock
**WING:** Bronze mallard with GP crest over
**HEAD:** Black

### BROWN TURKEY
**TAG:** Oval gold tinsel
**TAIL:** GP crest with GP tippet fibres over
**BODY:** In three parts; yellow, red & black seal's fur
**RIB:** Oval gold tinsel
**THROAT HACKLE:** Black cock or hen
**WING:** Mottled turkey or peacock quill
**HEAD:** Black

### BUMBLE, CLARET
**TAG:** Gold tinsel
**TAIL:** GP tippet
**BODY:** Dark claret seal's fur
**RIB:** Oval gold tinsel
**BODY HACKLE:** Two matched hackles, claret & black
**HEAD HACKLE:** Blue jay
**HEAD:** Black

### BUMBLE, GOLDEN OLIVE
**TAG:** Gold tinsel
**TAIL:** GP crest
**BODY:** Golden olive seal's fur
**RIB:** Oval gold tinsel
**BODY HACKLE:** Two matched hackles, golden olive & dark ginger
**HEAD HACKLE:** Blue jay
**HEAD:** Black

### BUMBLE, LEGGY CLARET
**TAG:** Silver tinsel
**TAIL:** GP tippet dyed hot orange
**BODY:** Dark claret seal's fur
**RIB:** Oval silver tinsel
**HEAD HACKLE:** Blue jay over blue peacock neck feather
**HEAD:** Black

### BULLDOG
**TAG:** Gold tinsel & ruby floss
**TAIL:** GP crest and chatterer
**BUTT:** Black chenille
**REAR BODY:** Flat silver tinsel veiled top & bottom with Indian crow
**CENTRE BUTT:** Black chenille
**FRONT BODY:** French blue floss
**RIB:** Oval silver tinsel
**BODY HACKLE:** Blue cock over front body
**THROAT:** Pintail or teal
**WING:** Married strips alternative yellow and black dyed swan; GP topping over
**CHEEKS:** Jungle cock with blue chatterer
**HEAD:** Black

### BURLAP
**TAIL:** Light brown or grey bucktail
**BODY:** Strands of burlap wound tight and then scored to give ragged appearance
**FRONT HACKLE:** Long grizzly
**HEAD:** Black

### BURTON
**TAG:** Silver tinsel
**TAIL:** GP crest
**BODY:** In three parts: yellow, red & black seal's fur
**RIB:** Flat silver tinsel
**THROAT:** Dark furnace hen
**WING:** Underwing of teal flank with cinnamon turkey tail strips over
**HEAD:** Black

# Catalogue of Dressings

| BRINDLE BUG | BROWN FAIRY | BROWN TURKEY |

| BUMBLE, CLARET | BUMBLE, GOLDEN OLIVE | BUMBLE, LEGGY CLARET |

| BULLDOG | BURLAP | BURTON |

# Catalogue of Dressings

### CAINS RIVER SCOTCH LASSIE
**TAIL:** Two paired strips of broad, barred wood duck flank
**BODY:** Flat silver tinsel
**WING:** Two bright French blue hackles back to back, outside these two yellow hackles
**CHEEKS:** Jungle cock
**COLLAR HACKLES:** Magenta followed by French blue hackle
**HEAD:** Black

### CAINS RIVER SILVER DOCTOR
**TAIL:** Two paired strips of broad, barred wood duck flank
**BODY:** Flat silver tinsel
**WING:** Two brown hackles back to back, outside these two grizzly hackles
**CHEEKS:** Jungle cock
**COLLAR HACKLES:** French blue followed by grizzly hackle
**HEAD:** Black

### CAMPBELL'S FANCY
**TAG:** Flat gold tinsel & fluorescent blue floss
**TAIL:** GP crest
**BODY:** Flat gold tinsel
**RIB:** Oval gold tinsel
**THROAT:** Furnace hackle
**WING:** Grey mallard flank
**HEAD:** Black

### CANDY MONTANA
**BODY:** Rear half: fluorescent lime floss
Front half: flame floss
**RIB:** Oval gold tinsel
**HACKLE:** Brown partridge
**HEAD:** Flame red

### CAR BODY
**BODY:** Black dubbing
**RIB:** Chartreuse Mylar tinsel
**BODY HACKLE:** Deep purple saddle
**THROAT:** Kingfisher blue hackle
**WING:** Two GP rump feathers dyed deep purple, back to back
**HEAD:** Black

### CASCADE VARIANT
**TAIL:** Red & yellow bucktail with strands of pearl Flashabou
**BODY:** Flat silver tinsel
**RIB:** Oval silver tinsel
**WING:** Purple hackle fibres
**SIDES:** Jungle cock
**FRONT HACKLE:** Red over yellow cock
**HEAD:** Black

### CASCAPEDIA
**TAG:** Fine oval gold tinsel & golden yellow floss
**TAIL:** Golden pheasant crest with red GP breast feather over
**BUTT:** Black ostrich herl
**RIB:** Oval gold tinsel
**BODY:** Embossed gold tinsel
**THROAT:** Golden pheasant red breast feather
**WING:** Sparse orange bucktail with one or two pairs of grizzly hackles back to back, GP crest over
**CHEEKS:** Spruce grouse with jungle cock
**HEAD:** Black

# Catalogue of Dressings

**CAINS RIVER SCOTCH LASSIE**  **CAINES RIVER SILVER DOCTOR**

**CAMPBELL'S FANCY**  **CANDY MONTANA**  **CAR BODY**

**CASCADE VARIANT**  **CASCAPEDIA**

# Catalogue of Dressings

### CATCH-A-ME-LODGE
**TAG:** Oval silver tinsel & fluorescent green wool
**BODY:** Black seal's fur
**RIB:** Oval silver tinsel
**BODY HACKLE:** Black silver pheasant body feather wound over front part of body
**THROAT:** Guinea fowl
**WING:** Two strips white goose tied short & splayed
**CHEEKS:** Jungle cock
**HEAD:** Black

### CERISE & CLARET SPEY
**REAR BODY:** Silver tinsel
**FRONT BODY:** Claret wool
**RIB:** Oval silver tinsel
**BODY HACKLE:** Cerise Spey hackle over claret wool
**FRONT HACKLE:** Mallard flank
**HEAD:** Black

### CHALEUR BAY SMELT
**TAIL:** Two peacock sword feathers with pintail flank over
**RIB:** Fine silver tinsel
**BODY:** Pearlescent Mylar tinsel, potbellied
**THROAT:** Pintail with peacock sword fibres over
**WING:** Underwing of two GP crests tied flat with sparse purple & blue dyed bucktail. Two sandy dun hackles back to back. GP crest over
**CHEEKS:** Tan ruffed grouse body feather with jungle cock
**HEAD:** Pearl cement

### CHAPPIE
**TAIL:** Two grizzly hackles, back to back
**BODY:** Orange wool
**RIB:** Oval silver tinsel
**THROAT:** Grizzly cock
**WING:** Two grizzly neck hackles, back to back set high
**HEAD:** Black

### CHARTREUSE SHRIMP
**TAIL:** Chartreuse bucktail with two strands pearl Crystal Hair
**BODY:** Underwind with flat silver tinsel, overwind with Lureflash pearl
**RIB:** Oval silver tinsel
**FRONT HACKLE:** Long chartreuse cock hackle fibres, top & bottom
**CHEEKS:** Jungle cock
**HEAD:** Yellow

### CHARTREUSE SPIDER
**TAG:** Silver tinsel
**TAIL:** Fluorescent green mallard flank fibres
**BODY:** Fluorescent chartreuse floss
**RIB:** Oval silver tinsel
**FRONT HACKLE:** Fluorescent green mallard flank
**HEAD:** White

### CINNAMON & GOLD
**TAG:** Gold tinsel
**TAIL:** GP crest
**BODY:** Flat gold tinsel
**RIB:** Oval gold tinsel
**WING:** Cinnamon slips
**HEAD HACKLE:** Cinnamon cock
**HEAD:** Black

### CINNAMON & GOLD (North American)
**TAG:** Orange floss
**TAIL:** Golden pheasant tippet
**BUTT:** Black ostrich
**BODY:** Flat gold tinsel
**RIB:** Oval gold
**THROAT:** Yellow cock
**WING:** Cinnamon turkey tail strips
**HEAD:** Black

# Catalogue of Dressings

| CATCH-A-ME-LODGE | CERISE & CLARET SPEY | CHALEUR BAY SMELT |

| CHAPPIE | CHARTREUSE SHRIMP |

| CHARTREUSE SPIDER | CINNAMON & GOLD | CINNAMON & GOLD (North American) |

# Catalogue of Dressings

## CLAN CHIEF
**TAG:** Silver tinsel
**TAIL:** Fluorescent floss, scarlet over yellow
**BODY:** Black seal's fur
**RIB:** Oval silver tinsel
**BODY HACKLE:** Black & scarlet cock wound together
**HEAD HACKLE:** Long black hen
**HEAD:** Black

## CLARET & BLACK
**TAG:** Fine oval gold tinsel & claret floss
**TAIL:** Small red-orange Indian crow substitute
**BUTT:** Black ostrich herl
**RIB:** Medium oval gold tinsel
**BODY:** Rear 1/3rd claret floss, front 2/3rds dark claret seal's fur
**BODY HACKLE:** Black cock from 2nd turn of rib
**THROAT:** Two turns widgeon or pintail flank
**WING:** Black goose
**CHEEKS (optional):** Jungle cock
**HEAD:** Black

## CLARET & JAY
**TAG:** Fine oval silver tinsel & orange floss
**TAIL:** GP tippets
**BODY:** Dark claret seal's fur
**RIB:** Oval silver tinsel
**BODY HACKLE:** Dark claret cock
**THROAT:** Blue jay
**WING:** GP tippet in strands, bronze mallard over
**CHEEKS (optional):** Jungle cock
**HEAD:** Black

## COMET
**TAIL:** Fluorescent orange polar bear at least as long as body
**RIB:** Oval gold tinsel
**BODY:** Orange chenille
**COLLAR HACKLE:** Fluorescent orange cock
**HEAD:** Silver bead chain eyes

## COMET, ORANGE
**TAIL:** Fluorescent orange polar bear at least as long as body
**BODY:** Flat silver tinsel
**COLLAR HACKLE:** Fluorescent orange cock
**HEAD:** Silver bead chain eyes

## CONNEMARA BLACK
**TAG:** Silver tinsel & orange floss
**TAIL:** GP crest & Indian crow substitute
**BODY:** Black seal's fur
**RIB:** Oval silver tinsel
**BODY HACKLE:** Black cock
**THROAT HACKLE:** Blue jay
**THROAT:** One turn of teal
**WING:** GP tippet under bronze mallard
**HEAD:** Black

## CONNEMARA CLARET
**TAG:** Silver tinsel
**TAIL:** GP crest
**BODY:** Claret seal's fur
**RIB:** Oval silver tinsel
**THROAT HACKLE:** Black cock with blue jay over
**WING:** Bronze mallard
**HEAD:** Black

## CONWAY BLUE
**TAG:** Silver tinsel & golden yellow floss
**TAIL:** GP crest
**BUTT:** Black ostrich herl
**BODY:** Royal blue seal's fur
**RIB:** Oval silver tinsel
**THROAT:** Blue cock with blue jay over
**WING:** GP tippet feathers, back to back, bronze mallard over; GP topping over all
**HEAD:** Black

# Catalogue of Dressings

**CLAN CHIEF**      **CLARET & BLACK**      **CLARET & JAY**

**COMET**      **COMET, ORANGE**

**CONNEMARA BLACK**      **CONNEMARA CLARET**      **CONWAY BLUE**

# Catalogue of Dressings

### COPPER MARCH BROWN
**TAG:** Silver tinsel
**TAIL:** Partridge hackle fibres
**BODY:** Flat copper tinsel
**RIB:** Oval gold tinsel
**THROAT:** Partridge hackle fibres
**WING:** Strips of hen pheasant tail, mottled turkey or similar
**HEAD:** Black

### COQUIHALLA ORANGE, DARK
**TAG:** Silver tinsel
**TAIL:** Golden pheasant tippet
**RIB:** Flat silver tinsel
**REAR BODY:** Orange floss
**FRONT BODY:** Orange polar bear underfur or seal's fur
**THROAT:** Scarlet cock
**WING:** Strands of orange polar bear with bronze mallard over
**HEAD:** Black

### COQUIHALLA ORANGE, LIGHT
**TAG:** Silver tinsel
**TAIL:** Golden pheasant tippet
**BUTT:** Black ostrich herl
**RIB:** Flat silver tinsel
**REAR BODY:** Orange floss
**FRONT BODY:** Orange polar bear underfur or seal's fur
**THROAT:** Scarlet cock
**WING:** Strands of orange polar bear with light mallard flank over
**HEAD:** Black

### COQUIHALLA RED
**TAG:** Yellow floss
**TAIL:** Red hackle tips
**BUTT:** Black ostrich herl
**RIB:** Flat silver tinsel
**BODY:** Orange floss, orange seal's fur, red seal's fur in equal sections
**THROAT:** Scarlet cock
**WING:** Peacock sword strands with grey mallard over
**HEAD:** Black

### CORNEILLE
**BODY:** Black wool
**THROAT:** Black cock
**WING:** Black crow
**HEAD:** Black

### COURTESAN
**BODY:** Orange seal's fur
**RIB:** Flat silver tinsel
**BODY HACKLE:** Long brown Spey hackle
**WING:** Two pairs hot orange hackle tips
**HEAD:** Black

### CRIMSON GLORY
**TAG:** Gold tinsel
**TAIL:** GP crest dyed orange
**REAR BODY:** Flat silver tinsel
**FRONT BODY:** Peacock herl
**RIB:** Oval gold tinsel
**THROAT:** Black hackle
**WING:** Two pairs GP tippet feathers dyed crimson, back to back. outer pair lined up to match black bars on inner pair. GP topping dyed orange over
**CHEEKS:** Jungle cock
**HEAD:** Black

### CROSFIELD
**TAG:** Oval silver tinsel
**TAIL:** GP crest
**BODY:** Flat silver tinsel
**RIB:** Oval silver tinsel
**THROAT:** Medium blue hackle
**WING:** Optional underwing of brown turkey, overwing of barred teal or grey mallard
**HEAD:** Black

### D'ANA MARIE
**TAIL:** GP crest dyed hot orange
**REAR BODY:** Hot orange floss
**FRONT BODY:** Red wool
**RIB:** Oval gold tinsel
**BODY HACKLE:** Orange hackle over front body
**THROAT:** Guinea fowl
**WING:** Pheasant tail
**CHEEKS:** Jungle cock
**HEAD:** Black

# Catalogue of Dressings

**COPPER MARCH BROWN**   **COQUIHALLA ORANGE, DARK**   **COQUIHALLA ORANGE, LIGHT**

**COQUIHALLA RED**   **CORNEILLE**   **COURTESAN**

**CRIMSON GLORY**   **CROSFIELD**   **D'ANA MARIE**

 # Catalogue of Dressings

### DANA MONTANA
**BODY:** Rear half: orange floss. Front half: red floss
**RIB:** Oval gold tinsel
**HACKLE:** Brown partridge
**HEAD:** Purple

### DANDY
**TAG:** Silver tinsel & yellow floss
**TAIL:** GP crest, summer duck & chatterer
**BUTT:** Black ostrich herl
**REAR BODY (2/3rds):** Flat silver tinsel
**FRONT BODY (1/3rd):** Light blue floss
**RIB:** Flat silver tinsel
**THROAT:** Light blue hackle with guinea fowl over
**WING:** Two long jungle cock, back to back enveloped by two GP tippet feathers; Outside this two barred summer duck feathers covering lower part of tippets
**CHEEKS:** Chatterer
**HORNS:** Blue macaw
**HEAD:** Black

### DARBEE'S SPATE FLY
**TAG:** Oval gold tinsel
**TAIL:** GP crest
**BODY:** Dark brown seal's fur
**RIB:** Oval gold tinsel
**THROAT:** Black hackle tied as collar then pulled down
**WING:** Natural brown bucktail to end of tail with wide strips of barred wood duck flank set each side. Two GP crests over
**HEAD:** Red or Black

### DARK MACKEREL
**TAIL:** GP tippet
**BODY:** Flat red Lurex
**RIB:** Oval silver tinsel
**BODY HACKLE:** Dark claret cock
**WING:** Bronze mallard
**COLLAR HACKLE:** Long dark claret hen
**HEAD:** Black

### DAWN
**TAG:** Oval silver tinsel
**TAIL:** Yellow hackle fibres
**BUTT:** Fluorescent orange floss
**RIB:** Oval silver tinsel & fluorescent green floss
**REAR BODY:** Flat silver tinsel
**FRONT BODY:** Black & gold crystal seal
**BODY HACKLE:** Black cock over front body
**THROAT:** Yellow hackle
**WING:** Two hot orange hackles back to back. Strand pearl flash each side. 1/4 white fox hair, 1/4 golden brown fox hair, 1/2 brown fox hair
**HEAD:** Black with fluorescent green stripe

### DAWN, BLACK
**TAG:** Oval gold tinsel
**TAIL:** Fire orange hackle fibres
**BUTT:** Fluorescent orange floss
**RIB:** Oval silver tinsel & fluorescent orange floss
**REAR BODY:** Flat gold tinsel
**FRONT BODY:** Black & gold crystal seal
**BODY HACKLE:** Black cock over front body
**THROAT:** Black heron
**WING:** Two fire orange hackles back to back. Strand red flash each side. golden brown fox hair
**HEAD:** Black with fluorescent orange stripe

### DAWN, BLUE
**TAG:** Flat gold tinsel
**TAIL:** Blue & orange hackle fibres
**BUTT:** Fluorescent red floss
**RIB:** Oval gold tinsel & fluorescent red floss
**REAR BODY:** Flat gold tinsel
**FRONT BODY:** Blue crystal seal
**BODY HACKLE:** Blue cock over front body
**THROAT:** Blue hackle
**WING:** Two blue hackles back to back. Strand pearl flash each side. 1/3 golden brown fox hair, 2/3 brown fox hair
**HEAD:** Black with fluorescent blue stripe

### DAWN, GREEN
**TAG:** Flat gold tinsel
**TAIL:** Green & orange hackle fibres
**BUTT:** Fluorescent green floss
**RIB:** Oval gold tinsel
**REAR BODY:** Flat gold tinsel
**FRONT BODY:** Green crystal seal
**BODY HACKLE:** Green cock over front body
**THROAT:** Green hackle
**WING:** Two yellow hackles back to back. Strand pearl flash each side. 1/4 white fox hair, 1/4 golden brown fox hair, 1/2 brown fox hair
**HEAD:** Black with fluorescent orange stripe

### DAWN, RED
**TAG:** Flat gold tinsel
**TAIL:** Red hackle fibres
**BUTT:** Fluorescent red floss
**RIB:** Oval gold tinsel & fluorescent red floss
**REAR BODY:** Flat gold tinsel
**FRONT BODY:** Black crystal seal
**BODY HACKLE:** Black cock over front body
**THROAT:** Red hackle
**WING:** Two red hackles back to back. Strand pearl flash each side. 1/3 golden brown fox hair, 2/3 black fox hair
**HEAD:** Black with fluorescent orange stripe

# Catalogue of Dressings

| DANA MONTANA | DANDY | DARBEE'S SPATE FLY |

| DARK MACKEREL | DAWN | DAWN, BLACK |

| DAWN, BLUE | DAWN, GREEN | DAWN, RED |

## Catalogue of Dressings

### DAWN, THUNDER
**TAG:** Oval gold tinsel and fluorescent orange floss
**TAIL:** Hot orange hackle fibres
**BUTT:** Fluorescent red floss
**RIB:** Oval gold tinsel
**REAR BODY:** Black floss
**FRONT BODY:** Black crystal seal
**BODY HACKLE:** Orange heron over front body
**THROAT:** Blue guinea hackle
**WING:** Two deep blue hackles back to back. Strand pearl flash each side. 1/3 green racoon, 2/3 brown fox hair
**HEAD:** Black with fluorescent orange stripe

### DAWN, YELLOW
**TAG:** Oval gold
**TAIL:** Yellow & green hackle fibres
**BUTT:** Fluorescent red floss
**RIB:** Oval gold tinsel
**REAR BODY:** Flat silver tinsel
**FRONT BODY:** Yellow crystal seal
**BODY HACKLE:** Yellow cock over front body
**THROAT:** Yellow hackle
**WING:** Two yellow hackles back to back. Strand pearl flash each side. 1/3 golden brown fox hair, 2/3 brown fox hair
**HEAD:** Black with fluorescent orange stripe

### DEAN RIVER LANTERN, GREEN
**TAIL:** Squirrel hair dyed black, as long as body
**BODY:** Underbody of flat silver tinsel. Overbody Edge Brite dyed fluorescent green
**HACKLE:** Fluorescent green cock
**HEAD:** Black

### DEAN RIVER LANTERN, ORANGE
**TAIL:** Squirrel hair dyed black, as long as body
**BODY:** Underbody of flat silver tinsel. Overbody Edge Brite dyed fluorescent orange
**HACKLE:** Fluorescent orange cock
**HEAD:** Black

### DEAN RIVER LANTERN, RED
**TAIL:** Squirrel hair dyed black, as long as body
**BODY:** Underbody of flat silver tinsel. Overbody Edge Brite dyed fluorescent red
**HACKLE:** Fluorescent red cock
**HEAD:** Black

### DEAN RIVER LANTERN, YELLOW
**TAIL:** Squirrel hair dyed black, as long as body
**BODY:** Underbody of flat silver tinsel. Overbody Edge Brite dyed fluorescent yellow
**HACKLE:** Fluorescent yellow cock
**HEAD:** Black

### DEEP PURPLE SPEY
**TAG:** Silver tinsel
**BODY:** Purple floss
**RIB:** Flat silver tinsel
**BODY HACKLE:** Brown Chinese pheasant
**THROAT:** Purple hackle
**WING:** Red golden pheasant body feathers
**HEAD:** Black

### DELPHI SILVER
**TAG:** Silver tinsel
**TAIL:** Two jungle cock eye feathers, back to back
**BODY:** Flat silver tinsel in two parts
**RIB:** Oval silver tinsel
**CENTRE HACKLE:** Black cock
**HEAD HACKLE:** Long black cock
**HEAD:** Black

### DENISE
**TAG:** Oval silver tinsel & ginger floss
**TAIL:** Amherst pheasant crest and teal fibres
**BUTT:** Black ostrich herl
**BODY:** Flat silver tinsel
**RIB:** Oval silver tinsel
**BODY HACKLE:** Dark ginger cock
**THROAT:** Kelly green hackle, tied as collar and then pulled down
**WING:** Long jungle cock flanked by a pair of GP tippet feathers and then shorter Amherst pheasant tippets
**CHEEKS:** Jungle cock & kingfisher
**HORNS:** Blue & yellow macaw
**HEAD:** Black

# Catalogue of Dressings

**DAWN, THUNDER**  **DAWN, YELLOW**  **DEAN RIVER LANTERN, GREEN**

**DEAN RIVER LANTERN, ORANGE**  **DEAN RIVER LANTERN, RED**  **DEAN RIVER LANTERN, YELLOW**

**DEEP PURPLE SPEY**  **DELPHI SILVER**  **DENISE**

## Catalogue of Dressings

### DENISE MONTANA
**BODY:** Red floss
**RIB:** Oval gold tinsel
**HACKLE:** Pheasant dyed black
**HEAD:** Purple

### DESCHUTES SKUNK
**TAG:** Flat silver tinsel & red floss
**BODY:** Black dubbing
**RIB:** Oval silver tinsel
**BODY HACKLE:** Chinese pheasant rump feather
**THROAT:** Teal flank
**WING:** Bronze mallard
**HEAD:** Black

### DESCHUTES SKUNK SPEY
**TAG:** Flat silver tinsel & red floss
**BODY:** Black dubbing
**RIB:** Oval silver tinsel
**BODY HACKLE:** Long chinese pheasant rump feather as Spey hackle
**THROAT:** Chinese pheasant rump with Teal flank in front
**WING:** Bronze mallard
**HEAD:** Black

### DICK'S FLY
**TAG:** Oval gold tinsel
**TAIL:** Golden pheasant crest
**RIB:** Oval gold tinsel
**BODY:** Black floss
**THROAT:** Yellow or coch-y-bonddu
**WING:** Bronze mallard
**CHEEKS:** Jungle cock
**HEAD:** Black

### DOC SPRATLEY
**TAIL:** Guinea fowl
**RIB:** Flat silver tinsel
**BODY:** Black floss, wool or chenille
**THROAT:** Guinea fowl
**WING:** Slender strips of centre tail feather from ring-necked pheasant
**HEAD:** Black

### DONEGAL BLUE
**TAG:** Silver tinsel
**BODY:** Light kingfisher blue seal's fur
**RIB:** Flat silver tinsel
**HACKLE:** Long black hen
**HEAD:** Black

### DRAGON
**TAG:** Silver tinsel
**BODY:** Underwound with flat silver tinsel, fluorescent green floss over
**RIB:** Black ostrich herl counterwound with silver wire
**COLLAR HACKLE:** Webby black saddle hackle
**HEAD:** Black

### DRAGON'S TOOTH
**TAG:** Silver tinsel
**BODY:** Purple dubbing or wool
**RIB:** Flat silver tinsel & oval silver tinsel
**BODY HACKLE:** Deep purple saddle
**THROAT:** Pintail flank
**WING:** Two red GP rump feathers back to back with shorter yellow GP rump feather each side.
**HEAD:** Black

### DREAM
**TAG:** Flat gold tinsel
**BUTT:** Black ostrich herl
**TAIL:** Golden pheasant tippet
**RIB:** Oval gold tinsel
**BODY:** Golden yellow floss
**BODY HACKLE:** Yellow cock
**THROAT:** Fire orange cock hackle
**WING:** Two fire orange hackles back to back, 1/2 golden brown fox hair, 1/2 brown fox hair
**HEAD:** Black

## Catalogue of Dressings

| DENISE MONTANA | DESCHUTES SKUNK | DESCHUTES SKUNK SPEY |

| DICK'S FLY | DOC SPRATLEY | DONEGAL BLUE |

| DRAGON | DRAGON'S TOOTH | DREAM |

# Catalogue of Dressings

### DUNKELD
**TAIL:** GP crest
**BODY:** Flat gold tinsel
**RIB:** Oval gold tinsel
**BODY HACKLE:** Orange cock
**THROAT:** Blue jay
**WING:** Bronze mallard
**CHEEKS:** Jungle cock
**HEAD:** Black

### DURHAM RANGER
**TAG:** Silver tinsel & gold floss
**TAIL:** GP crest
**BUTT:** Black ostrich herl
**BODY:** In four equal parts: yellow floss, orange seal's fur, brown seal's fur, black seal's fur
**RIB:** Oval silver tinsel
**BODY HACKLE:** Yellow dyed badger over front half of body
**THROAT:** Light blue hackle
**WING:** Pair of long jungle cock, back to back; two pairs of tippet feathers outside, GP topping over all
**CHEEKS:** Kingfisher
**HORNS:** Blue macaw
**HEAD:** Black

### DUSTY MILLER
**TAG:** Silver tinsel & yellow floss
**TAIL:** GP crest & Indian crow substitute
**BUTT:** Black ostrich herl
**BODY:** Rear 2/3rds embossed silver tinsel, front 1/3rd orange floss
**RIB:** Oval silver tinsel
**BODY HACKLE:** Golden olive over orange floss
**THROAT:** Guinea fowl
**WING:** Married strips of red, yellow & orange swan, bustard & golden pheasant tail; strips of barred summer duck; bronze mallard; GP topping over all
**CHEEKS:** Jungle cock
**HEAD:** Black

### DWYRYD RED & YELLOW
**TAIL:** GP crest
**REAR BODY:** Rear 1/3rd yellow wool, middle 1/3rd red wool. Front 1/3rd black wool
**THROAT:** Guinea fowl
**WING:** Dark brown turkey strips
**HEAD:** Black

### EAGLE, BLACK
**TAG:** Silver tinsel
**TAIL:** GP crest & Indian crow
**BODY:** Black seal's fur
**RIB:** Oval silver tinsel
**BODY HACKLE:** Black marabou
**THROAT:** Teal flank
**WING:** Two strips white tipped dark turkey tail
**HEAD:** Black

### EAGLE, EMERALD
**TAG:** Silver tinsel
**REAR BODY:** Chartreuse floss
**FRONT BODY:** Black seal's fur
**RIB:** Oval silver tinsel
**BODY HACKLE:** Emerald green marabou with black tips wound over front body. Counter rib with fine oval gold tinsel
**COLLAR:** Mallard flank dyed black
**WING:** Black goose quill
**HEAD:** Black

### EAGLE, GREY
**TAG:** Silver tinsel
**TAIL:** Golden pheasant red breast feather
**BODY:** Yellow, light blue & scarlet seal's fur
**RIB:** Flat silver tinsel & oval silver tinsel
**BODY HACKLE:** Grey eagle from blue seal's fur
**THROAT:** One turn of teal or widgeon
**WING:** Strips of grey mottled turkey with white tips
**HEAD:** Black

### EAGLE, YELLOW
**TAG:** Silver tinsel
**TAIL:** Golden pheasant red breast feather
**BODY:** Yellow, scarlet, & light blue seal's fur
**RIB:** Flat silver tinsel & oval silver tinsel
**BODY HACKLE:** Eagle dyed yellow from scarlet seal's fur
**THROAT:** One turn of teal or widgeon
**WING:** Strips of grey mottled turkey with white tips
**HEAD:** Black

# Catalogue of Dressings

| DUNKELD | DURHAM RANGER | DUSTY MILLER |

| DWYRYD RED & YELLOW | EAGLE, BLACK | EAGLE, EMERALD |

| EAGLE, GREY | EAGLE, YELLOW |

# Catalogue of Dressings

### EANY TAILFIRE
**TAIL:** Flame orange bucktail with two strands pearl Flashabou Accent
**TAG:** Lime green Globrite floss
**REAR BODY:** Flat gold Mylar tinsel
**RIB:** Oval gold tinsel
**CENTRE HACKLE:** Flame orange cock
**FRONT BODY:** Black floss
**RIB:** Oval silver tinsel
**FRONT HACKLE:** Silver badger dyed yellow
**HEAD:** Black

### EM TE FLUGOR
**TAG:** Gold tinsel
**TAIL:** GP crest
**BODY:** Mixed red-brown & green wool
**RIB:** Flat gold tinsel
**THROAT:** Black cock
**WING:** Cinnamon dyed polar bear with a furnace hackle either side. Peacock sword fibres over
**HEAD:** Black

### FATHER BILL
**TAIL:** Wood duck flank
**BUTT:** Black ostrich herl
**BODY:** Embossed silver tinsel
**BODY HACKLE:** Orange over front body
**WING:** Underwing: red goose quill, back to back. Overwing: Teal. GP topping dyed flame over.
**CHEEKS:** Jungle cock
**HEAD:** Black

### FIERY BROWN
**TAG:** Gold tinsel
**TAIL:** GP crest
**BODY:** Fiery brown seal's fur
**RIB:** Oval gold tinsel
**BODY HACKLE:** Fiery brown cock
**THROAT:** Black cock
**WING:** Bronze mallard
**HORNS:** Blue macaw
**HEAD:** Black

### FIERY BROWN STREAMER
**TAG:** Gold tinsel
**TAIL:** GP crest
**BODY:** Flat gold tinsel
**THROAT:** Red hackle fibres
**WING:** Dark badger hackles back to back. GP topping over
**CHEEKS:** Jungle cock
**HEAD:** Black

### GABY
**TAG:** Silver tinsel
**REAR BODY (2/3rds):** #18 green Krystal Flash wound over flat silver tinsel
**FRONT BODY (1/3rd):** Black ostrich herl
**BODY HACKLE:** Black heron over front body
**HEAD HACKLE:** Long chartreuse dyed mallard flank
**HEAD:** Black

### GAGEURE
**TAG:** Oval silver tinsel & golden yellow floss
**TAIL:** Golden pheasant yellow rump
**BUTT:** Black ostrich herl
**BODY:** Flat silver tinsel
**RIB:** Oval silver tinsel
**WING:** Pair black hackles back to back with a pair of long jungle cock feathers each side
**COLLAR HACKLE:** Grizzly hen hackle
**HEAD:** Black

### GAUDY FLY
**TAIL:** Peacock herl
**BODY:** Red ostrich herl
**RIB:** Oval gold tinsel
**BODY HACKLE:** Bright yellow
**THROAT:** Green peacock herl
**WING:** Pair of red dyed hackles back to back enclosed with guinea fowl feathers
**HEAD:** Black

146

# Catalogue of Dressings

**EANY TAILFIRE**      **EM TE FLUGOR**

**FATHER BILL**      **FIERY BROWN**      **FIERY BROWN STREAMER**

**GABY**      **GAGEURE**      **GAUDY FLY**

# Catalogue of Dressings

**GENERAL MONEY #1**
**TAG:** Oval silver tinsel
**TAIL:** Golden pheasant red breast fibres
**RIB:** Oval silver tinsel
**REAR BODY (2/5ths):** Oval silver tinsel
**FRONT BODY (3/5ths):** Black polar bear underfur or seal's fur
**HACKLE:** Long burgundy black fur
**THROAT:** Burgundy dyed guinea fowl
**WING:** Orange goose
**CHEEKS:** Jungle cock
**HEAD:** Black

**GENERAL MONEY #2**
**TAG:** Oval gold tinsel
**TAIL:** Golden pheasant crest
**RIB:** Oval gold tinsel
**BODY:** Black floss
**HACKLE:** Long yellow from 2nd turn of rib
**THROAT:** Yellow dyed badger
**WING:** Red goose with GP crest over (optional)
**CHEEKS:** Jungle cock
**HEAD:** Black

**GERMAN SNELDA**
**TAIL:** Three bunches bucktail equally spaced: black, red, yellow
**BODY:** Black wool
**RIB:** Oval silver tinsel
**FRONT HACKLE:** Short black cock
**HEAD:** Black

**GHOST**
**TAG:** Silver tinsel
**TAIL:** GP crest
**BODY:** White chenille
**RIB:** Oval silver tinsel
**THROAT:** White cock
**WING:** White goose
**HEAD:** Black

**GLASGOW RANGERS**
**TAG:** Globrite #4 floss (fluorescent orange-red)
**BODY:** Holographic silver tinsel
**RIB:** Oval silver tinsel
**WING:** Blue hackle fibres
**FRONT HACKLE:** Black cock
**HEAD:** Black

**GLED WING**
**TAG:** Silver tinsel
**TAIL:** Red GP body feather fibres
**BODY:** In two sections – 1/3rd orange-yellow seal's fur, 2/3rds claret seal's fur
**RIB:** Flat silver tinsel
**BODY HACKLE:** Lemon cock
**CENTRE BUTT:** Long black heron
**THROAT:** One turn of teal
**WING:** Red dun turkey strips
**HEAD:** Black

**GLEN GRANT**
**TAIL:** Yellow GP rump feather fibres
**BODY:** A few turns of yellow Berlin wool then black Berlin wool
**RIB:** Flat silver tinsel followed by oval silver tinsel
**BODY HACKLE:** Black Spey cock
**THROAT:** Teal flank
**WING:** Two long jungle cock eyes, back to back enclosed by another two pairs, in each case shorter. Teal flank over
**HEAD:** Yellow Berlin wool

# Catalogue of Dressings

**GENERAL MONEY #1**  **GENERAL MONEY #2**

**GERMAN SNELDA**  **GHOST**

**GLASGOW RANGERS**  **GLED WING**  **GLEN GRANT**

# Catalogue of Dressings

### GOAT'S TOE
**TAIL:** Tuft of red wool or floss
**BODY:** Peacock herl
**RIB:** Red floss
**FRONT HACKLE:** Blue peacock neck feather, long
**HEAD:** Black

### GOLD BUTCHER
**TAG:** Gold tinsel
**TAIL:** Red swan slip
**BODY:** Flat gold tinsel
**RIB:** Oval gold tinsel
**FRONT HACKLE:** Claret cock
**WING:** Blue mallard wing slips
**CHEEKS:** Jungle cock
**HEAD:** Black

### GOLD BUTCHER, HARDY'S
**TAG:** Gold tinsel
**TAIL:** Red hackle fibres
**BODY:** Flat gold tinsel
**RIB:** Oval gold tinsel
**FRONT HACKLE:** Hot orange hen
**WING:** Cinnamon turkey tail strips
**HEAD:** Black

### GOLD HILTON SPIDER
**TAIL:** Wood duck or widgeon flank fibres
**BODY:** Black chenille
**RIB:** Oval gold tinsel
**WING:** Grizzly hackle tips
**FRONT HACKLE:** Bronze mallard
**HEAD:** Black

### GOLD REEACH
**TAG:** Orange floss
**BODY:** Black wool
**RIB:** Flat gold tinsel with two strands fine oval gold tinsel between
**BODY HACKLE:** Natural red cock
**THROAT:** One turn of teal
**WING:** Bronze mallard
**HEAD:** Black

### GOLD SYLPH
**TAG:** Gold tinsel
**TAIL:** GP crest
**BODY:** Flat gold tinsel
**RIB:** Oval silver tinsel
**THROAT:** Lemon yellow hackle with golden pheasant yellow breast feather over
**WING:** Bronze mallard
**HEAD:** Black

### GOLDEN BUTTERFLY
**TAG:** Silver tinsel & gold floss
**TAIL:** GP crest with barred wood duck over
**BUTT:** Black ostrich herl
**BODY:** Yellow floss
**RIB:** Oval gold tinsel
**THROAT:** Three toppings, curved downwards
**WING:** A GP topping each side of body curving inwards. A large topping on top curving upwards
**CHEEKS:** Red cock-of-the-rock feather each side, a kingfisher feather each side tied low
**HEAD:** Black ostrich herl

### GOLDEN DEMON II
**TAG:** Silver tinsel
**TAIL:** GP crest
**BODY:** Flat gold or copper tinsel
**RIB:** Oval silver tinsel
**BODY HACKLE:** Long hot orange from centre body
**WING:** Furnace hackle tips with bronze mallard over
**TOPPING:** Six to eight GP toppings
**CHEEKS:** Jungle cock
**HEAD:** Black

### GOLDEN EDGE ORANGE
**TAG:** Silver tinsel
**TAIL:** GP crest
**BODY:** Orange seal's fur
**RIB:** Flat silver tinsel
**THROAT:** Guinea fowl
**WING:** Grey squirrel with bronze mallard over. GP topping over all
**CHEEKS:** Jungle cock
**HEAD:** Orange

# Catalogue of Dressings

| GOAT'S TOE | GOLD BUTCHER | GOLD BUTCHER, HARDY'S |

| GOLD HILTON SPIDER | GOLD REEACH | GOLD SYLPH |

| GOLDEN BUTTERFLY | GOLDEN DEMON II | GOLDEN EDGE ORANGE |

# Catalogue of Dressings

### GOLDEN EDGE YELLOW
**TAG:** Silver tinsel
**TAIL:** GP crest
**BODY:** Yellow seal's fur
**RIB:** Flat silver tinsel
**THROAT:** Guinea fowl
**WING:** Grey squirrel with bronze mallard over. GP topping over all
**CHEEKS:** Jungle cock
**HEAD:** Yellow

### GOLDEN GIRL
**TAIL:** Indian crow substitute or yellow hackle fibres
**BODY:** Flat gold tinsel
**THROAT:** Yellow cock
**WING:** Underwing, orange polar bear hair. Overwing golden pheasant tippet feathers back to back, golden pheasant crest over
**HEAD:** Black

### GOLDEN MALLARD
**TAG:** Gold tinsel
**TAIL:** GP crest & Indian crow
**BUTT:** Black floss
**REAR BODY:** Flat gold tinsel
**FRONT BODY:** Black floss
**RIB:** Oval gold tinsel
**BODY HACKLE:** Hot orange over black floss
**THROAT:** Guinea fowl
**WING:** GP tippet & cinnamon turkey with bronze mallard over. GP topping over all
**HEAD:** Black

### GOLDEN PURPLE SPEY
**TAG:** Flat gold tinsel & hot orange floss
**BODY:** Purple seal's fur
**RIB:** Fine oval gold tinsel
**BODY HACKLE:** Reddish-brown golden pheasant
**THROAT:** Guinea fowl
**WING:** Red golden pheasant body feathers
**HEAD:** Black

### GOLDEN RED
**TAG:** Silver tinsel & yellow floss
**TAIL:** GP crest and red hackle fibres
**BODY:** Oval gold tinsel
**THROAT:** Red cock
**WING:** Bronze mallard with GP crest over
**HEAD:** Black

### GOLDEN SPEY
**TAG:** Flat gold tinsel
**BODY:** Golden yellow seal's fur
**RIB:** Flat gold tinsel
**BODY HACKLE:** Grey heron dyed golden yellow
**THROAT:** Golden yellow hackle
**WING:** Matched pair of brown hackle tips; GP topping over
**HEAD:** Black

### GOLDEN SPEY, TAYLOR'S
**TAG:** Silver tinsel
**REAR BODY:** Hot orange floss
**FRONT BODY:** Hot orange seal's fur
**RIB:** Flat silver tinsel followed by oval silver tinsel
**BODY HACKLE:** Long grey heron
**THROAT:** Golden pheasant red breast feather or lemon wood duck flank
**WING:** Two golden pheasant red breast feathers, set flat over body
**HEAD:** Black

### GORBENMAC, BLACK
**TAG:** Silver tinsel & black floss
**TAIL:** GP crest dyed black with GP tippets dyed black over
**BODY:** Black seal's fur
**RIB:** Peacock herl
**BODY HACKLE:** Black cock
**THROAT:** Blue jay
**WING:** Natural black peacock wing feather
**SIDES:** GP tippet dyed black
**CHEEKS:** Jungle cock
**HEAD:** Black

### GORBENMAC, GREEN
**TAG:** Silver tinsel & green floss
**TAIL:** GP crest dyed green with GP tippets dyed green over
**BODY:** Green highlander seal's fur
**RIB:** Peacock herl
**BODY HACKLE:** Green cock
**THROAT:** Blue jay
**WING:** Natural black peacock wing feather
**SIDES:** GP tippet dyed green
**CHEEKS:** Jungle cock
**HEAD:** Black

# Catalogue of Dressings

**GOLDEN EDGE YELLOW**     **GOLDEN GIRL**     **GOLDEN MALLARD**

**GOLDEN PURPLE SPEY**     **GOLDEN RED**     **GOLDEN SPEY**

**GOLDEN SPEY, TAYLOR'S**     **GORBENMAC, BLACK**     **GORBENMAC, GREEN**

# Catalogue of Dressings

### GORBENMAC, ORANGE
**TAG:** Silver tinsel & orange floss
**TAIL:** GP crest dyed orange with GP tippets dyed orange over
**BODY:** Orange seal's fur
**RIB:** Peacock herl
**BODY HACKLE:** Orange cock
**THROAT:** Blue jay
**WING:** Natural black peacock wing feather
**SIDES:** GP tippet dyed orange
**CHEEKS:** Jungle cock
**HEAD:** Black

### GORBENMAC, PURPLE
**TAG:** Silver tinsel & purple floss
**TAIL:** GP crest dyed purple with GP tippets dyed purple over
**BODY:** Purple seal's fur
**RIB:** Peacock herl
**BODY HACKLE:** Black cock
**THROAT:** Blue jay
**WING:** Natural black peacock wing feather
**SIDES:** GP tippet dyed purple
**CHEEKS:** Jungle cock
**HEAD:** Black

### GORBENMAC, RED
**TAG:** Silver tinsel & red floss
**TAIL:** GP crest dyed red with GP tippets dyed red over
**BODY:** Red seal's fur
**RIB:** Peacock herl
**BODY HACKLE:** Red cock
**THROAT:** Blue jay
**WING:** Natural black peacock wing feather
**SIDES:** GP tippet dyed red
**CHEEKS:** Jungle cock
**HEAD:** Black

### GORBENMAC RANGER, BLACK
**TAG:** Silver tinsel
**TAIL:** GP crest with GP crest dyed black over
**BODY:** Black seal's fur
**RIB:** Peacock herl
**BODY HACKLE:** Black cock
**THROAT:** Blue jay
**WING:** Pair of long jungle cock back to back covered for 3/4 of their length by two pairs GP tippets dyed black. 2nd pair to match black bands on first pair. Black dyed GP topping over
**CHEEKS:** Jungle cock
**HEAD:** Black

### GORBENMAC RANGER, BLACK & GOLD
**TAG:** Silver tinsel
**TAIL:** GP crest dyed orange with GP crest dyed black over
**BODY:** Gold Lite-Brite dubbing
**RIB:** Peacock herl
**BODY HACKLE:** Orange cock
**THROAT:** Blue jay
**WING:** Pair of long jungle cock back to back covered for 3/4 of their length by pair of GP tippets dyed orange. 2nd pair of GP tippet dyed black to reach black bands on first pair. Black dyed GP topping over
**CHEEKS:** Jungle cock
**HEAD:** Black

### GORBENMAC RANGER, GREEN
**TAG:** Silver tinsel
**TAIL:** GP crest dyed with GP crest dyed green over
**BODY:** Green seal's fur
**RIB:** Peacock herl
**BODY HACKLE:** Green cock
**THROAT:** Blue jay
**WING:** Pair of long jungle cock back to back covered for 3/4 of their length by two pairs GP tippets dyed green. 2nd pair to match black bands on first pair. Green dyed GP topping over
**CHEEKS:** Jungle cock
**HEAD:** Black

### GOSHAWK
**TAG:** Silver tinsel & lemon floss
**BUTT:** Black ostrich
**TAIL:** Strip of red goose
**RIB:** Oval silver tinsel
**BODY:** Black floss
**THROAT:** Blue jay
**WING:** Married strips of goose in order yellow, red, yellow
**HEAD:** Black

### GOSLING, GREY
**TAG:** Gold tinsel
**TAIL:** Cock pheasant centre tail fibres
**BODY:** Golden olive seal's fur
**RIB:** Oval gold tinsel
**HEAD HACKLES:** Hot orange cock, long, sloping well back. Grey mallard flank sloping back over
**HEAD:** Black

### GOSLING, RUSH
**TAG:** Gold tinsel
**TAIL:** Cock pheasant centre tail fibres
**BODY:** Golden olive seal's fur
**RIB:** Oval gold tinsel
**HEAD HACKLES:** Yellow golden pheasant breast feather under long hot orange cock, sloping well back. Grey mallard flank sloping back over
**HEAD:** Black

# Catalogue of Dressings

**GORBENMAC, ORANGE**  **GORBENMAC, PURPLE**  **GORBENMAC, RED**

**GORBENMAC RANGER, BLACK**  **GORBENMAC RANGER, BLACK & GOLD**  **GORBENMAC RANGER, GREEN**

**GOSHAWK**  **GOSLING, GREY**  **GOSLING, RUSH**

## Catalogue of Dressings

### GOSLING, YELLOW
**TAIL:** Fibres of cock pheasant centre tail
**BODY:** Golden olive seal's fur
**RIB:** Oval gold tinsel
**HACKLES:** Hot orange with grey mallard flank over
**HEAD:** Black

### GREEN BEAUTY
**TAG:** Silver tinsel
**BODY:** Golden orange floss
**RIB:** Flat silver tinsel
**THROAT:** White bucktail & two golden pheasant crests
**WING:** Four strands of peacock herl under two pairs dark green saddle hackles
**SIDES:** Lemon wood duck flank
**CHEEKS:** Jungle cock
**HEAD:** Black

### GREEN BUTT SILVER HILTON
**TAG:** Silver tinsel
**TAIL:** Pintail flank
**REAR BODY (1/3rd):** Fluorescent green chenille
**FRONT BODY (2/3rds):** Black seal's fur
**RIB:** Oval silver tinsel
**THROAT:** Long pintail flank
**WING:** Two pairs grizzly hackle tips
**HEAD:** Black

### GREEN BUTT SPIDER
**TAIL:** Red hackle fibres
**BUTT:** Fluorescent green floss over silver tinsel
**BODY:** Black seal's fur
**RIB:** Oval silver tinsel
**HACKLE:** Pheasant rump dyed black
**HEAD:** Black

### GREEN DRAKE
**TAG:** Oval gold tinsel
**TAIL:** Yellow golden pheasant body feather
**BODY:** Greenish yellow floss
**RIB:** Black floss
**THROAT:** Brown hackle wound as collar then pulled down
**WING:** Underwing, red fibres of golden pheasant body feathers with greenish-yellow dyed mallard flank feathers
**HEAD:** Black

### GREEN HIGHLANDER
**TAG:** Silver tinsel
**TAIL:** GP crest
**BUTT:** Black ostrich
**REAR BODY:** Yellow floss
**FRONT BODY:** Green floss
**RIB:** Flat silver tinsel
**BODY HACKLE:** Green cock over front body
**THROAT:** Green cock
**WING:** Married strips of orange, yellow, green goose, hen pheasant tail; bronze mallard over; GP topping over all
**CHEEKS:** Jungle cock (optional)
**HEAD:** Black

### GREEN PETER
**TAG:** Gold tinsel
**BODY:** Green olive seal's fur
**RIB:** Oval gold tinsel
**BODY HACKLE:** Red game palmered & clipped along top of body
**WING:** Four slips hen pheasant secondary to lie flat, partially enveloping body
**HEAD HACKLE:** Red game
**HEAD:** Black

### GREEN SPEY
**BODY:** Green Mylar tinsel
**RIB:** Oval silver tinsel
**COLLAR HACKLE:** Long chartreuse dyed mallard flank
**HEAD:** Green

# Catalogue of Dressings

| GOSLING, YELLOW | GREEN BEAUTY |

| GREEN BUTT SILVER HILTON | GREEN BUTT SPIDER | GREEN DRAKE |

| GREEN HIGHLANDER | GREEN PETER | GREEN SPEY |

# Catalogue of Dressings

### GREY FLY
**TAG:** Oval silver tinsel
**RIB:** Oval silver tinsel
**BODY:** Grey wool
**THROAT:** Red cock
**WING:** Bronze mallard
**HEAD:** Black

### GREY GHOST
**TAG:** Silver tinsel
**BODY:** Orange floss
**RIB:** Flat silver tinsel
**THROAT:** Four strands peacock herl, white bucktail, GP crest
**WING:** Underwing: GP crest. Overwing: Four grey dun saddle hackles.
**SIDES:** Silver pheasant body feathers
**CHEEKS:** Jungle cock
**HEAD:** Black

### GROUSE & CLARET
**TAG:** Gold tinsel
**TAIL:** GP tippet fibres
**BODY:** Dark claret seal's fur
**RIB:** Oval gold tinsel
**WING:** Grouse tail feather
**HACKLE:** Long black hen
**HEAD:** Black

### GROUSE & CLARET, HAROLD'S
**TAG:** Gold tinsel
**TAIL:** Tuft of yellow wool or floss
**BODY:** Dark claret seal's fur
**RIB:** Oval gold tinsel
**THORAX:** Two or three turns of bronze peacock herl, full
**HACKLE:** Grouse neck feather, long
**HEAD:** Black

### GULLNOKK
**TAG:** Gold tinsel
**TAIL:** GP crest with red hackle fibres over
**BUTT:** Black ostrich herl
**REAR BODY:** Flat gold tinsel
**FRONT BODY:** Bronze peacock herl
**RIB:** Oval gold tinsel
**BODY HACKLE:** Hot orange cock over peacock herl
**THROAT:** Guinea fowl
**WING:** White tipped brown turkey tail strips. GP topping over
**HEAD:** Black

### HALLOWEEN MATUKA
**TAG:** Silver tinsel
**BODY:** Black chenille
**RIB:** Oval silver tinsel
**WING:** Two matched pairs of orange hackle tips
**FRONT HACKLE:** Orange cock
**HEAD:** Black

### HALLOWEEN SPEY
**TAG:** Silver tinsel
**BODY:** Black orange seal's fur
**RIB:** Oval silver tinsel
**BODY HACKLE:** Orange goose flank
**WING:** Black hackle tips
**FRONT HACKLE:** Dark guinea fowl
**HEAD:** Black

### HASLAM
**TAG:** Silver tinsel
**BUTT:** White wool or floss
**TAIL:** GP crest
**BODY:** Flat silver tinsel
**RIB:** Oval silver tinsel
**THROAT HACKLE:** Blue jay or guinea fowl dyed blue
**WING:** Hen pheasant tail
**HORNS:** Blue macaw, curving along wings and crossing at tail
**HEAD:** Black

### HEAVY BREATHER ORANGE
**TAG:** Gold tinsel
**REAR BODY:** Orange floss
**FRONT BODY:** Orange seal's fur
**RIB:** Oval gold tinsel
**WING:** Orange dyed grizzly hackles, back to back
**FRONT HACKLE:** Orange dyed teal
**HEAD:** Black

# Catalogue of Dressings

### GREY FLY        GREY GHOST        GROUSE & CLARET

### GROUSE & CLARET, HAROLD'S    GULLNOKK    HALLOWEEN MATUKA

### HALLOWEEN SPEY    HASLAM    HEAVY BREATHER ORANGE

## Catalogue of Dressings

### HEGGELI
**TAG:** Silver tinsel
**TAIL:** GP tippet
**BODY:** Flat silver tinsel
**RIB:** Oval silver tinsel
**THROAT:** Light brown cock
**WING:** Bronze mallard
**CHEEKS:** Jungle cock
**HEAD:** Black

### HELEN'S FANCY
**TAIL:** GP crest dyed orange
**REAR BODY:** Fluorescent lime floss
**FRONT BODY:** Fluorescent flame floss
**RIB:** Oval silver tinsel
**BODY HACKLE:** Fluorescent lime green over front body
**HACKLE:** Red golden pheasant rump feather
**WING:** Teal flank
**CHEEKS:** Jungle cock
**HEAD:** Red

### HERON, BLACK
**BODY:** Black Berlin wool
**RIB:** Flat gold tinsel with fine oval gold & silver tinsel between
**BODY HACKLE:** Black heron, extra long
**WING:** Bronze mallard
**HEAD:** Black

### HERON, BLACK & ORANGE
**TAG:** Gold tinsel
**BODY:** Rear 1/2 black floss. Front 1/2 hot orange seal's fur
**RIB:** Two strands oval silver tinsel with one strand fluorescent red floss between
**BODY HACKLE:** Orange Spey hackle with dyed black tips
**WING:** Two orange hackle tips flanked by two black hackle tips
**HEAD:** Red

### HERON, BLUE
**TAG:** Silver tinsel
**BODY:** Rear 1/2 blue floss. Front 1/2 blue seal's fur
**RIB:** Flat silver tinsel & oval silver tinsel
**BODY HACKLE:** Grey heron
**WING:** Two blue hackle tips
**HEAD:** Black

### HERON, BROWN (GLASSO)
**TAG:** Silver tinsel
**BODY:** Rear 1/3rd orange floss. Front 2/3rds hot orange seal's fur
**RIB:** Flat silver tinsel
**BODY HACKLE:** Long grey heron
**THROAT:** Teal flank
**WING:** Bronze mallard
**HEAD:** Red

### HERON, BROWN (McNEESE)
**TAG:** Gold tinsel
**BODY:** Rear 1/3rd orange floss. Front 2/3rds hot orange seal's fur
**RIB:** Flat silver tinsel & oval gold tinsel
**BODY HACKLE:** Grey heron over front body
**THROAT:** Teal flank
**WING:** Bronze mallard
**HEAD:** Red

### HERON, GOLD
**TAG:** Gold tinsel
**BODY:** Rear 2/3rds flat gold tinsel. Front 1/3rd hot orange seal's fur
**RIB:** Oval gold tinsel
**BODY HACKLE:** Grey or brown heron
**THROAT:** Widgeon flank
**WING:** Widgeon flank
**HEAD:** Black

### HERON, GOLDEN
**TAG:** Silver tinsel
**BODY:** Flat gold tinsel
**RIB:** Oval silver tinsel
**BODY HACKLE:** Long black heron
**THROAT:** Widgeon flank
**WING:** Four golden macaw orange breast feathers, Bronze mallard over
**HEAD:** Black

Note: Red Heron – identical but wing of red macaw

# Catalogue of Dressings

| HEGGELI | HELEN'S FANCY | HERON, BLACK |

| HERON, BLACK & ORANGE | HERON, BLUE | HERON, BROWN (GLASSO) |

| HERON, BROWN (McNEESE) | HERON, GOLD | HERON, GOLDEN |

# Catalogue of Dressings

### HERON, GREEN
**TAG:** Gold tinsel
**BODY:** Rear 1/2 fluorescent green floss. Front 1/2 green seal's fur
**RIB:** Flat gold tinsel & oval gold tinsel
**BODY HACKLE:** Black heron
**THROAT:** Teal or mallard flank
**WING:** Two green hackle tips
**HEAD:** Red

### HERON, GREY
**BODY:** One third lemon yellow Berlin wool, rest black Berlin wool
**RIB:** Flat silver tinsel with fine oval gold and silver tinsel between
**BODY HACKLE:** Long grey heron
**THROAT:** Guinea fowl
**WING:** Bronze mallard
**HEAD:** Black

### HERON, ORANGE
**TAG:** Gold tinsel
**BODY:** Rear 2/3rds fluorescent orange floss. Front 1/3rd hot orange seal's fur
**RIB:** Flat silver tinsel overlaid with oval silver tinsel
**BODY HACKLE:** Grey heron
**THROAT:** Teal flank
**WING:** Four matching hot orange hackle tips
**HEAD:** Black

### HERON, SILVER
**TAG:** Silver tinsel
**BODY:** Rear 1/2 flat silver tinsel. Front 1/2 black seal's fur
**RIB:** Oval silver tinsel
**BODY HACKLE:** Grey or black heron
**THROAT:** Guinea fowl or teal flank
**WING:** Grey or black
**HEAD:** Black

### HORNBERG
**BODY:** Flat silver tinsel
**RIB:** Oval silver tinsel
**WING:** Underwing – two yellow hackles. Overwing – pair of grey mallard breast feathers one each side, cupped over body and underwing
**CHEEKS:** Well marked barred wood duck feathers or jungle cock
**COLLAR HACKLE:** Grizzly hen
**HEAD:** Black

### IRISHMAN'S CLARET
**TAG:** Silver tinsel
**TAIL:** GP tippet fibres
**BODY:** Dark claret seal's fur
**RIB:** Oval gold tinsel
**BODY HACKLE:** Dark claret cock
**WING:** Bronze mallard
**HEAD HACKLE:** Long dark claret hen, in front of wing
**HEAD:** Black

### JACOB'S COAT
**TAIL:** Brown deer hair
**BODY:** Rope consisting of one strand of peacock herl and six different coloured strands of ostrich
**HEAD HACKLE:** Grizzly hen to match body colour
**HEAD:** Black

### JACOB'S LADDER
**TAG:** Silver tinsel
**TAIL:** GP tippet fibres
**BODY:** Magenta seal's fur
**RIB:** Oval silver tinsel
**WING:** Bronze mallard
**HEAD HACKLE:** Black cock
**HEAD:** Black

### JEANNIE
**TAG:** Silver tinsel
**TAIL:** GP crest
**REAR BODY:** Yellow floss
**FRONT BODY:** Black floss
**RIB:** Oval silver tinsel
**THROAT:** Black cock
**WING:** Bronze mallard or mottled brown turkey
**HEAD:** Black

# Catalogue of Dressings

| HERON, GREEN | HERON, GREY | HERON, ORANGE |

| HERON, SILVER | HORNBERG | IRISHMAN'S CLARET |

| JACOB'S COAT | JACOB'S LADDER | JEANNIE |

# Catalogue of Dressings

### JOHNSON M.D.
**TAIL:** GP crest dyed flame
**BUTT:** Black ostrich herl
**BODY:** Claret floss
**RIB:** Flat silver tinsel
**HACKLE:** Red palmered
**WING:** White tipped mallard secondary
**CHEEKS:** Jungle cock
**HEAD:** Black

### JUNGLE COCK & SILVER
**TAG:** Silver tinsel
**TAIL:** GP tippet fibres
**BODY:** Flat silver tinsel
**RIB:** Oval silver tinsel
**WING:** Paired jungle cock eye feathers
**FRONT HACKLE:** Black hen
**HEAD:** Black

### KATE
**TAG:** Silver tinsel & lemon floss
**TAIL:** GP crest & blue chatterer
**BODY:** Rear 1/4 ruby floss, rest ruby seal's fur
**RIB:** Flat silver tinsel & oval silver tinsel
**BODY HACKLE:** Ruby cock over seal's fur
**THROAT:** Rich yellow cock
**WING:** GP tippet feathers back to back; married strips golden pheasant tail, bustard, red & yellow swan. Bronze mallard; GP topping over all
**CHEEKS:** Jungle cock
**HORNS:** Blue macaw
**HEAD:** Black chenille

### KATE (GARRETT)
**TAG:** Silver tinsel
**BODY:** Red over silver Mylar tinsel
**RIB:** Oval silver tinsel
**BODY HACKLE:** Red cock over front body
**WING:** Underwing: pair Golden pheasant rump feathers, back to back. Overwing: Green-wing teal flank
**CHEEKS:** Jungle cock
**HEAD:** Claret

### KATE McLAREN
**TAG:** Silver tinsel
**TAIL:** GP crest
**BODY:** Black seal's fur
**RIB:** Oval silver tinsel
**BODY HACKLE:** Open turns of black cock
**HEAD HACKLE:** Ginger or natural red hen, long & full
**HEAD:** Black

### KING'S FISHER
**BODY:** Deep green mohair
**RIB:** Light green silk
**BODY HACKLE:** Lemon cock
**THROAT:** Blue jay
**WING:** Peacock eye feather
**HEAD:** Black

### KINGSMILL
**TAG:** Silver tinsel & gentian blue floss
**TAIL:** GP crest
**BODY:** Black ostrich herl
**RIB:** Oval silver tinsel
**HACKLE:** Black cock
**WING:** Crow secondary with GP topping over
**CHEEKS:** Jungle cock
**HEAD:** Black

### KNOUSE
**TAG:** Silver tinsel & fluorescent red floss
**TAIL:** GP crest dyed purple with Indian crow substitute
**REAR BODY:** Hot pink seal's fur
**FRONT BODY:** Hot purple seal's fur
**RIB:** Oval silver tinsel
**BODY HACKLE:** Long hot pink over front body
**THROAT:** Long purple pintail flank
**WING:** Purple dyed pintail flank. GP topping dyed purple over
**CHEEKS:** Jungle cock
**HEAD:** Black

### LADY AMHERST
**TAG:** Oval silver tinsel & golden yellow floss
**TAIL:** GP crest and teal fibres
**BUTT:** Black ostrich
**BODY:** Flat silver tinsel
**RIB:** Oval silver tinsel
**BODY HACKLE:** Silver badger, palmered
**THROAT:** Barred teal flank
**WING:** Two long jungle cock back to back veiled by two large Amherst pheasant tippet feathers, these flanked by two shorter ones. Golden pheasant crest over
**CHEEKS:** Jungle cock veiled with kingfisher
**HEAD:** Black

# Catalogue of Dressings

| JOHNSON M.D. | JUNGLE COCK & SILVER | KATE |

| KATE (GARRETT) | KATE McLAREN | KING'S FISHER |

| KINGSMILL | KNOUSE | LADY AMHERST |

# Catalogue of Dressings

### LADY CAROLINE
**TAIL:** Strands of red GP breast feather
**BODY:** Mixed strands of olive-green and brown wool wound together
**RIB:** Flat gold tinsel with oval gold and oval silver tinsel between
**BODY HACKLE:** Long grey heron
**THROAT:** Long red breast feather from golden pheasant
**WING:** Bronze mallard
**HEAD:** Black

### LAERDAL
**TAIL:** GP crest
**BUTT:** Black ostrich
**BODY:** Grey seal's fur
**RIB:** Oval silver tinsel
**THROAT:** Black cock hackle
**WING:** Brown turkey tail strips. GP topping over
**CHEEKS:** Jungle cock
**HEAD:** Black

### LAMQUI
**TAG:** Silver tinsel & claret floss
**TAIL:** GP crest with barred wood duck over
**BUTT:** Black ostrich
**BODY:** Rear one third, yellow floss. Front two thirds, black seal's fur
**RIB:** Oval silver tinsel
**BODY HACKLE:** Black hackle over black fur
**THROAT:** Claret dyed guinea fowl
**WING:** Married strips of red, yellow & blue dyed goose. Bronze mallard Veiled with strips of barred wood duck. GP crest over
**CHEEKS:** Jungle cock with kingfisher
**HEAD:** Black

### LANCTOT
**TAG:** Silver tinsel & yellow floss
**TAIL:** GP crest
**BUTT:** Black ostrich
**REAR BODY:** Yellow floss veiled top & bottom with yellow hackle tips
**RIB:** Oval silver tinsel
**BODY HACKLE:** Lemon cock
**CENTRE BUTT:** Black ostrich herl
**FRONT BODY:** Black floss
**RIB:** Oval silver tinsel
**THROAT:** Guinea fowl
**WING:** Yellow goose. GP crest over
**HEAD:** Black

### LANSDALE PARTRIDGE
**TAG:** Silver tinsel
**TAIL:** Cock pheasant tail fibres
**BODY:** Brown wool or seal's fur
**RIB:** Oval silver tinsel
**HEAD HACKLES:** Ginger cock with natural French partridge in front
**HEAD:** Black

### LAXFORD
**TAG:** Gold tinsel
**TAIL:** GP crest
**BODY:** Gold floss
**RIB:** Flat silver tinsel & oval gold tinsel
**BODY HACKLE:** Bright yellow cock
**THROAT:** Dark blue cock hackle
**WING:** Large bunch peacock herl with bustard over. GP topping overall
**HEAD:** Black

### LEE BLUE
**TAG:** Silver tinsel & yellow wool
**TAIL:** GP crest
**BUTT:** Black ostrich herl
**BODY:** Blue seal's fur
**RIB:** Oval silver tinsel
**BODY HACKLE:** Blue cock from 2nd turn of ribbing
**THROAT:** Rich yellow hackle
**WING:** GP tippet; married strands golden pheasant tail, mottled turkey, swan dyed yellow & blue; bronze mallard
**HORNS:** Blue macaw
**HEAD:** Black ostrich herl

### LEMON GREY
**TAG:** Silver tinsel & yellow floss
**TAIL:** GP crest
**BUTT:** Black ostrich herl
**BODY:** Grey rabbit fur
**RIB:** Oval silver tinsel
**BODY HACKLE:** Natural blue-dun cock from 2nd turn of ribbing
**THROAT:** Claret hackle with lemon yellow hackle over
**WING:** GP tippet; married strands teal, guinea fowl; bronze mallard; GP topping over
**HORNS:** Blue macaw
**HEAD:** Black

### LIBBY'S BLACK
**BODY:** Rear half: black floss. Front half: black ostrich
**RIB:** Oval silver tinsel over black floss
**HACKLE:** Soft pheasant dyed black
**HEAD:** Purple

# Catalogue of Dressings

| LADY CAROLINE | LAERDAL | LAMQUI |

| LANCTOT | LANSDALE PARTRIDGE | LAXFORD |

| LEE BLUE | LEMON GREY | LIBBY'S BLACK |

# Catalogue of Dressings

### LOCH LOMOND
**BODY:** Flat gold tinse
**WING:** White tipped turkey
**HEAD:** Black

### LOCH ORDIE
**BODY HACKLES:** Hen hackles, tied to slope backwards in order from rear – black, dark ginger, white
**HEAD:** Black

### LOGIE
**TAG:** Silver tinsel
**TAIL:** GP crest
**BODY:** Rear 2/5ths yellow floss. Front 3/5ths red floss
**THROAT:** Dark blue or cobalt hackle fibres
**WING:** Yellow swan or goose with bronze mallard over
**HEAD:** Black

### LORD IRIS
**TAG:** Silver tinsel
**TAIL:** GP crest
**BODY:** Flat silver tinsel
**RIB:** Oval silver tinsel
**THROAT:** Orange
**WING:** Underwing: two orange saddle hackles, peacock sword fibres, two badger hackles. Overwing: married strips of red, orange, green & blue goose. GP topping over all
**CHEEKS:** Jungle cock
**HEAD:** Black

### LOW & CLEAR SPIDER
**TAG:** Gold tinsel & yellow floss
**TAIL:** Lemon wood duck fibres & GP crest dyed red
**BUTT:** Bronze peacock
**REAR BODY:** Flat gold tinsel
**FRONT BODY:** Sienna brown seal's fur
**WING:** Pine squirrel hair with pair of jungle cock
**FRONT HACKLE:** Lemon wood duck
**HEAD:** Black

### MAC GARRETT
**TAIL:** GP crest dyed flame
**BUTT:** Black ostrich herl
**REAR BODY:** Fluorescent lime floss over silver Mylar tinsel
**FRONT BODY:** Black ostrich herl
**RIB:** Oval silver tinsel
**BODY HACKLE:** Natural black over front body
**WING:** Underwing: purple goose quill, back to back. Overwing: Teal. GP topping dyed flame over
**SIDES:** Small GP tippet feathers dyed flame
**CHEEKS:** Jungle cock
**HEAD:** Black

### MACARTAIR
**TAG:** Gold tinsel, yellow & claret floss
**TAIL:** GP crest & blue kingfisher
**BUTT:** Orange ostrich herl
**REAR BODY:** Golden yellow seal's fur
**FRONT BODY:** Claret seal's fur
**RIB:** Oval gold tinsel
**BODY HACKLE:** Yellow cock over claret fur
**THROAT:** Yellow cock with orange cock over
**WING:** Pair GP tippet feathers back to back; married strips peacock & claret, yellow, claret, yellow goose
**CHEEKS:** Large blue kingfisher with shorter jungle cock
**HEAD:** Black

### MACHAIR CLARET
**TAG:** Gold tinsel
**TAIL:** Jungle cock eye feather, shiny side down
**BODY:** Dark claret seal's fur
**RIB:** Oval golder tinsel
**BODY HACKLES:** Pair claret & black cock hackles, wound together
**HEAD HACKLE:** Long black hen
**HEAD:** Black

### MADAME HAZEL
**TAG:** Silver tinsel & gold floss
**TAIL:** GP topping
**BUTT:** Black ostrich herl
**BODY:** Flat silver tinsel
**RIB:** Oval silver tinsel
**BODY HACKLE:** Badger over front third of body
**THROAT:** Extra turns badger hackle
**WING:** Strips of Amherst pheasant tail. GP topping over
**CHEEKS:** Jungle cock
**HEAD:** Black

# Catalogue of Dressings

| LOCH LOMOND | LOCH ORDIE | LOGIE |

| LORD IRIS | LOW & CLEAR SPIDER | MAC GARRETT |

| MACARTAIR | MACHAIR CLARET | MADAME HAZEL |

# Catalogue of Dressings

## MAJOR
**TAG:** Silver tinsel & ruby floss
**TAIL:** GP crest, GP tippet fibres
**BODY:** Seal's fur as follows – two turns medium blue, two turns dark orange, four or five turns bright claret, two turns of blue, well picked out, at shoulder
**RIB:** Flat silver tinsel followed by oval gold tinsel
**BODY HACKLE:** Claret from orange fur
**THROAT:** Bustard hackle
**WING:** Pair white tipped snipe feathers back to back, long GP tippet each side; married fibres bustard, pheasant tail, red, blue & yellow swan; GP topping over
**FRONT HACKLE:** Yellow cock
**HEAD:** Black

## MALLARD & CLARET SPIDER
**HOOK:** Silver Salar
**BODY:** None
**HACKLES:** Claret hackle, long
**WING:** Strands of grey mallard flank
**HEAD:** Black

## MAR LODGE
**TAG:** Silver tinsel
**TAIL:** GP crest with a pair of small jungle cock back to back
**BUTT:** Black ostrich herl
**BODY:** In three parts, rear & front, flat silver tinsel, middle 1/4 black floss
**THROAT:** Guinea fowl
**WING:** GP tippet; married fibres of white swan, bustard, grey & brown turkey tail; summer duck; GP topping over
**CHEEKS:** Jungle cock
**HEAD:** Black

## MARCH BROWN
**TAG:** Silver tinsel
**TAIL:** GP topping
**BODY:** Hare's mask, picked out
**RIB:** Oval gold tinsel
**THROAT:** Partridge hackle fibres
**WING:** Strips of hen pheasant tail, mottled turkey or similar
**HEAD:** Black

## MARIGOLD
**TAG:** Flat copper tinsel
**TAIL:** Two GP toppings
**BUTT:** Red seal's fur or wool
**BODY:** Flat silver tinsel
**RIB:** Oval gold tinsel
**THROAT:** Long hot orange hackle
**WING:** Four bright red hackles
**HEAD:** Red

## MATEPEDIA SPEY
**TAG:** Silver tinsel & chartreuse floss about twice normal length
**BODY:** Peacock herl
**RIB:** Oval silver tinsel
**COLLAR HACKLE:** Golden pheasant red body feather
**WING:** Bronze mallard
**FRONT COLLAR HACKLE:** Long teal flank
**HEAD:** Black

## MICKEY SPEY
**TAG:** Silver tinsel
**BODY:** Black floss
**RIB:** Flat silver tinsel followed by oval silver tinsel. Counterwrap body hackle with extra fine oval silver tinsel
**BODY HACKLE:** Black schlappen
**THROAT:** One turn of teal flank
**WING:** Married goose strips, yellow, red, yellow
**HEAD:** Black

## MIDNIGHT CANYON
**TAG:** Gold tinsel
**BODY:** Rear 1/2 flat silver tinsel. Front half black seal's fur.
**RIB:** Oval silver tinsel
**BODY HACKLE:** Black marabou over front body. Counter rib with fine oval silver tinsel
**COLLAR HACKLE:** Mallard, teal or gadwall flank
**WING:** Married strips of goose in order from bottom: orange, black, orange, black. Orange strips narrow
**CHEEKS:** Jungle cock
**HEAD:** Black

## MIKE'S PRAWN
**TAIL:** Top: Black bucktail with pearl Crystal Hair. Bottom: Red cock hackle fibres over red Arctic fox hair
**REAR HACKLE:** Long black cock
**BODY:** Bright red wool
**RIB:** Black body wrap
**FRONT HACKLE:** Short black cock
**HEAD:** Black

170

# Catalogue of Dressings

| MAJOR | MALLARD & CLARET SPIDER | MAR LODGE |

| MARCH BROWN | MARIGOLD | MATEPEDIA SPEY |

| MICKEY SPEY | MIDNIGHT CANYON | MIKE'S PRAWN |

# Catalogue of Dressings

### MITCHELL
**TAG:** Oval silver tinsel & yellow floss
**TAIL:** GP topping & kingfisher blue hackle fibres
**BUTT:** Black ostrich herl
**REAR BODY:** Yellow floss
**BUTT (2):** Red ostrich herl
**FRONT BODY:** Black floss
**RIB:** Oval silver tinsel
**THROAT:** Yellow hackle fibres with black hackle over
**WING:** Black crow
**CHEEKS:** Jungle cock with kingfisher
**HEAD:** Red or black

### MORRUM
**TAG:** Oval silver tinsel & orange floss
**RIB:** Oval silver tinsel
**BODY:** Black dubbing
**BODY HACKLE:** GP red breast feather or orange cock
**THROAT:** GP red breast feather with teal or pintail over
**WING:** Underwing of GP tippets, overwing pheasant tail slips
**HEAD:** Black

### MORRUM SPEY
**TAG:** Oval silver tinsel & orange floss
**RIB:** Oval silver tinsel
**BODY:** Black dubbing
**BODY HACKLE:** Long brown heron
**THROAT:** GP red breast feather with teal or pintail over
**WING:** Underwing of GP tippets, overwing pheasant tail slips
**HEAD:** Black

### Mr GLASSO
**TAG:** Silver tinsel
**BODY:** Rear half, hot orange floss. Front half, hot orange seal's fur
**RIB:** Oval silver tinsel
**BODY HACKLE:** Black heron
**THROAT:** Guinea fowl dyed orange
**WING:** Matched hot orange hackle tips; GP topping dyed hot orange over
**HEAD:** Black

### NAMSEN #1
**TAG:** Silver tinsel
**TAIL:** GP crest and teal fibres
**BODY:** Brown seal's fur
**RIB:** Oval silver tinsel
**THROAT:** Black cock
**WING:** White goose with broad strips of barred teal each side
**CHEEKS:** Jungle cock
**HEAD:** Black

### NAMSEN #2
**TAG:** Silver tinsel & yellow floss
**TAIL:** GP crest and red swan or goose
**BODY:** Seal's fur in four equal parts. From rear – yellow, red-brown, blue-green, black
**RIB:** Oval silver tinsel
**BODY HACKLE:** Black cock from 2nd turn of ribbing
**THROAT:** Extra turns of black cock
**WING:** Married strips of yellow, red & dark blue goose, speckled turkey tail; over this each side bronze mallard & teal
**HEAD:** Black

### NEPTUNE
**TAG:** Oval silver tinsel
**TAIL:** Yellow floss
**REAR BODY:** Flat silver tinsel
**FRONT BODY:** Peacock herl
**RIB:** Oval silver tinsel
**THROAT:** Long brown hackle tied as collar
**WING:** Black turkey quill
**CHEEKS:** Jungle cock
**COLLAR HACKLE:** Long guinea fowl
**HEAD:** Black

### NessC
**TAG:** Pearl tinsel
**TAIL:** Green, yellow & purple bucktail with four strands pearl Lureflash Mobile
**BODY:** Purple floss (globrite #15)
**RIB:** Oval silver tinsel
**HEAD HACKLES:** Orange over yellow cock
**HEAD:** Red

 ## Catalogue of Dressings

| MITCHELL | MORRUM | MORRUM SPEY |

| Mr GLASSO | NAMSEN #1 | NAMSEN #2 |

| NEPTUNE | NessC |

# Catalogue of Dressings

### NIGHT HAWK
**TAG:** Oval silver tinsel & yellow floss
**TAIL:** GP crest with kingfisher over
**BUTT:** Red wool
**BODY:** Flat silver tinsel
**RIB:** Oval silver tinsel
**THROAT:** Black hackle
**WING:** Black turkey quill, tied low. GP topping over
**CHEEKS:** Jungle cock & kingfisher
**HEAD:** Black

### NIGHT TRAIN
**TAIL:** Amherst pheasant crest over GP tippet with single long strand red goose
**REAR BODY:** Fluorescent orange floss
**FRONT BODY:** Black ostrich herl
**RIB:** Oval silver tinsel
**BODY HACKLE:** Red cock over front body
**HACKLE:** Natural black hen
**WING:** Teal flank
**HEAD:** Red

### NIPISIGUIT GREY
**TAG:** Silver tinsel & yellow floss
**TAIL:** GP crest
**BUTT:** Black ostrich or peacock herl
**BODY:** Grey wool
**RIB:** Oval silver tinsel
**THROAT:** Guinea fowl or grizzly hackle
**WING:** Bronze mallard
**HEAD:** Black

### NITRO SHRIMP
**TAG:** Silver tinsel
**TAIL:** Golden pheasant breast feather dyed fluorescent red
**REAR BODY:** Orange Mylar tinsel
**CENTRE HACKLE:** Dyed amber cock
**FRONT BODY:** Red seal's fur
**RIB:** Oval silver tinsel
**HEAD HACKLE:** Well-marked badger cock
**CHEEKS:** Jungle cock
**HEAD:** Red

### NORTHEAST SMELT
**TAG:** Silver tinsel & red floss
**TAIL:** White polar bear hair with olive Fly Fur over
**BODY:** Braided silver tinsel
**THROAT:** Red hackle fibres
**WING:** White goat hair with olive Fly Fur over. Matched pair grizzly hackles outside
**CHEEKS:** Jungle cock
**HEAD:** Black

### NUPTIALE
**TAG:** Oval silver tinsel
**TAIL:** Chartreuse crystal flash
**BUTT:** Black ostrich herl
**BODY:** Flat silver tinsel
**RIB:** Oval silver tinsel
**BODY HACKLE:** White
**WING:** White turkey
**CHEEKS:** Jungle cock
**COLLAR HACKLE:** White cock
**HEAD:** Black

### OCTOBER CADDIS SPEY
**TAG:** Gold tinsel
**BODY:** Rusty orange seal's fur
**RIB:** Oval gold tinsel
**BODY HACKLE:** Red-brown golden pheasant
**WING:** Bronze mallard
**FRONT HACKLE:** Yellow-brown golden pheasant
**HEAD:** Black

### OCTOBER SPEY
**TAG:** gold tinsel
**REAR BODY:** Orange floss
**FRONT BODY:** Orange seal's fur
**RIB:** Oval gold tinsel
**BODY HACKLE:** Brown schlappen over seal's fur
**COLLAR HACKLE:** Orange dyed guinea fowl
**WING:** Mottled brown turkey
**HEAD:** Black

# Catalogue of Dressings

**NIGHT HAWK**  **NIGHT TRAIN**  **NIPISIGUIT GREY**

**NITRO SHRIMP**  **NORTHEAST SMELT**

**NUPTIALE**  **OCTOBER CADDIS SPEY**  **OCTOBER SPEY**

# Catalogue of Dressings

### OLA
**TAG:** Silver tinsel & pink floss
**TAIL:** GP crest
**BUTT:** Black ostrich
**REAR BODY:** Light grey seal's fur
**FRONT BODY:** Black seal's fur
**RIB:** Flat silver tinsel
**BODY HACKLE:** Black cock over front body
**THROAT:** Guinea fowl
**WING:** White tipped turkey tail sheathed with broad strip of blue goose and bronze mallard. Teal flank. GP topping over
**CHEEKS:** Jungle cock
**HEAD:** Black

### ORANGE ANGEL
**TAG:** Gold tinsel
**BODY:** Rear 1/2 orange floss. Front half orange seal's fur.
**RIB:** Flat gold tinsel followed by oval gold tinsel
**BODY HACKLE:** Orange marabou with tips dyed black over front body. Counter rib with fine oval gold tinsel
**WING:** White goose
**HEAD:** Black

### ORIOLE
**TAG:** Oval gold tinsel
**TAIL:** Red golden pheasant breast fibres
**BODY:** Black wool
**RIB:** Oval gold tinsel
**THROAT:** Brown hackle wound as collar then pulled down
**WING:** mallard flank feathers dyed green drake
**HEAD:** Black

### OTTESON
**TAG:** Silver tinsel & pink floss
**TAIL:** GP crest
**BUTT:** Black ostrich
**BODY:** White floss
**RIB:** Red floss
**BODY HACKLE:** Orange cock
**THROAT:** Widgeon
**WING:** Two GP tippets, back to back; married strands of yellow, red & blue goose, brown mottled turkey tail; teal flank. GP topping over
**CHEEKS:** Jungle cock
**HEAD:** Black

### PAINT BRUSH
**BODY:** Flat gold tinsel
**RIB:** Oval gold tinsel
**BODY HACKLE:** Orange hackle
**FRONT HACKLE:** Purple with light blue over
**HEAD:** Black

### PALSBU
**TAG:** gold tinsel & yellow floss
**TAIL:** Red ibis and brown speckled turkey fibres
**BODY:** Bronze peacock herl
**RIB:** Oval gold tinsel
**THROAT:** Natural red cock
**WING:** Brown mottled turkey tail. GP topping over
**CHEEKS:** Jungle cock
**HEAD:** Black

### PARSON #1
**TAG:** Silver tinsel
**TAIL:** GP crest
**BODY:** Yellow floss
**RIB:** Oval silver tinsel
**BODY HACKLE:** Lemon cock
**THROAT:** Yellow cock
**WING:** GP tippet feathers back to back strips; five or six GP toppings over
**CHEEKS:** Cock-of-the-rock
**HEAD:** Yellow pig's wool

### PEER GYNT
**TAG:** Gold tinsel & yellow floss
**TAIL:** GP crest and red hackle fibres
**BUTT:** Black ostrich herl
**BODY:** Flat silver tinsel
**RIB:** Oval silver tinsel
**BODY HACKLE:** Crimson cock
**THROAT:** Guinea fowl
**WING:** Brown mottled turkey tail with bronze mallard over. GP topping over all
**CHEEKS:** Jungle cock
**HEAD:** Black

### PENYBONT
**TAG:** Silver tinsel
**TAIL:** GP tippet fibres
**BODY:** Yellow floss
**RIB:** Oval silver tinsel
**THROAT:** Brown hen
**WING:** GP tippet with grey heron wing over
**HEAD:** Black

# Catalogue of Dressings

| OLA | ORANGE ANGEL | ORIOLE |

| OTTESON | PAINT BRUSH | PALSBU |

| PARSON #1 | PEER GYNT | PENYBONT |

# Catalogue of Dressings

### PETER ROSS SPIDER
**HOOK:** Silver Salar
**BODY:** Extremely short, red tying thread
**FRONT HACKLE:** Long black cock
**WING:** Grey mallard fibres
**HEAD:** Black

### PETERSON M.D.
**BODY:** Red floss over silver Mylar
**RIB:** Flat silver tinsel
**HACKLE:** Black palmered
**WING:** Midnight blue mallard
**CHEEKS:** Jungle cock
**HEAD:** Black

### PETERSON'S PENNELL
**TAG:** Silver tinsel
**TAIL:** Slip of yellow goose
**BODY:** Black seal's fur
**RIB:** Oval silver tinsel
**BODY HACKLE:** Black cock
**HEAD HACKLE:** Bottle green peacock neck feather
**HEAD:** Black

### PINK SHRIMP, DARK
**TAG:** Gold tinsel
**BODY:** Rear 1/3rd hot pink seal's fur. Front 2/3rds claret seal's fur
**RIB:** Oval gold tinsel
**BODY HACKLE:** Grey heron dyed hot pink
**WING:** Bronze mallard
**HEAD:** Black

### PINK SHRIMP, LIGHT
**TAG:** Silver tinsel
**BODY:** Hot pink seal's fur.
**RIB:** Oval silver tinsel
**BODY HACKLE:** White heron dyed hot pink
**WING:** Bronze mallard
**HEAD:** Black

### POLAR BEAR SPEY
**TAG:** Silver tinsel
**BODY:** Rear 1/2 hot orange floss. Middle 1/4 purple seal's fur. Front 1/4 hot orange seal's fur
**RIB:** Oval silver tinsel
**BODY HACKLE:** Orange polar bear hair over front 1/4 body
**THROAT:** Bleached golden pheasant dyed purple
**WING:** Mallard flank dyed purple
**HEAD:** Black

### POLAR SHRIMP, BLUMREICH
**TAG:** Silver tinsel
**BODY:** Magenta seal's fur
**RIB:** Flat silver tinsel with two stands oval silver tinsel between
**BODY HACKLE:** Red Spey hackle
**THROAT:** White hackle with red hackle over
**WING:** White goose quill
**HEAD:** Red

### POLAR SHRIMP, DARK
**TAG:** Silver tinsel
**BUTT:** Black ostrich
**REAR BODY:** Rose red floss
**FRONT BODY:** Rose red seal's fur
**RIB:** Flat silver tinsel & narrow oval silver tinsel
**BODY HACKLE:** Rose red
**THROAT:** Guinea fowl
**WING:** Bronze mallard
**HEAD:** Black

### POLAR SHRIMP, LIGHT
**TAG:** Silver tinsel
**BUTT:** Black ostrich
**REAR BODY:** Orange floss
**FRONT BODY:** Hot orange seal's fur
**RIB:** Oval silver tinsel
**BODY HACKLE:** Hot orange
**THROAT:** Pintail flank
**WING:** White goose
**HEAD:** Black

# Catalogue of Dressings

**PETER ROSS SPIDER**  **PETERSON M.D.**  **PETERSON'S PENNELL**

**PINK SHRIMP, DARK**  **PINK SHRIMP, LIGHT**  **POLAR BEAR SPEY**

**POLAR SHRIMP, BLUMREICH**  **POLAR SHRIMP, DARK**  **POLAR SHRIMP, LIGHT**

# Catalogue of Dressings

### POT BELLY PIG
**TAIL (FEELERS):** Six Chinese boar bristles curving upwards. Sparse bunch of brown bucktail with a few strands gold Flashabou or similar. Follow with brown hackle
**BODY:** Brown seal's fur
**BODY HACKLE:** Dark natural red cock
**RIB:** Oval gold tinsel
**WING:** Pair of jungle cock feathers tied in a flat 'vee'
**HEAD:** Red

### PRAWN FLY
**TAG:** Silver tinsel
**RIB:** Flat silver tinsel
**BODY HACKLE:** Lemon cock
**CENTRE BUTT:** Red cock, palmered
**COLLAR HACKLE:** Extra turns of body hackle
**HEAD:** Black

### PRISMATIC SPEY
**TAG:** Gold tinsel
**REAR BODY:** Hot orange floss
**FRONT BODY:** Mix 50% red & 50% orange seal's fur
**RIB:** Flat gold tinsel
**BODY HACKLE:** Yellow schlappen
**COLLAR HACKLE:** Hot orange
**WING:** Underwing (as support to main wing) hot orange goose. Overwing – married strips from bottom: magenta, purple, green, blue, orange
**HEAD:** Flame red

### PROFESSOR
**TAG:** Flat gold tinsel
**TAIL:** GP crest
**BUTT:** Black ostrich herl
**BODY:** Yellow floss
**RIB:** Oval gold tinsel
**THROAT:** Brown hackle wound as collar then pulled down
**WING:** Mallard flank feathers
**CHEEKS:** Jungle cock
**HEAD:** Black

### PURCELL'S PETER
**TAG:** Gold tinsel
**BODY:** Green olive, golden olive & a pinch of yellow seal's fur mixed. Well picked out
**RIB:** Oval gold tinsel
**THROAT:** Long ginger cock
**WING:** Hen pheasant secondary feather
**HEAD:** Black

### PURPLE & ORANGE MARABOU SPEY
**TAG:** Silver tinsel
**BODY:** Purple seal's fur
**RIB:** Oval silver tinsel
**HACKLES:** Purple over orange marabou Spey hackle
**COLLAR:** Purple dyed guinea fowl
**HEAD:** Black

### PURPLE GHOST
**TAG:** Silver tinsel
**TAIL:** European blue jay
**BUTT:** Black ostrich herl
**REAR BODY:** Purple floss veiled with GP
**FRONT BODY:** Black ostrich herl
**BODY HACKLE:** Purple & black Spey hackle over front body
**THROAT:** Guinea fowl
**WING:** Purple goose quill
**HEAD:** Black

### PURPLE GOOSE SPEY
**TAG:** Silver tinsel & hot pink floss
**BODY:** Black seal's fur
**RIB:** Oval silver tinsel
**BODY HACKLE:** Purple goose
**WING:** Two matched pairs of hot pink hackle tips
**FRONT HACKLE:** Guinea fowl dyed red
**HEAD:** Black

# Catalogue of Dressings

**POT BELLY PIG**  **PRAWN FLY**

**PRISMATIC SPEY**  **PROFESSOR**  **PURCELL'S PETER**

**PURPLE & ORANGE MARABOU SPEY**  **PURPLE GHOST**  **PURPLE GOOSE SPEY**

# Catalogue of Dressings

### PURPLE GUINEA SPEY
**REAR BODY:** Purple Krennick braid
**FRONT BODY:** Peacock herl
**WING:** Black hackle tips
**COLLAR HACKLE:** Purple saddle hackle, black guinea fowl over
**HEAD:** Black

### PURPLE HEART
**TAG:** Silver tinsel
**TAIL:** Amherst pheasant crest
**REAR BODY:** Purple floss
**FRONT BODY:** Red seal's fur
**RIB:** Flat silver tinsel
**BODY HACKLE:** Red over front body
**THROAT:** Black
**WING:** Two pairs red hackle tips, back to back. One purple hackle tip each side, 3/4 as long. Amherst pheasant topping over
**HEAD:** Black

### PURPLE HEART SPEY
**TAG:** Silver tinsel
**TAIL:** Amherst pheasant crest
**REAR BODY:** Fluorescent red floss
**FRONT BODY:** Purple seal's fur
**RIB:** Flat silver tinsel
**BODY HACKLE:** Purple over front body
**THROAT:** Black
**WING:** Two red hackle tips, back to back. One purple hackle tip each side, 3/4 as long
**HEAD:** Black

### PURPLE HILTON
**TAG:** Silver tinsel
**TAIL:** GP crest dyed red
**REAR BODY (1/3rd):** rear half fluorescent orange floss, front half hot orange seal's fur
**FRONT BODY (2/3rds):** Hot purple seal's fur
**RIB:** Oval silver tinsel
**HACKLE:** Hot purple dyed mallard flank
**WING:** Four purple dyed grizzly hackle tips
**HEAD:** Black

### PURPLE KING
**BODY:** Light purple seal's fur
**RIB:** Oval gold & oval silver tinsel
**BODY HACKLE:** Brownish-black Spey cock, counterwound with fine oval silver tinsel
**THROAT:** One turn of teal
**WING:** Grey mallard
**HEAD:** Black

### PURPLE MATUKA
**TAG:** Silver tinsel
**BODY:** Black seal's fur
**RIB:** Oval silver tinsel
**WING:** Two matched pairs of purple hackle tips
**HEAD:** Black

### PURPLE MATUKA, TINSEL
**TAG:** Silver tinsel
**BODY:** Flat silver tinsel
**RIB:** Oval silver tinsel
**WING:** Two matched pairs of purple hackle tips
**HEAD:** Black

### PURPLE OCTOBER
**TAG:** Silver tinsel
**BODY:** Purple seal's fur
**RIB:** Oval silver tinsel
**HACKLES:** 1st Purple burnt goose. 2nd orange dyed pheasant rump
**COLLAR:** Purple dyed guinea fowl
**WING:** Purple arctic fox
**HEAD:** Black

### PURPLE PRINCE
**TAG:** Silver tinsel
**TAIL:** GP crest & Indian crow substitute
**REAR BODY:** Fluorescent red floss
**FRONT BODY:** Fluorescent orange seal's fur
**RIB:** Oval silver tinsel
**BODY HACKLE:** Hot purple pintail flank
**THROAT:** Long pintail flank
**WING:** Underwing of hot oange hackle tips. Overwing, GP flank dyed purple. Two GP toppings over
**CHEEKS:** Jungle cock
**HEAD:** Black

# Catalogue of Dressings

| PURPLE GUINEA SPEY | PURPLE HEART | PURPLE HEART SPEY |

| PURPLE HILTON | PURPLE KING | PURPLE MATUKA |

| PURPLE MATUKA, TINSEL | PURPLE OCTOBER | PURPLE PRINCE |

# Catalogue of Dressings

### PURPLE SOL DUC SPEY
**REAR BODY:** Fluorescent red floss
**FRONT BODY:** Purple seal's fur
**RIB:** Flat silver tinsel
**BODY HACKLE:** Purple over front body
**THROAT:** Purple
**WING:** Two red hackle tips, back to back. One purple hackle tip each side, 3/4 as long
**HEAD:** Black

### PURPLE SPEY (LeBLANC)
**TAG:** Fine copper tinsel
**TAIL:** Sparse purple bucktail
**BODY:** Burnt orange floss
**RIB:** Oval gold tinsel
**COLLAR HACKLES:** Purple marabou followed by barred teal followed by black Spey hackle
**WING:** Narrow strips of Amherst pheasant centre tail
**CHEEKS:** Jungle cock
**HEAD:** Blue

### PURPLE SPEY (McNEESE)
**TAG:** Silver tinsel
**BODY:** Rear 1/2 orange floss. Front half purple seal's fur
**RIB:** Oval silver tinsel
**BODY HACKLE:** Black heron
**THROAT:** Pintail flank
**WING:** Matched purple hackle tips with purple dyed GP topping over
**CHEEKS:** Jungle cock
**HEAD:** Red

### PURPLE SPEY (MOOTRY)
**TAG:** Silver tinsel
**BODY:** Rear 1/2 orange floss. Front half purple seal's fur
**RIB:** Oval silver tinsel
**BODY HACKLE:** Black heron
**THROAT:** Guinea fowl or grey mallard
**WING:** Matched purple hackle tips
**CHEEKS:** Jungle cock (optional)
**HEAD:** Black

### PURPLE SPIDER
**TAIL:** Fuzzy purple hackle from base of feather
**REAR BODY:** Flat silver tinsel
**FRONT BODY:** Purple seal's fur
**SHOULDER HACKLE:** Deep purple hackle followed by pheasant rump dyed black
**HEAD:** Black

### QE3
**TAG:** Gold tinsel
**TAIL:** GP crest dyed flame
**REAR BODY:** Fluorescent cerise floss over silver Mylar tinsel
**FRONT BODY:** Peacock herl
**RIB:** Oval gold tinsel
**BODY HACKLE:** Pheasant rump over front body
**THROAT:** Red golden pheasant rump
**WING:** Teal flank
**CHEEKS:** Jungle cock
**HEAD:** Claret

### QUACK
**TAG:** Silver tinsel & yellow floss
**TAIL:** GP crest
**BUTT:** Red wool
**BODY:** Black floss
**RIB:** Oval silver tinsel
**THROAT:** Red cock
**WING:** GP tippet; red, blue & yellow swan; bronze mallard; GP topping over
**HEAD:** Red

### QUEEN OF WATERS
**TAG:** Oval gold tinsel & fluorescent yellow floss
**TAIL:** Barred mallard flank
**BODY:** Orange floss
**RIB:** Oval gold tinsel
**BODY HACKLE:** Dark ginger
**THROAT:** Extra turns dark ginger hackle
**WING:** Mallard flank
**CHEEKS:** Jungle cock
**HEAD:** Black

### QUILLAYUTE
**TAIL:** Red hackle fibres
**REAR BODY:** Orange floss
**FRONT BODY:** Hot orange seal's fur
**RIB:** Flat silver tinsel
**BODY HACKLE:** Teal flank
**THROAT:** One turn of black heron
**WING:** Two pairs GP red breast feathers back to back
**HEAD:** Black

## Catalogue of Dressings

| PURPLE SOL DUC SPEY | PURPLE SPEY (LeBLANC) | PURPLE SPEY (McNEESE) |

| PURPLE SPEY (MOOTRY) | PURPLE SPIDER | QE3 |

| QUACK | QUEEN OF WATERS | QUILLAYUTE |

## Catalogue of Dressings

### QUINSAM HACKLE
**TAG:** Yellow floss
**BODY:** Black wool or seal's fur
**RIB:** Oval gold tinsel
**HACKLE:** From mid-point of body – yellow
**COLLAR HACKLES:** Claret followed by scarlet cock
**HEAD:** Black

### RAINBOW
**REAR BODY:** Black wool
**FRONT BODY:** Fiery brown wool
**RIB:** Oval gold tinsel
**WING:** Bronze mallard
**HEAD:** Black

### RED ARROW
**TAG:** Silver tinsel
**TAIL:** GP tippet fibres
**REAR BODY:** Red seal's fur
**FRONT BODY:** Black seal's fur
**RIB:** Oval silver tinsel
**HACKLE:** Natural black hen
**CHEEKS:** Jungle cock (optional)
**HEAD:** Black

### RED DEMON
**TAG:** Silver tinsel
**BODY:** Flat red tinsel
**RIB:** Oval silver tinsel
**HACKLE:** Golden pheasant red breast feather
**HEAD:** Black

### RED DOG
**TAG:** Silver tinsel
**BODY:** Bright red wool
**RIB:** Wide flat silver tinsel & medium oval silver tinsel
**BODY HACKLE:** Brown dyed heron or brown Spey hackle
**COLLAR HACKLE:** Teal
**WING:** Bronze mallard
**HEAD:** Red

### RED GUINEA SPEY
**REAR BODY:** Red floss
**FRONT BODY:** Claret dubbing
**HACKLES:** Long red saddle under red dyed guinea
**HEAD:** Black

### RED SANDY
**TAG:** Silver tinsel
**TAIL:** GP crest & Indian crow
**BUTT:** Scarlet wool
**REAR BODY:** Oval silver tinsel veiled top & bottom with Indian crow
**CENTRE BUTT:** Scarlet wool
**FRONT BODY:** Oval silver tinsel
**BODY HACKLE:** Scarlet cock along front body
**THROAT:** Extra turns scarlet hackle
**WING:** Two long jungle cock, back to back enveloped by two pairs Indian crow feathers: two GP toppings over
**HORNS:** Red macaw
**HEAD:** Scarlet wool

### RED SANDY, VARIANT
**TAG:** Oval silver tinsel
**TAIL:** GP crest with red hackle fibres
**REAR BODY:** Oval silver tinsel veiled top & bottom with red-orange hackle fibres
**CENTRE BUTT:** Red wool
**FRONT BODY:** Oval silver tinsel
**BODY HACKLE:** Red hackle over front body
**THROAT:** Extra turns red hackle, pulled down
**WING:** Golden pheasant tippet feathers dyed red. Overwing pair of matched red hackle tips. GP topping over
**HEAD:** Red

### RED TURKEY
**TAG:** Silver tinsel & yellow floss
**TAIL:** GP crest & red feather
**BODY:** Hares fur
**RIB:** Oval gold tinsel
**THROAT:** Ginger cock with blue jay over
**WING:** Brown mottled turkey tail strips
**HEAD:** Black

# Catalogue of Dressings

**QUINSAM HACKLE**  **RAINBOW**  **RED ARROW**

**RED DEMON**  **RED DOG**  **RED GUINEA SPEY**

**RED SANDY**  **RED SANDY, VARIANT**  **RED TURKEY**

# Catalogue of Dressings

### REDWING
**TAG:** Silver tinsel
**TAIL:** GP crest
**REAR BODY (1/3rd):** Flat silver tinsel
**FRONT BODY (2/3rds):** Four to six bunches of red feathers (macaw breast or dyed hackle tips etc.) tied in around body to cover hook
**WING:** Pair GP tippet feathers back to back; GP topping over
**CHEEKS:** Jungle cock
**HEAD:** Black

### RELIABLE
**TAG:** Oval silver tinsel
**TAIL:** Red golden pheasant body feather fibres
**REAR BODY (1/3rd):** Bright yellow floss
**FRONT BODY (2/3rds):** Black floss
**THROAT:** Black hackle applied as collar then pulled down
**WING:** Bronze mallard
**HEAD:** Black

### RVI
**TAG:** Silver tinsel
**TAIL:** Golden pheasant red breast feather
**BODY:** Rear 1/3rd silver tinsel or pearl Flashabou. Front 2/3rds orange seal's fur
**RIB:** Flat silver tinsel
**BODY HACKLE:** Teal flank
**WING:** Two pairs golden pheasant red breast feathers tied low & tented over body
**HEAD:** Red

### SAN JUAN SPIDER
**TAG:** Silver tinsel
**TAIL:** Fluorescent yellow hackle fibres
**BODY:** Fluorescent orange sparkle chenille
**SHOULDER HACKLE:** Fluorescent yellow
**FRONT HACKLE:** Mallard flank dyed yellow
**TOPPING:** Cinnamon turkey tail strips
**CHEEKS:** Red hair
**HEAD:** Black

### SANDY SPIDER
**TAG:** Silver tinsel
**BUTT:** Black ostrich
**REAR BODY:** Hot orange Edge Bright over flat silver tinsel
**FRONT BODY:** Hot orange dubbing
**BODY HACKLE:** Fluorescent yellow saddle over front body
**COLLAR HACKLE:** Mallard flank
**HEAD:** Black

### SARA TEEN
**TAIL:** GP crest dyed hot orange
**REAR BODY:** Embossed silver tinsel
**FRONT BODY:** Black chenille
**RIB:** Oval gold tinsel
**HACKLE:** Guinea fowl
**WING:** Two pairs white hackle tips, back to back. Amherst pheasant crest over
**CHEEKS:** Jungle cock
**HEAD:** Claret

### SEPTOBER CANDY
**TAIL:** GP crest dyed flame
**BODY:** Flame floss tied over underbody of silver Mylar
**RIB:** Oval gold tinsel
**BODY HACKLE:** Lime green over front half of body
**THROAT:** Red
**WING:** White tipped mallard
**CHEEKS:** Jungle cock
**HEAD:** Black

### SEPTOBER ORANGE
**TAIL:** GP crest dyed flame
**BODY:** Embossed gold tinsel
**RIB:** Oval gold tinsel
**BODY HACKLE:** Brown over front half of body
**WING:** Orange goose
**CHEEKS:** Jungle cock
**HEAD:** Black

### SEPTOBER PHEASANT
**TAIL:** GP crest dyed flame
**BODY:** Rear half claret floss. Front half black ostrich herl
**RIB:** Oval gold tinsel
**BODY HACKLE:** Fluorescent orange over front half of body
**WING:** Matched sections from back feather of ring-necked pheasant
**HEAD:** Black

# Catalogue of Dressings

| REDWING | RELIABLE | RVI |
|---|---|---|

| SAN JUAN SPIDER | SANDY SPIDER | SARA TEEN |
|---|---|---|

| SEPTOBER CANDY | SEPTOBER ORANGE | SEPTOBER PHEASANT |
|---|---|---|

# Catalogue of Dressings

### SHERIFF
**TAG:** Gold tinsel
**TAIL:** GP crest with guinea fowl fibres over
**BUTT:** Black ostrich herl
**REAR BODY:** Flat gold tinsel
**FRONT BODY:** Black ostrich herl
**RIB:** Oval gold tinsel
**BODY HACKLE:** Yellow cock over ostrich herl
**THROAT:** Guinea fowl
**WING:** White tipped turkey with bronze mallard over. GP topping over all
**CHEEKS:** Jungle cock
**HEAD:** Black

### SILVER BROWN
**TAIL:** Indian crow
**BODY:** Flat silver tinsel
**THROAT:** Natural dark red hackle
**WING:** Golden pheasant centre tail
**HEAD:** Black

### SILVER DOCTOR
**TAG:** Silver tinsel & yellow floss
**TAIL:** GP crest & kingfisher blue hackle tip
**BUTT:** Red wool
**BODY:** Flat silver tinsel
**RIB:** Oval silver tinsel
**THROAT:** Pale kingfisher blue with widgeon over
**WING:** GP tippet; married red, blue & yellow swan; Bronze mallard; GP topping over
**HEAD:** Red

### SILVER GREY
**TAG:** Silver tinsel & yellow floss
**TAIL:** GP crest
**BUTT:** Black ostrich herl
**BODY:** Flat silver tinsel
**RIB:** Oval silver tinsel
**BODY HACKLE:** Badger cock from 2nd turn of ribbing
**THROAT:** Widgeon or teal
**WING:** GP tippet; married white, yellow & green swan, bustard, peacock wing; barred summer duck; Bronze mallard; GP topping over
**CHEEKS:** Jungle cock
**HEAD:** Black

### SILVER HILTON
**TAG:** Silver tinsel
**TAIL:** Mallard flank fibres
**BODY:** Black chenille
**RIB:** Oval silver tinsel
**THROAT HACKLE:** Grizzly cock
**WING:** Grizzly hackle tips
**HEAD:** Black

### SILVER LADY #1
**TAG:** Silver tinsel
**TAIL:** GP tippet
**BODY:** Flat silver tinsel
**THROAT:** Badger hackle
**WING:** Four fibres bronze peacock herl. Two badger hackles back to back, strips of teal each side. GP topping over
**HEAD:** Black

### SILVER LADY #2
**TAG:** Silver tinsel
**TAIL:** GP tippet
**BODY:** Flat silver tinsel
**THROAT:** Badger hackle
**WING:** Two blue hackles back to back, strips of golden pheasant centre tail, teal and barred wood duck each side. GP topping over
**CHEEKS:** Blue chatterer
**HEAD:** Black

### SILVER SHRIMP
**TAIL:** Black squirrel with two strands silver Twinkle
**BODY:** Holographic silver tinsel
**HEAD HACKLE:** Long black cock
**CHEEKS:** Jungle cock
**HEAD:** Black

# Catalogue of Dressings

**SHERIFF**  **SILVER BROWN**  **SILVER DOCTOR**

**SILVER GREY**  **SILVER HILTON**  **SILVER LADY #1**

**SILVER LADY #2**  **SILVER SHRIMP**

# Catalogue of Dressings

### SILVER WILKINSON
**TAG:** Silver tinsel & golden yellow floss
**TAIL:** GP crest with Indian crow substitute
**BUTT:** Red wool
**BODY:** Flat silver tinsel
**RIB:** Oval silver tinsel
**THROAT:** Magenta cock with widgeon in front
**WING:** GP tippet; married strands of red, blue & yellow swan, peacock wing, bustard, mottled turkey tail; bronze mallard over; GP topping over all
**HEAD:** Black

### SILVER WILKINSON SPEY
**TAG:** Silver tinsel
**TAIL:** GP tippet fibres
**BODY:** Flat silver tinsel
**RIB:** Oval silver tinsel
**BODY HACKLE:** Magenta & light blue cock from 2nd turn of ribbing
**THROAT:** Magenta cock
**WING:** Bronze mallard
**CHEEKS:** Jungle cock
**HEAD:** Black

### SKAGIT SPEY, BLACK
**TAG:** Gold tinsel
**REAR BODY (1/4):** Orange floss over flat gold tinsel. Sparse strands orange polar bear hair over
**FRONT BODY (3/4):** Black seal's fur
**RIB:** Oval silver tinsel over seal's fur
**BODY HACKLE:** Black marabou over front body
**THROAT:** Teal
**WING:** Bronze mallard
**CHEEKS:** Jungle cock
**HEAD:** Black

### SKAGIT SPEY, ORANGE
**TAG:** Gold tinsel
**REAR BODY (1/4):** Orange floss over flat gold tinsel. Sparse strands orange polar bear hair over
**FRONT BODY (3/4):** Hot orange seal's fur
**RIB:** Oval gold tinsel over seal's fur
**BODY HACKLE:** Orange marabou over front body with one turn of red marabou at front
**THROAT:** Red GP breast feather with pintail over
**WING:** Bronze mallard
**CHEEKS:** Jungle cock
**HEAD:** Red

### SKAGIT SPEY, WHITE
**TAG:** Gold tinsel
**REAR BODY (1/4):** Red floss. Sparse strands white polar bear hair over
**FRONT BODY (3/4):** Light grey seal's fur
**RIB:** Oval gold tinsel over seal's fur
**BODY HACKLE:** Light grey marabou over front body
**THROAT:** Mallard flank
**WING:** Bronze mallard
**CHEEKS:** Jungle cock
**HEAD:** Black

### SKAGIT SPEY, YELLOW
**TAG:** Gold tinsel
**REAR BODY (1/4):** Hot orange floss over flat gold tinsel. Sparse strands white polar bear hair over
**FRONT BODY (3/4):** Yellow seal's fur
**RIB:** Oval silver tinsel over seal's fur
**BODY HACKLE:** Light grey marabou over front body with one turn yellow marabou in front
**THROAT:** Magenta hackle fibres with mallard flank over
**WING:** Bronze mallard
**CHEEKS:** Jungle cock
**HEAD:** Black

### SKYKOMISH DARK
**TAG:** Gold tinsel
**REAR BODY:** Orange floss
**FRONT BODY:** Red seal's fur
**RIB:** Oval silver
**BODY HACKLE:** Long yellow hackle
**THROAT:** Pheasant rump dyed black
**WING:** Bronze mallard
**HEAD:** Red

### SKYKOMISH LIGHT
**TAG:** Gold tinsel
**REAR BODY:** Orange floss
**FRONT BODY:** Red seal's fur
**RIB:** Oval silver
**BODY HACKLE:** Long yellow hackle
**THROAT:** GP red breast feather
**WING:** Bronze mallard
**HEAD:** Red

### SNELDA
**TAIL:** Black bucktail with strands silver Flashabou
**BODY:** Black wool
**RIB:** Oval silver tinsel
**FRONT HACKLE:** Short black cock
**HEAD:** Black

# Catalogue of Dressings

**SILVER WILKINSON**  **SILVER WILKINSON SPEY**  **SKAGIT SPEY, BLACK**

**SKAGIT SPEY, ORANGE**  **SKAGIT SPEY, WHITE**  **SKAGIT SPEY, YELLOW**

**SKYKOMISH DARK**  **SKYKOMISH LIGHT**  **SNELDA**

# Catalogue of Dressings

### SOFT HACKLE SPEY
**TAG:** Silver tinsel
**BODY:** Orange seal's fur
**RIB:** Oval silver tinsel
**BODY HACKLE:** Purple Spey hackle
**FRONT HACKLE:** Orange dyed guinea fowl
**HEAD:** Black

### SOL DUC SPEY
**TAG:** Silver tinsel
**BODY:** Rear 1/2 fluorescent orange floss. Front half hot orange seal's fur
**RIB:** Oval silver tinsel
**BODY HACKLE:** Long yellow Spey hackle
**THROAT:** Black heron
**WING:** Two matched pairs of hot orange hackle tips
**HEAD:** Black

### SOLDIER PALMER
**TAG:** Gold tinsel
**TAIL:** Long tuft red wool
**BODY:** Red seal's fur or wool
**RIB:** Oval gold tinsel
**BODY HACKLE:** Light ginger cock
**HEAD HACKLE:** Two turns lighter ginger cock
**HEAD:** Black

### SOUL DUCK
**TAIL:** Wood duck flank
**BUTT:** Yellow ostrich herl
**BODY:** Yellow floss
**RIB:** Oval gold tinsel
**BODY HACKLE:** Fluorescent yellow over front body
**THROAT HACKLE:** Teal flank
**WING:** Underwing: red goose quill, back to back. Overwing: Teal.
**SIDES:** Small GP tippet feathers dyed flame
**CHEEKS:** Jungle cock
**HEAD:** Black

### SPADE
**TAIL:** Natural brown deer hair
**BODY:** Black chenille
**FRONT HACKLE:** Grizzly hen
**HEAD:** Black

### SPADE, BLUE
**TAIL:** Natural brown deer hair
**BODY:** Rear 1/2: fluorescent orange dubbing. Front 1/2: iron blue dun dubbing
**FRONT HACKLE:** Grizzly hen
**HEAD:** Black

### SPADE, FANCY
**TAIL:** Dark brown mink or fitchtail
**BODY:** Rear half: peacock herl. Front half: Black ostrich rope with built-in silver rib
**FRONT HACKLE:** Grizzly cock
**HEAD:** Black

### SPADE, FANCY RED
**TAIL:** Dark brown mink or fitchtail
**BODY:** Rear half: peacock herl. Front half: Red ostrich rope with built-in silver rib
**FRONT HACKLE:** Grizzly cock
**HEAD:** Black

### SPADE, FARRAR
**TAIL:** Dark brown bucktail
**BODY:** Black seal's fur
**FRONT HACKLE:** Long, soft grizzly hen
**HEAD:** Black

# Catalogue of Dressings

### SOFT HACKLE SPEY     SOL DUC SPEY     SOLDIER PALMER

### SOUL DUCK     SPADE     SPADE, BLUE

### SPADE, FANCY     SPADE, FANCY RED     SPADE, FARRAR

# Catalogue of Dressings

### SPADE, GREEN BUTT
**TAIL:** Natural brown deer hair
**BODY:** Rear 1/4: fluorescent green dubbing. Front 3/4: black dubbing
**FRONT HACKLE:** Grizzly hen
**HEAD:** Black

### SPADE, ORANGE BUTT
**TAIL:** Natural brown deer hair
**BODY:** Rear 1/4: fluorescent orange dubbing. Front 3/4: black dubbing
**FRONT HACKLE:** Grizzly hen
**HEAD:** Black

### SPADE, POLAR
**TAIL:** White polar bear
**BODY:** Rear 1/2: green-blue dubbing. Front 1/2: black dubbing
**FRONT HACKLE:** Grizzly hen
**HEAD:** Black

### SPADE, RED GUINEA
**TAG:** Red Gantron Firefuzz
**TAIL:** Dark brown mink or fitchtail
**BODY:** Black chenille with built-in silver rib
**FRONT HACKLE:** Grizzly cock with claret dyed guinea fowl over
**HEAD:** Black

### SPADE, YELLOW GUINEA
**TAG:** Yellow Gantron Firefuzz
**TAIL:** Dark brown mink or fitchtail
**BODY:** Black chenille with built-in silver rib
**FRONT HACKLE:** Grizzly cock with yellow dyed guinea fowl over
**HEAD:** Black

### SPAWNING PURPLE
**TAG:** Silver tinsel
**TAIL:** Orange polar bear
**BODY:** Hot orange seal's fur
**RIB:** Oval silver tinsel
**BODY HACKLE:** Hot orange
**CENTRE BUTT:** Black ostrich herl
**THROAT:** Hot orange
**WING:** Matched purple hackle tips
**FRONT HACKLE:** Dark guinea fowl
**HEAD:** Black

### SPAWNING SPEY
**TAG:** Silver tinsel
**REAR BODY (1/3rd):** Half fluorescent orange floss, half fluorescent red floss
**FRONT BODY (2/3rds):** Fluorescent orange seal's fur
**RIB:** Oval silver tinsel
**BODY HACKLE:** Hot orange heron from 2nd turn of ribbing
**THROAT:** Long hot purple pintail
**WING:** Two pairs hot purple hackle tips; three or four GP toppings dyed purple over
**CHEEKS:** Jungle cock
**HEAD:** Black

### SPECTRAL SPIDER
**TAIL:** Fluorescent yellow yarn
**BODY:** Pearl Mylar
**RIB:** Flat silver tinsel
**WING:** From bottom: small tufts of yarn as follows: cerise, orange, green, blue. Cream badger hackle set each side
**FRONT HACKLE:** Grizzly cock with long mallard flank over
**CHEEKS:** Blue kingfisher
**HEAD:** Black

### SPIDER, GOLD
**BUTT:** Peacock herl
**REAR BODY:** Flat silver tinsel
**FRONT BODY:** Gold seal's fur
**SHOULDER HACKLES:** Golden pheasant flank followed by brown pheasant
**FRONT HACKLE:** Lemon wood duck
**HEAD:** Black

# Catalogue of Dressings

**SPADE, GREEN BUTT**  **SPADE, ORANGE BUTT**  **SPADE, POLAR**

**SPADE, RED GUINEA**  **SPADE, YELLOW GUINEA**  **SPAWNING PURPLE**

**SPAWNING SPEY**  **SPECTRAL SPIDER**  **SPIDER, GOLD**

# Catalogue of Dressings

### SPIRIT FLY #1
**TAG:** Gold tinsel & puce floss
**TAIL:** Two GP toppings
**BUTT:** Black ostrich herl
**BODY:** Five joints of red floss, each butted with two turns gold tinsel, a scarlet hackle & black ostrich herl
**THROAT:** Purple or dark blue cock hackle
**WING:** Six GP toppings with a broad strip of wood duck each side. A Himalayan pheasant crest over all
**CHEEKS:** Cock-of-the-rock feathers with blue kingfisher
**HORNS:** Yellow & blue macaw
**HEAD:** Black

### SPIRIT FLY #2
**TAG:** Silver tinsel & gold floss
**TAIL:** GP crest with wood duck over
**BUTT:** Black ostrich herl
**REAR BODY:** Puce floss
**FRONT BODY:** Orange seal's fur
**RIB:** Flat silver tinsel
**BODY HACKLE:** Guinea hen rump over front body
**WING:** Yellow macaw body feathers back to back; married strips of bustard, scarlet macaw, mallard, yellow macaw & silver pheasant. strips of barred wood duck each side; bronze mallard; GP topping over
**HEAD HACKLE:** Blue jay
**HORNS:** Yellow & blue macaw
**HEAD:** Black ostrich herl

### SPIRIT FLY #3
**TAG:** Silver tinsel & puce floss
**TAIL:** GP crest with red & green parrot fibres over
**BUTT:** Black ostrich herl
**BODY:** Four equal joints. From rear - puce butted with gold tinsel & a brown hackle. Red butted with gold tinsel & a green hackle. Green & yellow butted with gold tinsel & a puce hackle. Blue & orange
**WING:** GP tippet; married strips of bustard, wood duck, teal, red macaw, yellow macaw; bronze mallard; GP topping over
**SIDES:** Blue kingfisher
**HORNS:** Yellow & blue macaw
**HEAD:** Black ostrich herl

### SPITFIRE
**TAIL:** Red turkey or goose
**BODY:** Black floss or chenille
**RIB:** Oval gold tinsel
**BODY HACKLE:** Fiery brown cock
**FRONT HACKLE:** Guinea fowl
**CHEEKS:** Jungle cock
**HEAD:** Black

### SPRING FLY, HANSARD'S
**BODY:** Orange silk
**RIB:** Broad oval gold tinsel
**WING:** Dark mottled brown bittern feathers, back to back
**HACKLE:** Smokey dun cock
**HEAD:** Black

### SQUIRREL & TEAL
**TAG:** Gold tinsel
**TAIL:** GP crest
**BODY:** Dark grey seal's fur
**RIB:** Oval gold tinsel
**THROAT:** Blue dun
**WING:** Grey squirrel with teal over
**CHEEKS:** Jungle cock
**HEAD:** Black

### STEEL WOOLLY, BLACK
**TAIL:** Black bucktail
**BODY:** Braided silver tinsel
**BODY HACKLE:** Black saddle hackle
**FRONT HACKLE:** Three or four turns of black saddle
**HEAD:** Black

### STEEL WOOLLY, RED
**TAIL:** Red bucktail
**BODY:** Braided silver tinsel
**BODY HACKLE:** Red saddle hackle
**FRONT HACKLE:** Three or four turns of red saddle
**HEAD:** Black

# Catalogue of Dressings

### SPIRIT FLY #1  SPIRIT FLY #2  SPIRIT FLY #3

### SPITFIRE  SPRING FLY, HANSARD'S  SQUIRREL & TEAL

### STEEL WOOLLY, BLACK  STEEL WOOLLY, RED

# Catalogue of Dressings

### STEELHEAD CAREY
**TAG:** Cerise floss
**BODY:** Black seal's fur
**FRONT HACKLE:** Grey-green pheasant rump
**HEAD:** Black

### STEELHEAD PETITE, BLACK
**TAG:** Flat gold tinsel
**RIB:** Flat gold tinsel
**BODY:** Black uni-stretch
**THORAX:** Peacock herl
**WING:** Antron yarn, chartreuse
**HACKLE:** Hoffman chickabou black
**HEAD:** Black

### STEELHEAD PETITE, BLUE
**TAG:** Flat gold tinsel
**RIB:** Flat gold tinsel
**BODY:** Blue uni-stretch
**THORAX:** Peacock herl
**WING:** Antron yarn, clear
**HACKLE:** Hoffman chickabou blue
**HEAD:** Black

### STEELHEAD PETITE, GRIZZLY
**TAG:** Flat gold tinsel
**RIB:** Flat gold tinsel
**BODY:** Wine uni-stretch
**THORAX:** Peacock herl
**WING:** Antron yarn, yellow
**HACKLE:** Hoffman chickabou grizzly
**HEAD:** Black

### STEELHEAD PETITE, OLIVE
**TAG:** Flat gold tinsel
**RIB:** Flat gold tinsel
**BODY:** Olive uni-stretch
**THORAX:** Peacock herl
**WING:** Antron yarn, olive
**HACKLE:** Hoffman chickabou olive
**HEAD:** Black

### STEELHEAD PETITE, PINK
**TAG:** Flat gold tinsel
**RIB:** Flat gold tinsel
**BODY:** Pink uni-stretch
**THORAX:** Peacock herl
**WING:** Antron yarn, clear
**HACKLE:** Hoffman chickabou pink
**HEAD:** Black

### STEELHEAD PETITE, PURPLE
**TAG:** Flat gold tinsel
**RIB:** Flat gold tinsel
**BODY:** Purple uni-stretch
**THORAX:** Peacock herl
**WING:** Antron yarn, clear
**HACKLE:** Hoffman chickabou purple
**HEAD:** Black

### STEELHEAD SPEY
**TAG:** Gold tinsel & hot orange floss
**BODY:** Hot orange seal's fur
**RIB:** Oval gold tinsel
**BODY HACKLE:** Red Spey hackle
**THROAT:** Grey heron
**WING:** Bronze mallard
**HEAD:** Black

### STEELHEAD STICK
**TAIL:** Fluorescent green yarn
**BODY:** Black chenille or black sparkle chenille
**HACKLE:** Long black, extending to end of body
**HEAD:** Black

# Catalogue of Dressings

**STEELHEAD CAREY**  **STEELHEAD PETITE, BLACK**  **STEELHEAD PETITE, BLUE**

**STEELHEAD PETITE, GRIZZLY**  **STEELHEAD PETITE, OLIVE**  **STEELHEAD PETITE, PINK**

**STEELHEAD PETITE, PURPLE**  **STEELHEAD SPEY**  **STEELHEAD STICK**

# Catalogue of Dressings

### STUART'S KILLER
**TAG:** Gold tinsel
**TAIL:** Red dyed hackle fibres
**BODY:** Flat silver tinsel
**RIB:** Oval gold tinsel
**THROAT:** Dyed red hen
**WING:** GP tippets with bronze mallard over
**CHEEKS:** Jungle cock
**HEAD:** Black

### SUMMER DEEP PURPLE SPEY
**TAG:** Silver tinsel
**REAR BODY:** Purple diamond braid
**FRONT BODY:** Purple chenille
**RIB:** Oval silver tinsel
**BODY HACKLE:** Purple dyed golden pheasant
**COLLAR HACKLE:** 1st: Purple dyed golden pheasant. 2nd: Purple dyed pheasant rump
**HEAD:** Black

### SUMMER FRONTIER
**TAG:** Silver tinsel
**REAR BODY:** Red floss
**FRONT BODY:** Purple dubbing
**RIB:** Flat silver tinsel & oval silver tinsel
**BODY HACKLE:** Purple schlappen
**WING:** Pair purple hackle tips back to back, enclosed by a pair of red hackle tips
**COLLAR HACKLE:** Guinea fowl
**HEAD:** Black

### SUMMER LADY CAROLINE
**TAIL:** Burnt orange saddle hackle fibres
**TAG:** Silver tinsel
**BODY:** Brown dubbing
**RIB:** Oval gold tinsel
**BODY HACKLE:** Long grey dyed Chinese chicken hackle. Counter rib with oval silver tinsel
**COLLAR HACKLE:** Burnt orange saddle hackle
**WING:** Mallard flank dyed wood duck
**HEAD:** Black

### SUMMER MIDNIGHT EXPRESS
**TAG:** Silver tinsel
**REAR BODY:** Purple braided Mylar tinsel
**FRONT BODY:** Black chenille
**RIB:** Oval silver tinsel
**BODY HACKLE:** Black dyed golden pheasant
**COLLAR HACKLE:** 1st Black dyed golden pheasant, 2nd Purple dyed pheasant rump
**HEAD:** Black

### SUMMER SUNRISE
**TAG:** Silver tinsel
**REAR BODY:** Red braided Mylar tinsel
**FRONT BODY:** Pink chenille
**RIB:** Oval silver tinsel
**BODY HACKLE:** Black dyed golden pheasant
**COLLAR HACKLE:** 1st Orange dyed golden pheasant, 2nd Orange dyed pheasant rump
**HEAD:** Black

### SUNDOWNER, BLACK
**TAG:** Silver tinsel
**TAIL:** Orange hackle fibres
**BODY:** Fluorescent green wool
**RIB:** Oval silver tinsel
**BODY HACKLE:** Black palmered
**WING:** Orange Krystal Flash
**COLLAR HACKLE:** Black
**HEAD:** Black

### SUNDOWNER, ORANGE
**TAG:** Silver tinsel
**TAIL:** Black hackle fibres
**BODY:** Fluorescent green wool
**RIB:** Oval silver tinsel
**BODY HACKLE:** Orange palmered
**WING:** Black Krystal Flash
**COLLAR HACKLE:** Orange
**HEAD:** Black

### SUNDOWNER, PINK
**TAG:** Silver tinsel
**TAIL:** Fluorescent pink hackle fibres
**BODY:** Fluorescent red wool
**RIB:** Oval silver tinsel
**BODY HACKLE:** Fluorescent pink palmered
**WING:** Pearl Krystal Flash
**COLLAR HACKLE:** Fluorescent pink
**HEAD:** Black

# Catalogue of Dressings

### STUART'S KILLER  SUMMER DEEP PURPLE SPEY  SUMMER FRONTIER

### SUMMER LADY CAROLINE  SUMMER MIDNIGHT EXPRESS  SUMMER SUNRISE

### SUNDOWNER, BLACK  SUNDOWNER, ORANGE  SUNDOWNER, PINK

# Catalogue of Dressings

### SUNDOWNER, PURPLE
**TAG:** Silver tinsel
**TAIL:** Purple hackle fibres
**BODY:** Fluorescent orange wool
**RIB:** Oval silver tinsel
**BODY HACKLE:** Purple palmered
**WING:** Pearl Krystal Flash
**COLLAR HACKLE:** Purple
**HEAD:** Black

### SUNDOWNER, RED
**TAG:** Silver tinsel
**TAIL:** Red hackle fibres
**BODY:** Fluorescent red wool
**RIB:** Oval silver tinsel
**BODY HACKLE:** Red palmered
**WING:** Pearl Krystal Flash
**COLLAR HACKLE:** Red
**HEAD:** Black

### SUNSET, BLUE & BRONZE
**BODY:** Flat silver tinsel veiled above & below with GP crest
**HACKLE:** Blue with claret over
**THROAT:** Golden pheasant body feather
**WING:** Bronze mallard
**HEAD:** Black

### SUNSET, ORANGE
**BODY:** Flat gold tinsel veiled above & below with GP crest.
**HACKLE:** Yellow with orange over
**THROAT:** Golden pheasant body feather
**WING:** Orange goose
**HEAD:** Black

### SUNSET, STEELHEAD
**BODY:** Flat silver tinsel veiled above & below with GP crest.
**HACKLE:** Magenta with claret over
**THROAT:** Golden pheasant body feather
**WING:** Claret goose
**HEAD:** Black

### SWEEP
**TAG:** Oval gold tinsel
**TAIL:** GP crest
**BUTT:** Black ostrich herl
**BODY:** Black floss
**RIB:** Oval gold tinsel
**THROAT:** Long black hackle wound as collar then pulled down
**WING:** Black goose quill
**CHEEKS:** Kingfisher
**HEAD:** Black

### SWEET LORETTA
**TAG:** Short tuft of flame yarn
**BODY:** Black seal's fur – very ragged
**BODY HACKLE:** Black long with extra turns at head
**HEAD:** Black

### TAILFIRE
**TAIL:** Hot orange bucktail with two strands pearl Flashabou Accent
**TAG:** Lime green Globrite floss
**REAR BODY:** Flat gold Mylar tinsel
**RIB:** Oval gold tinsel
**CENTRE HACKLE:** Hot orange cock
**FRONT BODY:** Black floss
**RIB:** Oval silver tinsel
**FRONT HACKLE:** Black cock
**HEAD:** Black

# Catalogue of Dressings

**SUNDOWNER, PURPLE**  **SUNDOWNER, RED**  **SUNSET, BLUE & BRONZE**

**SUNSET, ORANGE**  **SUNSET, STEELHEAD**  **SWEEP**

**SWEET LORETTA**  **TAILFIRE**

# Catalogue of Dressings

### TANA
**TAG:** Gold tinsel
**TAIL:** GP crest
**BUTT:** Black ostrich herl
**BODY:** Flat silver tinsel
**RIB:** Oval gold tinsel
**BODY HACKLE:** Yellow cock over front half of body
**THROAT:** Guinea fowl
**WING:** Mottled brown turkey tail strips
**CHEEKS:** Jungle cock
**HEAD:** Black

### TARTAN
**TAG:** Gold tinsel
**TAIL:** Golden pheasant red rump feather
**BODY:** Red-orange seal's fur
**RIB:** Oval gold tinsel
**BODY HACKLE:** Grey heron
**THROAT:** Teal
**WING:** Strips of silver-grey turkey
**HEAD:** Black

### TC3
**TAIL:** GP crest dyed flame
**REAR BODY:** Fluorescent white floss
**FRONT BODY:** Fluorescent flame floss
**RIB:** Oval gold tinsel
**BODY HACKLE:** White cock over front body
**WING:** Green-wing teal flank
**CHEEKS:** Jungle cock
**HEAD:** Flame

### TEAL, BLUE & SILVER SPIDER
**HOOK:** Silver Salar
**BODY:** None
**FRONT HACKLES:** Grey mallard flank over light blue cock
**HEAD:** Black

### TERESA'S TEASE
**TAIL:** GP crest dyed hot orange
**REAR BODY:** Red floss
**FRONT BODY:** Peacock herl
**RIB:** Oval gold tinsel
**BODY HACKLE:** Soft black hackle over front body
**THROAT:** Guinea fowl
**WING:** Green-wing teal flank
**HEAD:** Black

### THUNDER & LIGHTNING
**TAG:** Silver tinsel & golden yellow floss
**TAIL:** GP crest and Indian crow
**BUTT:** Black ostrich
**BODY:** Black floss
**RIB:** Oval gold tinsel
**BODY HACKLE:** Orange cock
**THROAT:** Blue jay
**WING:** Bronze mallard with GP topping over
**CHEEKS:** Jungle cock
**HEAD:** Black

### THUNDER SHRIMP
**TAIL:** Orange bucktail with GP tippet over
**BODY:** Pearl tinsel
**RIB:** Oval silver tinsel
**FRONT HACKLE:** Guinea fowl over orange cock
**HEAD:** Black

### TOPPY
**BUTT:** Crimson wool with small red hackle
**TAIL:** Tuft of yellow wool
**BODY:** Black seal's fur
**RIB:** Oval gold tinsel
**BODY HACKLE:** Black cock
**THROAT:** Extra turns of black cock
**WING:** White tipped black turkey
**HEAD:** Black

# Catalogue of Dressings

| TANA | TARTAN | TC3 |

| TEAL, BLUE & SILVER SPIDER | TERESA'S TEASE | THUNDER & LIGHTNING |

| THUNDER SHRIMP | TOPPY |

# Catalogue of Dressings

### TRAFFIC TICKET
**TAG:** Gold tinsel
**TAIL:** Lemon wood duck fibres
**BODY:** Peacock herl
**WING:** Lemon wood duck flank
**FRONT HACKLE:** Badger hackle
**HEAD:** Black

### TRINITY BROWN
**TAIL:** Brown hackle fibres
**BODY:** Brown chenille
**RIB:** Oval silver tinsel
**FRONT HACKLE:** Brown cock
**HEAD:** Black

### TRINITY GREY
**TAIL:** Grizzly hackle fibres
**BODY:** Grey chenille
**RIB:** Oval silver tinsel
**FRONT HACKLE:** Grizzly cock
**HEAD:** Black

### TROPHY HUNTER
**TAG:** Gold tinsel & hot orange floss
**BODY:** Red seal's fur
**RIB:** Oval gold tinsel
**BODY HACKLE:** Black heron
**THROAT:** Dark guinea fowl
**WING:** Golden pheasant red body feather
**HEAD:** Black

### TURKEY TRACKER
**BODY:** Black wool or dubbing
**RIB:** Embossed gold tinsel
**BODY HACKLE:** Brown turkey
**THROAT:** Purple saddle with pintail flank over
**WING:** Two green highlander hackle tips, back to back. Veil each side with short GP red breast feather
**HEAD:** Black

### VALDUM
**TAG:** Silver tinsel & red floss
**TAIL:** Red hackle fibres
**BUTT:** Black ostrich herl
**BODY:** Flat silver tinsel
**RIB:** Black floss
**THROAT:** Black cock hackle
**WING:** Black dyed goose
**CHEEKS:** Jungle cock
**HEAD:** Black

### VI MENN FLUA
**TAG:** Silver tinsel
**TAIL:** GP crest with red hackle fibres over
**BUTT:** Red ostrich herl
**BODY:** Black floss
**RIB:** Flat silver tinsel
**BODY HACKLE:** Red cock over front body
**THROAT:** Black cock hackle
**WING:** Married strips of mottled turkey, dark red swan, white swan. GP topping over
**CHEEKS:** Jungle cock
**HEAD:** Black

### WASP GRUB
**TAG:** Silver tinsel
**TAIL:** Yellow toucan feather
**BODY:** Yellow & black chenille in alternate bands (not spiral)
**HACKLE:** Dark brown coch-y-bonddu over front half of body
**THROAT:** Extra turns of body hackle
**WING:** Cinnamon turkey tail strips
**HEAD:** Black

### WATSON'S FANCY
**TAG:** Silver tinsel
**TAIL:** GP crest
**REAR BODY:** Red seal's fur
**FRONT BODY:** Black seal's fur
**RIB:** Oval silver tinsel
**THROAT:** Black hackle
**WING:** Crow slips
**CHEEKS:** Jungle cock
**HEAD:** Black

# Catalogue of Dressings

| TRAFFIC TICKET | TRINITY BROWN | TRINITY GREY |

| TROPHY HUNTER | TURKEY TRACKER | VALDUM |

| VI MENN FLUA | WASP GRUB | WATSON'S FANCY |

## Catalogue of Dressings

### WET SPIDER
**BODY:** Yellow chenille
**FRONT HACKLE:** Grizzly cock with mallard flank over
**HEAD:** Black

### WHAKA BLONDE
**TAIL:** Purple cock hackle fibres
**BODY:** Purple ostrich rope with built-in silver rib
**FRONT HACKLE:** Purple hen
**HEAD:** Black

### WHITEWING
**TAG:** Silver tinsel
**TAIL:** GP crest and tippet in strands
**REAR BODY:** Red seal's fur
**FRONT BODY:** Black seal's fur
**RIB:** Oval silver tinsel
**BODY HACKLE:** Black cock over front body
**THROAT:** Blue cock
**WING:** White swan strips set horizontally
**HEAD:** Black

### WIL HARRY
**TAG:** Silver tinsel
**TAIL:** Peacock sword fibres
**BODY:** Rear 1/3rd orange wool, rest black floss
**RIB:** Oval silver tinsel
**THROAT:** Olive cock
**WING:** Married strips of blue & red swan with peacock herl over
**HEAD:** Black

### WILD TURKEY ORANGE
**TAG:** Gold tinsel
**REAR BODY:** Fluorescent orange floss
**RIB:** Flat gold tinsel
**FRONT BODY:** Hot orange seal's fur
**RIB:** Oval gold tinsel
**BODY HACKLE:** Wild turkey marabou over front body
**COLLAR:** Orange dyed mallard flank
**WING:** Hot orange goose
**HEAD:** Black

### WINTER CANDLELIGHT
**TAG:** Silver tinsel
**REAR BODY:** Fluorescent orange floss
**FRONT BODY:** Medium dark orange seal's fur
**RIB:** Oval silver tinsel
**BODY HACKLE:** Long dyed yellow Chinese hackle
**COLLAR HACKLE:** Black marabou
**WING:** Orange goose quill
**HEAD:** Black

### WINTER EXPRESSION
**TAG:** Silver tinsel
**REAR BODY:** Fuschia floss
**FRONT BODY:** Medium dark orange seal's fur
**RIB:** Oval silver tinsel
**BODY HACKLE:** Long dyed yellow Chinese hackle
**COLLAR HACKLE:** Guinea fowl
**WING:** White goose quill
**HEAD:** Black

### WINTER GREEN BUTT SKUNK
**TAG:** Silver tinsel
**TAIL:** Red saddle hackle fibres
**REAR BODY:** Fluorescent chartreuse floss
**FRONT BODY:** Black seal's fur
**RIB:** Oval silver tinsel
**BODY HACKLE:** Long dyed yellow Chinese hackle
**COLLAR HACKLE:** Guinea fowl
**WING:** White goose quill
**HEAD:** Black

### WINTER JACK O'LANTERN
**TAG:** Gold tinsel
**TAIL:** Red saddle hackle fibres
**REAR BODY (1/3rd):** Gold floss
**FRONT BODY (2/3rds):** Orange floss
**RIB:** Oval gold tinsel
**BODY HACKLE:** Long dyed orange Chinese hackle
**COLLAR HACKLE:** Black marabou with guinea fowl over
**WING:** Orange goose quill
**HEAD:** Black

# Catalogue of Dressings

**WET SPIDER**  **WHAKA BLONDE**  **WHITEWING**

**WIL HARRY**  **WILD TURKEY ORANGE**  **WINTER CANDLELIGHT**

**WINTER EXPRESSION**  **WINTER GREEN BUTT SKUNK**  **WINTER JACK O'LANTERN**

# Catalogue of Dressings

**WINTER PUNCH SPEY**
**TAG:** Silver tinsel
**BODY:** Rear 1/2 fuchia floss. Front 1/2 lime green seal's fur
**RIB:** Oval silver tinsel
**BODY HACKLE:** Hot pink from 2nd turn of ribbing
**THROAT:** Lime green hackle, long as collar
**WING:** Mallard dyed wood duck
**HEAD:** Black

**WINTER SUNKIST**
**TAG:** Gold tinsel
**TAIL:** Red saddle hackle fibres
**REAR BODY:** Hot orange floss
**FRONT BODY:** Red seal's fur
**RIB:** Oval gold tinsel
**BODY HACKLE:** Orange marabou
**COLLAR HACKLE:** Red dyed guinea fowl
**WING:** White goose quill
**HEAD:** Black

**WINTER'S HOPE**
**BODY:** Flat silver tinsel
**WING:** Two pairs of hackle tips, orange over yellow
**FRONT HACKLES:** Deep blue then purple cock
**HEAD:** Black

**WINTER'S HOPE SPEY**
**TAG:** Yellow floss
**TAIL:** GP crest
**BUTT:** Yellow ostrich herl
**BODY:** Bright blue floss
**RIB:** Oval silver tinsel
**BODY HACKLE:** Kingfisher blue schlappen
**THROAT:** Mallard flank dyed hot purple
**WING:** Narrow strips of hot orange goose
**HEAD:** Black

**WOOLLY BUGGER, BLACK**
**TAIL:** Two matching black marabou blood hackle tips with a few strands of black Krystal Flash
**BODY:** Black Crystal chenille
**BODY HACKLE:** Black saddle hackle
**FRONT HACKLE:** Three or four turns of black saddle
**HEAD:** Black

**WOOLLY BUGGER, ORANGE**
**TAIL:** Two matching orange marabou blood hackle tips with a few strands of orange Krystal Flash
**BODY:** Orange Crystal chenille
**BODY HACKLE:** Orange saddle hackle
**FRONT HACKLE:** Three or four turns of orange saddle
**HEAD:** Black

**WOOLLY BUGGER, PEACOCK**
**TAIL:** Kelly green marabou with dark olive flash
**BODY:** Peacock herl
**RIB:** Green wire
**BODY HACKLE:** Grizzly dyed olive
**HEAD:** Black

# Catalogue of Dressings

### WINTER PUNCH SPEY     WINTER SUNKIST     WINTER'S HOPE

### WINTER'S HOPE SPEY     WOOLLY BUGGER, BLACK

### WOOLLY BUGGER, ORANGE     WOOLLY BUGGER, PEACOCK

## Catalogue of Dressings

### WOOLLY BUGGER, PURPLE
**TAIL:** Two matching purple marabou blood hackle tips with a few strands of purple Krystal Flash
**BODY:** Purple Crystal chenille
**BODY HACKLE:** Purple saddle hackle
**FRONT HACKLE:** Three or four turns of purple saddle
**HEAD:** Black

### WOOLLY BUGGER, RED
**TAIL:** Two matching red marabou blood hackle tips with a few strands of red Krystal Flash
**BODY:** Red Crystal chenille
**BODY HACKLE:** Red saddle hackle
**FRONT HACKLE:** Three or four turns of red saddle
**HEAD:** Black

### WOOLLY WORM
**TAIL:** Tuft of red or orange wool or floss
**BODY:** Black chenille
**BODY HACKLE:** Grizzly cock
**THROAT:** One turn of teal
**HEAD:** Black

### WYE GRUB
**TAG:** Silver tinsel & red floss
**TAIL:** Yellow macaw with ibis over
**BUTT:** Coch-y-bonddu hackle dyed yellow cheeked with a pair of jungle cock, back to back
**REAR BODY:** Yellow seal's fur
**CENTRE BUTT:** Coch-y-bonddu hackle dyed yellow cheeked with a pair of jungle cock larger than rear, back to back
**FRONT BODY:** Yellow seal's fur
**RIB:** Oval silver tinsel
**THROAT:** Coch-y-bonddu hackle dyed yellow cheeked with a pair of jungle cock, back to back, larger than centre. Guinea fowl hackle dyed orange over
**HEAD:** Black

### ZULU
**TAG:** Silver tinsel
**TAIL:** Fluorescent red wool
**BODY:** Black seal's fur
**RIB:** Oval silver tinsel
**BODY HACKLE:** Black cock
**HEAD HACKLE:** Long black hen
**HEAD:** Black

### ZULU, BLUE
**TAG:** Silver tinsel
**TAIL:** Fluorescent red wool
**BODY:** Black seal's fur
**RIB:** Flat silver tinsel
**BODY HACKLE:** Black cock
**HEAD HACKLE:** Long kingfisher blue hen
**HEAD:** Black

# Catalogue of Dressings

**WOOLLY BUGGER, PURPLE**  **WOOLLY BUGGER, RED**

**WOOLLY WORM**  **WYE GRUB**  **ZULU**

**ZULU, BLUE**

# Bibliography

## BOOKS

**Bachmann, Troy**
*Frontier Flies*, Frank Amato Publications 1998

**Bates, Col. Joseph D**
*Atlantic Salmon Flies & Fishing*, Stackpole Books 1970
*The Art of the Atlantic Salmon Fly*, D. R. Godine 1987

**Buckland, John**
*The Pocket Guide to Trout & Salmon Flies*, Mitchell Beazley Publishers 1986

**Buckland, John and Oglesby, Arthur**
*A Guide to Salmon Flies*, The Crowood Press 1990

**Combs, Trey**
*Steelhead Fly Fishing*, Lyons Press 1991, Paperback Edition 1999
*Steelhead Fly Fishing & Flies*, Salmon Trout Steelheader 1976

**Dunham, Judith**
*The Atlantic Salmon Fly - The Tyers and Their Art*, Chronicle Books 1991

**Francis, Francis**
*A Book on Angling*, London 1867

**Frodin, Mikael**
*Classic Salmon Flies - History & Patterns*, Bonanza Books 1991

**Fulsher, Keith and Krom, Charles**
*Hair-Wing Atlantic Salmon Flies*, Fly Tyer Inc. 1981

**Haig-Brown, Roderick**
*The Western Angler, Vols I & II*, Derrydale Press, New York 1939
*A River Never Sleeps*, William Morrow & Co. New York 1946

**Hale, J. H.**
*How to Tie Salmon Flies*, London 1892 & 1919

**Headley, Stan**
*Trout & Salmon Flies of Scotland*, Merlin Unwin Books 1997

**Inland Empire Fishing Club**
*Flies of the Northwest*, Frank Amato Publications, 1998

**Jorgensen, Poul**
*Salmon Flies - Their Character, Style and Dressing*, Stackpole Books, 2nd Ed. 1999

**Kelson, Geoge Mortimer**
*The Salmon Fly*, London 1895

**Knox, Arthur Edward**
*Autumns on the Spey*, London 1892

**Lingren, Arthur James**
*Fly Patterns of British Columbia*, Frank Amato Publications 1996

**McKenzie, Gordon**
*Hair-Hackle Tying Techniques & Fly Patterns*, Frank Amato Publications 2001

# Bibliography

**Malone, E. J.**
*Irish Trout & Salmon Flies*, Coch-y-Bonddu Books Paperback Ed. 1998

**Mann, Christopher and Gillespie, Robert**
*Shrimp & Spey Flies for Salmon*, Merlin Unwin Books 2001

**Mann, Christopher**
*Hairwing & Tube Flies for Salmon*, Merlin Unwin Books 2004

**Marriner, Paul C.**
*Modern Atlantic Salmon Flies*, Frank Amato Publications 1998

**Meyer, Deke**
*Advanced Fly Fishing For Steelhead*, Frank Amato Publications 1992

**Morgan, Moc**
*Trout & Salmon Flies of Wales*, Merlin Unwin Books 1996

**O'Reilly, Peter**
*Trout & Salmon Flies of Ireland*, Merlin Unwin Books 1995

**Patrick, Roy A.**
*Pacific Northwest Fly Patterns*, Patrick's Fly Shop 1948, Rev. 1953, 1958

**Pryce-Tanatt, Dr. Thomas**
*How to Dress Salmon Flies*, London 1914

**Radencich, Michael D.**
*Tying the Classic Salmon Fly*, Stackpole Books 1997

**Shewey, John & Maxwell, Forrest**
*Fly Fishing For Summer Steelhead*, Frank Amato Publications 1996

**Stetzer, Randle Scott**
*Flies - The Best One Thousand*, Frank Amato Publications 1992

**Stewart, Dick & Allen, Farrow**
*Flies for Atlantic Salmon*, Northland Press 1991

**Supinski, Matt**
*Steelhead Dreams*, Frank Amato Publications 2001

Almost all of the classic books on British fly fishing and flies (Francis, Kelson, Hales, Knox, Pryce-Tannatt etc.) are available as reprints from The Fly Fisher's Classic Library

## PERIODICALS

**Trout and Salmon**, EMAP Active Ltd. Peterborough, UK
**Fly Fishing & Fly Tying**, Rolling River Publications, Kenmore, Perthshire, UK

# Index

## A

Abe Munn Killer  54, 116-117
Aguanus  68, 116-117
Akroyd, Reverse (Halyk's)  84, 116-117
    Steelhead (Yarnot)  84, 116-117
Alexandra  59, 116-117
All Night Spey  116-117
Arnold, Bob  90
As Specified #1  106, 116-117
Assassin  29, 116-117

## B

Bachmann, Troy  77-79
Bainbridge, Geogre  7
Ballyshannon  14, 116-117
Baron  55, 118-119
Bastard Dose  57, 118-119
Bates, Joseph D.  51
Beauly Snow Fly  105, 118-119
Beresford's Fancy  16, 118-119
Bibio  29, 118-119
Blacker, William  12, 14, 17
Black & Blue  103, 118-119
Black & Gold Gorbenmac Ranger  42, 154-155
Black & Orange Heron  81, 160-161
Black & Silver  101, 118-119
Black & Teal  8, 118-119
Black Boar  39, 118-119
Black Dawn  45, 138-139
Black Diamond  104, 120-121
Black Doctor  21, 120-121
Black Dog (Mackintosh)  6, 120-121
    (Kelson)  12, 120-121
Black Eagle  64, 120-121, 144-145
Black Fairy  58, 120-121
Black Gorbenmac  43, 152-153
Black Gorbenmac Ranger  42, 154-155
Black Hawk  55, 120-121
Black Heron  61, 81, 160-161
Black KeHe  37, 122-123
Black Labrador  66, 122-123
Black, Orange & Jungle Cock  Pl.14 (p100), 122-123
Black Pennell  17, 122-123
Black Ranger  9, 122-123
Black Reeach (Shewey)  76, 122-123
Black Skagit Spey  63, 192-193
Black Sky  108, 122-123
Black Spey  105, 122-123
Black Steel Woolly  99, 198-199
Black Steelhead Petite  Pl.10 (p95), 200-201
Black Sundowner  Pl.9 (p94), 202-203
Black, Tippet & Yellow  Pl.14 (p100), 122-123
Black Turkey  25, 124-125
Black Woolly Bugger  Pl.13 (p98), 212-213
Blackville  56, 124-125
Bladnoch Shrimp  38, 124-125
Blue & Bronze Sunset  85, 204-205
Blue Charm  20, 124-125
Blue Charm, Double  20, 124-125
Blue Charm Spider  Pl.12 (p97), 124-125
Blue Dawn  45, 138-139
Blue Doctor  21, 124-125
Blue Elver  23, 126-127
Blue Heron  81, 160-161
Blue Sandy  57, 126-127
Blue Sapphire  44, 126-127
Blue Sky  108, 122-123
Blue Spade  Pl.6 (p91), 194-195
Blue Steelhead Petite  Pl.10 (p95), 200-201
Blue Zulu  30, 214-215
Bobbie Jean  111, 126-127
Børre Flua  50, 126-127
Boss  99, 126-127
Boulder Creek  Pl.15 (p106), 126-127
Branchu  68, 126-127
Brayshaw, Thomas  101
Brigg's Pennell  29, 126-127
Brindle Bug  89, 128-129
Brown Fairy  59, 128-129
Brown Heron (McNeese)  82, 160-161
    (Glasso)  62, 160-161
Brown Turkey  22, 128-129
Bulldog  16, 128-129
Bumble, Claret  32, 128-129
    Golden Olive  32, 128-129
    Leggy Claret  32, 128129
Burlap  89, 128-129
Burton  35, 128-129

## C

Cains River Scotch Lassie  52, 130-131
Cains River Silver Doctor  52, 130-131
Campbells Fancy  67, 130-131
Candy Montana  Pl.8 (p93), 130-131
Car Body  Pl.15 (p106), 130-131
Cascade Variant  40, 130-131
Cascapedia  53, 130-131
Catch-A-Me-Lodge  61, 132-133
Cerise & Claret Spey  75, 132-133
Chaleur Bay Smelt  53, 132-133
Chappie  103, 132-133
Chartreuse Shrimp (MacDonald)  40, 132-133
Chartreuse Spider  65, 132-133
Cinnamon & Gold (North American)  35, 132-133
Clan Chief  36, 134-135
Claret & Black  105, 134-135
Claret & Jay  26, 134-135
Claret Bumble  32, 128-129
Combs, Trey  103-104, 111
Comet  99, 134-135
    Orange  99, 134-135
Connemara Black  26, 134-135
Connemara Claret  31, 134-135
Conway Blue  24, 134-135
Copper March Brown  60, 136-137
Coquihalla Orange Dark  101, 136-137
    Light  101, 136-137
Coquihalla Red  101, 136-137
Corneille  66, 136-137
Courtesan  62, 136-137
Crimson Glory  58, 136-137
Crosfield  44, 136-137

## D

D'Ana Marie  111, 136-137
Dana Montana  Pl.8 (p93), 138-139
Dandy  9, 138-139
Darbee's Spate Fly  59, 138-139
Dark Mackerel  33, 138-139
Dawn  45, 138-139
Dawn, Black  45, 138-139
    Blue  45, 138-139
    Green  45, 138-139
    Red  45, 138-139
    Thunder  45, 140-141
    Yellow  45, 140-141
Dean River Lantern, Green  Pl.11 (p96) 140-141
    Orange  Pl.11 (p96), 140-141
    Red  Pl.11 (p96), 140-141
    Yellow  Pl.11 (p96) 140-141
Deep Purple Spey  72, 140-141
Delphi Silver  38, 140-141
Denise  58, 140-141
Denise Montana  Pl.8 (p93) 142-143
Deschutes Skunk  109, 142-143
    Spey  109, 142-143
Dick's Fly  Pl.14 (p100), 142-143
Doc Spratley  104, 142-143
Doctor, Black  21, 120-121
    Blue  21, 124-125
    Silver  21, 190-191
Donegal Blue  31, 142-143
Dragon  66, 142-143
Dragons Tooth  Pl.15 (p106), 142-143
Dream  46, 142-143
Dunkeld  31, 144-145
Durham Ranger  57, 144-145
Dusty Miller  27, 144-145
Dwyryd Red & Yellow  26, 144-145

## E

Eagle, Black  64, 120-121, 144-145
    Emerald  85, 144-145

# Index

Grey 63, 144-145
Yellow 63, 144-145
Eany Tailfire 40, 146-147
Em Te Flugor 50, 146-147
Emerald Eagle 85, 144-145

## F

Fancy Red Spade Pl.7 (p92), 194-195
Fancy Spade Pl.7 (p92), 194-195
Farrar Spade Pl.6 (p91), 194-195
Father Bill Pl.16 (p112), 146-147
Fiery Brown 16, 146-147
Fiery Brown Streamer 54, 146-147

## G

Gaby 65, 146-147
Gageure 69, 146-147
Garrett, Jim 111-113
Gaudy Fly 7, 146-147
General Money #1 77, 148-149
General Money #2 77, 148-149
German Snelda 41, 148-149
Ghost 22, 148-149
Glasgow Rangers 41, 148-149
Glasso, Sydney 61-62, 71
Gled Wing 11, 148-149
Glen Grant 11, 148-149
Goat's Toe 30, 150-151
Gold Butcher 37, 150-151
    Hardy's 37, 150-151
Gold Heron (Glasso) 62, 160-161
Gold Hilton Spider 87, 150-151
Gold Reeach 10, 150-151
Gold Spider 87, 196-197
Gold Sylph 28, 150-151
Golden Butterfly 8, 150-151
Golden Demon II 110, 150-151
Golden Edge Orange 104, 150-151
Golden Edge Yellow 104, 152-153
Golden Girl 102, 152-153
Golden Heron (McNeese) 82, 160-161
Golden Mallard 48, 152-153
Golden Olive Bumble 32, 128-129
Golden Purple Spey 75, 152-153
Golden Red Pl.14 (p100), 152-153
Golden Spey 73, 152-153
Golden Spey (Taylor) 108, 152-153
Gorbenmac, Black 43, 152-153
    Green 43, 152-153
    Orange 43, 154-155
    Purple 43, 154-155
    Red 43, 154-155
Gorbenmac Ranger, Black 42, 154-155
    Black & Gold 42, 154-155
    Green 42, 154-155
Goshawk 27, 154-155
Gosling, Grey 28, 154-155
    Rush 32, 154-155
    Yellow 32, 156-157
Green Beauty 54, 156-157
Green Butt Silver Hilton 103, 156-157
Green Butt Spade Pl.6 (p91), 196-197
Green Butt Spider 88, 156-157
Green Dawn 45, 138-139
Green Drake 68, 156-157
Green Gorbenmac 43, 152-153
Green Gorbenmac Ranger 42, 154-155
Green Heron 81, 162-163
Green Highlander 23, 156-157
Green Peter 33, 156-157
Green Spey 65, 156-157
Grey Eagle 63, 144-145
Grey Fly Pl.14 (p100), 158-159
Grey Ghost 53, 158-159
Grey Gosling 28, 154-155
Grey Heron 11, 61, 162-163
Grizzly Steelhead Petite Pl.10 (p95), 200-201
Grouse & Claret 36, 158-159
    Harold's 36, 158-159
Gullnokk 48, 158-159

## H

Haig-Brown, Roderick 89, 101-102
Halloween Matuka 109, 158-159
Halloween Spey 74, 158-159
Hansard's Spring Fly 7, 198-199
Hardy's Gold Butcher 37, 150-151
Harold's Grouse & Claret 36, 158-159
Haslam 25, 158-159
Headley, Stan 22
Heavy Breather Orange 76, 158-159
Heggeli 46, 160-161
Helens Fancy Pl.16 (p112), 160-161
Heron, Black 61, 160-161
    Black & Orange 81, 160-161
    Blue 81, 160-161
    Brown (Glasso) 62, 160-161
    Brown (McNeese) 82, 160-161
    Gold (Glasso) 62, 160-161
    Golden (McNeese) 82, 160-161
    Green 81, 162-163
    Grey 11, 61, 162-163
    Orange 62, 162-163
    Silver (Glasso) 62, 162-163
Hilton, Gold Spider 87, 150-151
    Green Butt Silver 103, 156-157
    Purple 73, 182-183
    Silver 103, 190-191
Hornberg 69, 162-163

## I

Irishman's Claret 33, 162-163

## J

Jacob's Coat Pl.7 (p92), 162-163
Jacob's Ladder 34, 162-163
Jackson, Alec 92-93
Jeannie 20, 162-164
Johnson M.D. Pl.17 (p113), 164-165
Jungle Cock & Silver 34, 164-165

## K

Kate 15, 164-165
Kate (Garrett) Pl.16 (p112), 164-165
Kate McLaren 34, 164-165
Kelson, George 15
King's Fisher 6, 164-165
Kingsmill 35, 164-165
Knouse 111, 164-165

## L

Lady Amherst 56, 164-165
Lady Caroline 61, 166-167
Laerdal 47, 166-167
Lamqui 57, 166-167
Lanctôt 58, 166-167
Lansdale Partridge 34, 166-167
Laxford 12, 166-167
Lee Blue 13, 166-167
Leggy Claret Bumble 32, 128-129
Lemon Grey 13, 166-167
Libby's Black Pl.8 (p93), 166-167
Lingren, Arthur 89, 104-105
Loch Lomond 66, 168-169
Loch Ordie 37, 168-169
Logie 20, 168-169
Lord Iris 107, 168-169
Low & Clear Spider 86, 168-169

## M

Mac Garrett Pl.16 (p112), 168-169
Macartair 28, 168-169
MacDonald's Chartreuse Shrimp 40, 132-133
Machair Claret 36, 168-169
Madame Hazel 68, 168-169
Major 13, 170-171
Mallard & Claret Spider Pl.12 (p97), 170-171
Mar Lodge 22, 170-171
March Brown 60, 170-171
Marigold 67, 170-171
Marriner, Paul 65
Matepedia Spey 64, 170-171
Meyer, Deke 73-74, 87
McKay, Pat 8

# Index

McNeese, Dave  72-3, 81, 110
Mickey Spey  61, 170-171
Midnight Canyon  76, 170-171
Mike's Prawn  41, 170-171
Mitchell  60, 172-173
Money, General Noel  77, 89, 100-101
Morgan, Moc  25
Mörrum  70, 172-173
      Mörrum Spey  70, 172-173
Mr Glasso  72, 172-173

## N

Namsen #1  48, 172-173
Namsen #2  48, 172-173
Neptune  59, 172-173
NessC  39, 172-173
Night Hawk  54, 174-175
Night Train  Pl.16 (p112), 174-175
Nipisiguit Grey  55, 174-175
Nitro Shrimp  39, 174-175
Northeast Smelt  53, 174-175
Nuptiale  69, 174-175

## O

October Caddis Spey  75, 174-175
October Spey  84, 174-175
Ola  49, 176-177
Olive Steelhead Petite  Pl.10 (p95),
    200-201
Orange Angel  76, 176-177
Orange Butt Spade  Pl.6 (p91), 196-197
Orange Comet  99, 134-135
Orange Gorbenmac  43, 154-155
Orange Heron (Glasso)  62, 162-163
Orange Skagit Spey  63, 192-193
Orange Sundowner  Pl.9 (p94), 202-203
Orange Sunset  85, 204-205
OrangeWoolly Bugger  Pl.13 (p98),
    212-213
O'Reilly, Peter  21
Oriole  55, 176-177
Otteson  49, 176-177

## P

Paint Brush  88, 176-177
Pålsbu  50, 176-177
Parson #1  9, 176-177
Peacock Woolly Bugger  98, 212-213
Peer Gynt  47, 176-177
Pennell, Black  17, 122-123
Pennell, Briggs  29, 126-127
Pennell, Peterson's  30, 178-179
Penybont  24, 176-177
Peter Ross Spider  Pl.12 (p97), 178-179

Peterson M.D.  Pl.17 (p113), 178-179
Peterson's Pennell  30, 178-179
Pink Shrimp, Dark  80, 178-179
Pink Shrimp,Light  80, 178-179
Pink Steelhead Petite  Pl.10 (p95),
    200-201
Pink Sundowner  Pl.9 (p94), 202-203
Polar Bear Spey  73, 178-179
Polar Shrimp, Blumreich  80, 178-179
      Dark  80, 178-179
      Light  80, 178-179
Polar Spade  Pl.6 (p91), 196-197
Pot Belly Pig  18, 180-181
Prawn Fly  89, 180-181
Prismatic Spey  82, 180-181
Professor  56, 180-181
Purcell's Peter  33, 180-181
Purple & Orange Marabou Spey  83,
    180-181
Purple Ghost  180-181
Purple Goose Spey  74, 180-181
Purple Gorbenmac  43, 154-155
Purple Guinea Spey  85, 182-183
Purple Heart  107, 182-183
Purple Heart Spey  106, 182-183
Purple Hilton  73, 182-183
Purple King  64, 182-183
Purple Matuka  109, 182-183
Purple Matuka, Tinsel  109, 182-183
Purple October  83, 182-183
Purple Prince  72, 182-183
Purple Sol Duc Spey  107, 184-185
Purple Spey (Leblanc)  65, 184-185
    (McNeese)  72, 184-185
    (Mootry)  72, 184-185
Purple Spider  87, 184-185
Purple Steelhead Petite  Pl.10 (p95),
    200-201
Purple Sundowner  Pl.9 (p94), 202-203
Purple Woolly Bugger  Pl.13 (p98),
    214-215

## Q

QE3  Pl.16 (p112), 184-185
Quack  21, 184-185
Queen of Waters  68, 184-185
Quillayute  72, 184-185
Quinsam Hackle  89, 186-187

## R

Radencich, Michael  15
Rainbow  Pl.14 (p100), 186-187
Red Arrow  35, 186-187
Red Dawn  45, 138-139
Red Demon  41, 186-187
Red Dog  81, 186-187
Red Gorbenmac  43, 154-155

Red Guinea Spade  Pl.7 (p92),
    196-197
Red Guinea Spey  75, 186-187
Red Sandy  10, 186-187
Red Sandy, variant  67, 186-187
Red Steel Woolly  99, 198-199
Red Sundowner  Pl.9 (p94), 202-203
Red Turkey  25, 186-187
Red Woolly Bugger  Pl.13 (p98),
    214-215
Redwing  110, 188-189
Reliable  56, 188-189
Reverse Akroyd (Halyk's)  84, 116-117
Rush Gosling  32, 154-155
Rusty Sky  108, 122-123
RVI Orange  81, 188-189

## S

San Juan Spider  87, 188-189
Sandy Spider  88, 188-189
Sara Teen  111, 188-189
September Candy  Pl.17 (p113), 188-189
    Orange  Pl.17 (p113), 188-189
    Pheasant  Pl.17 (p113), 188-189
Sheriff  47, 190-191
Silver Brown  102, 190-191
Silver Doctor  21, 190-191
Silver Grey  27, 190-191
Silver Heron (Glasso)  62, 162-163
Silver Hilton  103, 190-191
Silver Lady #1  102, 190-191
    #2  102, 190-191
Silver Shrimp  39, 190-191
Silver Wilkinson  28, 192-193
Silver Wilkinson Spey  44, 192-193
Skagit Spey, Black  63, 192-193
    Orange  63, 192-193
    White  63, 192-193
    Yellow  63, 192-193
Sky, Blue  108, 122-123
    Black  108, 122-123
    Rusty  108, 122-123
Skykomish Dark  83, 192-193
    Light  83, 192-193
Snelda  41, 192-193
Soft Hackle Spey  74, 194-195
Sol Duc Spey  62, 194-195
Soldier Palmer  38, 194-195
Soul Duck  Pl.16 (p112), 194-195
Spade  Pl.6 (p91), 194-195
    Blue  Pl.6 (p91), 194-195
    Fancy  Pl.7 (p92), 194-195
    Fancy Red  Pl.7 (p92), 194-195
    Farrar  Pl.6 (p91), 194-195
    Green Butt  Pl.6 (p91), 196-197
    Orange Butt  Pl.6 (p91), 196-197
    Polar  Pl.6 (p91), 196-197
    Rcd Guinea  Pl.7 (p92), 196-197
    Yellow Guinea  Pl.7 (p92), 196-197

# Index

Spawning Purple 110, 196-197
Spawning Spey 73, 196-197
Spectral Spider 86, 196-197
Spider, Gold 87, 196-197
Spirit Fly #1 14, 198-199
Spirit Fly #2 14, 198-199
Spirit Fly #3 14, 198-199
Spitfire 49, 198-199
Spring Fly, Hansard's 7, 198-199
Squirrel & Teal 104, 198-199
Steel Woolly, Black 99, 198-199
    Steel Woolly, Red 99, 198-199
Steelhead Akroyd (Yarnot) 84, 116-117
Steelhead Carey 88, 200-201
Steelhead Petite, Black Pl.10 (p95), 200-201
    Blue Pl.10 (p95), 200-201
    Grizzly Pl.10 (p95), 200-201
    Olive Pl.10 (p95), 200-201
    Pink Pl.10 (p95), 200-201
    Purple Pl.10 (p95), 200-201
Steelhead Spey 78, 200-201
Steelhead Stick 97, 200-201
Steelhead Sunset 85, 204-205
Stuart's Killer 24, 202-203
Summer Deep Purple Spey 7, 202-203
Summer Frontier 77, 202-203
Summer Lady Caroline 77, 202-203
Summer Midnight Express 78, 202-203
Summer Sunrise 78, 202-203
Sundowner, Black Pl.9 (p94), 202-203
    Orange Pl.9 (p94), 202-203
    Pink Pl.9 (p94), 202-203
    Purple Pl.9 (p94), 204-205
    Red Pl.9 (p94), 204-205
Sunset, Blue & Bronze 85, 204-205
    Orange 85, 204-205
    Steelhead 85, 204-205
Sweep 46, 204-205
Sweet Loretta 95, 204-205

## T

Tailfire 40, 204-205
    Eany 40, 204-205
Tana 46, 206-207
Tartan 62, 206-207
Taylors Golden Spey 108, 152-153
TC3 Pl.16 (p112), 206-207
Teal, Blue & Silver Spider Pl.12 (p97), 206-207
Teresa's Tease 111, 206-207
Thunder & Lightning 23, 206-207
Thunder Dawn 45, 140-141
Thunder Shrimp 38, 206-207
Toppy 6, 206-207
Traffic Ticket 69, 208-209
Trinity Brown 90, 208-209
    Grey 90, 208-209

Trophy Hunter 75, 208-209
Turkey Tracker Pl.15 (p106), 208-209
Turkey, Black 25, 124-125
    Brown 22, 128-129
    Red 25, 186-187

## V

Valdum 47, 208-209
Veverka, Bob 11, 106
Vi Menn Flua 49, 208-209

## W

Wasp Grub 7, 208-209
Watson's Fancy 24, 208-209
Wet Spider 86, 210-211
Whaka Blonde Pl.7 (p92), 210-211
White Skagit Spey 63, 192-193
Whitewing 22, 210-211
Wil Harry 26, 210-211
Wild Turkey Orange 84, 210-211
Winter Candlelight 78, 210-211
Winter Expression 78, 210-211
Winter Green Butt Skunk 78, 210-211
Winter Jack O'Lantern 78, 210-211
Winter Punch Spey 78, 212-213
Winter Sunkist 78, 212-213
Winter's Hope 67, 212-213
    Spey 82, 212-213
Woolly Bugger, Black Pl.13 (p98), 212-213
    Orange Pl.13 (p98), 212-213
    Peacock 98, 212-213
    Purple Pl.13 (p98), 214-215
    Red Pl.13 (p98), 214-215
Woolly Worm 90, 214-215
Wye Grub 7, 214-215

## Y

Yellow Dawn 45, 140-141
Yellow Eagle 63, 144-145
Yellow Gosling 32, 156-157
Yellow Guinea Spade Pl.7 (p92), 196-197
Yellow Skagit Spey 63, 192-193

## Z

Zulu 30, 214-215
Zulu, Blue 30, 214-215